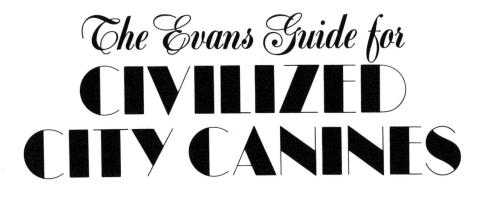

The Evans Guide for CIVILIZED CITY CANINES

Job Michael Evans

Photographs by Charles Hornek
Foreword by Myrna Milani, D.V.M.

First Edition—First Printing
1988

HOWELL BOOK HOUSE INC.

230 Park Avenue
New York, N.Y. 10169

Library of Congress Cataloging-in-Publication Data

Evans, Job Michael.
   The Evans guide for civilized city canines.
      1. Dogs.   2. Dogs—Training.   3. City and town life.
I. Title.   II. Title: Civilized city canines.
SF426.E9   1988   636.7'088   88-13264
ISBN 0-87605-543-9

Some of the materials in this book appeared in *Dog Fancy, Dog World* and *The American Kennel Gazette* in different form.

Note on gender terms:
Throughout this book I alternately refer to dogs as he, she or it. I mean nothing demeaning by occasionally referring to a dog as "it." Nor do I mean any harm to males or females if "he" or "she" is used separately or together when the terms apply to people or dogs. I realize this issue is sensitive with some readers, but I do not feel bound to "de-genderize" each sentence. I hope the reader will understand.

To
Charles Hornek,
my friend and photographer,
and to
Jody Milano,
my friend and typist,
native New Yorkers
who welcomed me to
this city with love,
support and encouragement

Contents

Foreword

IF JOB EVANS had called five years ago asking me to write an introduction to a book on living with a dog in the city, I surely would have questioned his judgment. True, I had lived in major, bustling metropolises most of my life, but I fled to the serenity of the New Hampshire woods about the same time Job found himself in a monastery on top of a mountain in a remote area of New York state.

I still live on a dirt road in the middle of the woods, but now the almost constant rumble of dump trucks and construction equipment heralds the arrival of an instant city in the form of a housing development nearby. As references to the whole state of New Hampshire as a "suburb" of Boston creep more and more frequently into realtors' sales pitches, once sleepy hamlets like mine feel the need to enforce long on the books but rarely enforced leash laws. (In some towns as many as 60 percent of the police calls are complaints of one sort or another about dogs.) My two dogs, whom I trusted to remain in their own area and out of trouble for the first half of their lives, must now learn a whole new set of rules. For the first time I must deal with my (often considerable) irritation as one of the "new" people daily jogs down our once almost uninhabited road, her macho black Lab free ranging over my yard, lifting his leg and sending my confined pets into a frenzy of frantic barking. In the veterinary practice where I work, the once ubiquitous dogs with a muzzle full of porcupine quills have been replaced by those hit by cars or attacked by other dogs. And rather surprisingly (or, sadly, perhaps not) in this day and age when access to poisonous substances is much more restricted, it seems more and more people suspect their neighbors of attempting to do in their dogs; they look at me in confusion when I ask the obvious question, "Why?"

I suspect Job and I have remained such good friends for so long because our orientations toward the human/canine relationship compliment each other's so well. It's often said in scientific circles that the more we know about a large population, the less we can know about individuals within that population. Many dog books miss that crucial point. City dogs—and their owners—do not have the same needs as country dogs and owners, or even suburbanites. To be sure, the same basic urges and instincts still exist in both species, but the environment exerts a potent influence on how these will manifest. Country dogs may urinate and defecate to mark their territories literally hundreds of times and never encounter another canine who challenges them; city dogs, on the other hand, may be routinely walked where thousands of other dogs proclaim via their various secretions and wastes, "Keep out! This space belongs to *me!*" And even though both logic and experience tell us such differences exist, most guides for dog owners propose methods that supposedly work anytime and anywhere.

The more we know about dogs and their owners, the more we know that isn't true; the larger the population addressed by any method, the more general that method must be. For example, as the number of employed dog owners in my practice skyrocketed in the 1970s and 1980s, I realized that the needs of working owners and their dogs are quite different from those of someone who is home with the dog most of the time. The insights gained from these working owners and pets led me to write *The Weekend Dog.* Once I recognized that dogs often play a most intimate, often highly emotional and symbolic role in their owners lives, *The Invisible Leash* and *The Body Language and Emotion of Dogs* quickly followed, filling the void of more specific information relating to the psychological interplay of human and canine. Simultaneously, I saw Job's focus shifting from the almost poetic treatment of training in *How to Be Your Dog's Best Friend* to the more intimate, nitty-gritty orientation of *The Evans Guide for Counseling Dog Owners* and his all inclusive *The Evans Guide to Housetraining Your Dog.*

In the pages ahead we see the culmination of Job's ability to integrate his profound knowledge of training basics with his firsthand knowledge of the specific trials and tribulations encountered by every dog owner in the ever-changing complex city environment. We see some of those same techniques that seemed so beyond our (and our dog's) capacities when presented in the context of distraction-free, ever serene Smalltown, U.S.A. given new meaning applicable to life in the heart of Manhattan, Chicago, San Francisco, or any city.

More importantly, in the pages ahead we see a celebration of the unique relationship between city owner and dog. No hint of making the best of a bad lot exists; no reference to the inferior quality of such a life slips in to evoke fear or guilt in the reader. Indeed not, for Job realizes, as do you and I, that while the city may pose its own special problems and challenges for dog and owner, it also provides a most special opportunity to form a particularly strong relationship. Almost anyone can properly train a dog in a quiet neighborhood with a fenced-in yard, state-of-the-art dog door, and someone home all day to monitor the dog's activities. But when owning a dog means going out in all kinds of weather at all hours and threading one's way through an ever-changing sea of human, animal, and environmental distractions, a very special—and intense—form of love and commitment comes into play. Gone are the days when those who kept dogs in the city were viewed as selfish and uncaring. For those, like Job Evans, who truly know and appreciate the magnitude and capacity of the bond between owner and dog, living in the city provides exciting and fun opportunities to utilize aspects of human and canine potential that often lie dormant in less challenging environments.

The Evans Guide for Civilized City Canines not only speaks to the specific needs of a specific group of people, but also provides valuable insights for *all* dog lovers into the versatility and flexibility of one of our most treasured animal companions.

MYRNA M. MILANI, DVM

Fitzwilliam, New Hampshire
Past-president, New
Hampshire Veterinary
Medical Association

Acknowledgments

THIS IS MY fourth dog book and in some ways my most ambitious project. I was aided along the way by many friends and colleagues in the dog fancy and wish to thank them here. First, I am grateful to the Monks of New Skete, who educated me in dogs and in discipline, and with whom I was privileged to live for over a decade. I have not forgotten our time together. Sincere thanks and much love to my parents, who encouraged me to start my own business and try city life.

I am particularly grateful to the staff at Howell Book House and especially to the late founder, Elsworth S. Howell (1915-1987), who encouraged me with fatherly concern and advice. In a world of high-tech publishing and fast-buck schemes, Howell Book House remains a publishing house of integrity and quality—a "family" of authors who admire animals.

Thanks also to the staff at the American Kennel Club library and the staff at the Cornell University Animal Health Newsletter. Their resources greatly aided my research.

Without my friends in the veterinary community there would be no *Patience of Job: Training for Dogs and People,* and my life would be less full. I am grateful to Dr. Lewis Berman and Dr. Gene Solomon at Park East Animal Hospital and Dr. Sally Haddock at St. Mark's Veterinary Hospital, both in New York. My thanks also to these veterinarians who refer clients my way or work with me on other levels: Dr. Thomas DeVincentis, Dr. Peter Kross, Dr. Stuart Brodsky, Dr. Stephen Kritsick, Dr. Malcolm Kram, Dr. Paul Schwartz, Dr. Stephanie Hazen and Dr. Jane Bicks—my speaking partner for several years, who continues to educate me on canine nutrition. Thanks also to Lynn Levo, CSJ, Ph.D. for her psychological insights and support.

My participation in the Society of New York Dog Trainers has been rewarding and I would like to thank the members, as well as fellow trainers Marie Ehrenberg, Jack and Wendy Volhard, Don Arner and Debra Feliziani.

I am privileged to serve on the advisory boards of both the Humane Society of New York, and the Hearing Ear Dog Program in West Boylston, Massachusetts. My interaction with both organizations has helped me to understand more fully the tremendous services shelters and service organizations provide to dogs and those who love and need them. I am also grateful to Roberta Kaman at the Fidelco Foundation Guide-Dog School in Bloomfield, Connecticut for photographs and support.

Evelyn Danko at Hanlan's Realty in New York provided the perfect hideaway from my hectic office/home in New York City to complete sections of this book—especially those dealing with city canines who "migrate" weekly to the countryside. Evelyn, thanks for finding a house with *no phone!*

In Canada, special thanks goes to Judy Emmert of Campbellville, Ontario, my organizer in that province who has staged many seminars for me there. Through her efforts and the efforts of local clubs across Canada I was able to teach in Victoria, Vancouver, Calgary, Regina, Sault Ste. Marie, Thunder Bay, Toronto, Montreal, Halifax and St. John's—literally coast to coast in Canada—in less than three years! In this way, I was able to see firsthand the life of Canadian city dogs. Thanks also to Susan Pearce, Elizabeth Dunn, Alice Bixler and Dorothy Johnson at *Dogs in Canada* for support—and fine dinner company!

I have served as book reviewer for *Dog Fancy* for almost five years and I'm grateful to Linda Lewis, my editor there, as well as to Micky (Enid) Bergstrom at *Dog World,* where I often freelance. I am a proud member of the Dog Writers' Association of America and my contacts in that group greatly aided researching this book.

Finally, my thanks to Beverly Higgins at SUNY–New York for use of her dog, Bundy, as well as to Michelle Siegal and her Collie, Brandy, and to the other canine models and their owners who withstood endless photography sessions in order to help others. My thanks to a special person in New York who, when I came to this city, disoriented, jobless, broke but full of hope, fostered that hope, pushed me forward, and inspired me. You know who you are, and I thank you.

JOB MICHAEL EVANS

The *urbane* dog is polite in a smooth, polished way. This dog has poise, grace and fabulous eyes!

Chip Simons

1

Introduction:
The Urbane Dog—
A Civilized City Canine

ur-bane (ûr bān') adj. 1. Having the polish and suavity regarded as characteristic of sophisticated social life in major cities, 2. reflecting sophistication, elegance, etc. in manners and training.
"Manners are a means of getting what we want without appearing to be absolute swine."

—Quentin Crisp in *Manners from Heaven*

THE TROUBLE WITH many dogs is they lack manners. Even if they are "obedience-trained" they are often without poise, grace and tact—all qualities a dog can and should have to live in a city, for that matter, anywhere. In other words, to paraphrase Mr. Crisp, these dogs *do* act like absolute swine and *still* manage to get what they want. Of course, their owners have never taught them manners, so it's hardly the dogs' fault. This book tries to remedy this situation and help you create a civilized city canine.

Some owners might laugh at the notion of manners for dogs, remarking that obedience training to the come, sit, stay, down and stand level is certainly enough to secure decent behavior from any dog. That once was true. In the early days of obedience training, instructors stressed practical application of these exercises in the *home* environment, even if the recalcitrant pooch had to be hauled off to obedience school to learn the commands. All owners were expected to apply the methods at home in a practical way, and this was usually mapped out for the owner: down-stays during dinner (to stop begging), a sit-stay in front of every door (to prevent the dog from rudely crashing its way through) and so on. But with the advent of heavy ring training this emphasis has decreased and few trainers stress home application to the degree it should be stressed, concentrating instead on minute points of ringcraft. The result has been hordes of dogs who are obedience trained but not at all mannerly. And much of what gets taught in many classes doesn't address the complexity of city life.

The trained, urban dog is polite in a smooth, polished way. This dog has manners. The urban dog must also be *urbane,* perhaps more so than its country counterpart because life in a large city requires mounds of manners. Some may say the opposite is true, that big-city dwellers are insufferably rude. I would answer that this is just not so, that curtness is not always rudeness, and that moving quickly can be done in a courteous way. But I would also agree to an element of truth in that criticism. Studies show surprising evidences of kindness between large city residents, but they also show city denizens to be, true to stereotype, selfish, rude to strangers, more often than not in a hurry, unhelpful and, in a word, unmannerly.

Rather than try to prove this thesis one way or another, can't we just say that *if* this is the case, why don't we try to *improve* our manners, and why don't we insist that our dogs be mannerly—since manners are especially needed when time and space are conscriped. All too often, there will be an unpleasant correlation between the rude person and the rude dog. So, every urban dweller who wants an urbane dog must first examine his or her own behavior for signs of bad manners. Remember, even if you train your dog to be urbane, poised, controlled and gracious and *you* remain "an absolute swine" the juxtaposition will be more than many people can take. You must train both yourself and your dog to be urbane. To accomplish the first task, turn to Mr. Crisp's book; to accomplish the task with your dog, please continue with this book.

Now, I am going to begin the book by doing one of the most unmannerly things a person could do: I am going to talk about myself. I'll tell you a bit about my past as it relates to dogs, and how I came to become a trainer of civilized city canines. I hope through the prism of my experience that you will take heart and see that cities can be wonderful places for dogs—and persons, even persons who once hated cities and, yes, dogs. Like myself.

Although I didn't like dogs when I entered New Skete monastery, I grew to love them. But I still hated cities and lived surrounded by wilderness. I'm pictured here in 1978 with "Zanta" and one of her pups.

2

Offing Old Vows, Taking New Ones

WHEN I CAME TO NEW YORK CITY in 1983 to start my dog training business I was penniless and dogless. Fresh out of the monastery, I had eleven years of skills as a dog trainer. I also had eleven years with a vow of poverty. I could hardly afford to feed myself, let alone a dog. Because none of the monastery dogs belonged to me (the vow extends that far), I had left three dogs behind that were beloved pets. The emptiness of my heart was great. I hasten to add that I am not complaining, it was I who had left monastic life. I knew what I was sacrificing. I knew what I might have to face. Or did I?

I scoured the city for training jobs, pinning up my card everywhere, visiting pet stores, presenting my portfolio to veterinarians. The monastery was surrounded by 500 acres of wilderness and was reachable by a two-mile dirt road that dead-ended at the church and monastic buildings. My dogs lived with lush green fields and rolling hills.

Now I lived in a small apartment where the landlord forbade dogs, and I couldn't afford one anyway. I hated the noise and litter of New York, the hurried pace, the pushiness of the people—and to a degree, I still do. I was disoriented, as many out-of-towners tend to be when they come to this city. I didn't like New York at all. Why would people live here? Why would people keep dogs here?

Yet, I had made a demographic study by my own research and by consulting trainers who had practiced in New York. I determined that the largest concentration of dogs living in the smallest amount of space is on the island of Manhattan. Since I hated to drive, and since I had a lot of catching up to do financially, I decided on a business there. I could walk to most clients, see several a day and maintain the quality of my work. I might as well give it a try.

There was another inner conflict that I had to take a square look at in myself—one you too might harbor within. Back then I believed that dogs just didn't belong in cities—certainly not *this* city—and that life for a city dog (not to mention the people) was simply an ongoing torture that could only be eased, never eradicated. I transposed my feelings onto the face of every dog I saw—in my view, for dogs, as well as for people, Manhattan island was simply Devil's Island—people and dogs doomed to incarceration, with little or no hope of escape. What a way to start a business!

Maybe that's why I didn't get any jobs that first month. Slowly my attitude changed and I stopped transposing my own alienation onto the dogs. I learned the street plan. I went to the parks and saw dogs cavorting and playing everywhere. I saw trained dogs strolling proudly by their owners, very much at ease. As my own tension, alienation and nervousness eased, the pinched expressions I *thought* I had witnessed on the faces of the dogs I passed disappeared.

As I grew in confidence (I am told the process was very fast), I began to make a lot of personal promises to myself and to set goals—I even took private "vows" to myself. I vowed that I would start a business in New York and that it would succeed. I vowed that I would do everything I could to be sure that the dogs owned by my clients and, by extension all city dogs, led happy lives, as pleasurable as possible. Writing this book is part of fulfilling that vow.

It was then that I began to notice, *really* notice the many techniques city owners used to make life in the city more bearable. I passed playgrounds and would notice play groups of dogs with owners supervising their frolic. I noticed the different types of coats worn by dogs, which I first thought were "fruity" and unnecessary, but which I came to see really did help dogs constantly walked on concrete. I'd see park-type obedience courses being held and other private trainers at work. I began to reevaluate many aspects of my thinking.

Some of my first clients lived near Times Square. When you are a private trainer in New York, your appointments tend to be in the late afternoon or evening. Now, if your client happens to live near Times Square you must learn to train dogs there at night. There's no sense journeying to a quieter location—you'd waste half your client's lesson time and maybe not find an area much quieter. So there I was, training dogs in the madness of Manhattan in its most hectic area. Trainers often talk about the difficulty of getting a dog to concentrate on learning a given exercise because of *distractions.* I learned a lot about distractions in Times Square, even though, frankly, I was in culture-shock.

Vowless and now beardless I took to the streets of New York after starting Patience of Job, my training business. At first I was scared to even put the dog on the ground! Note the perplexed expression on the human's face.

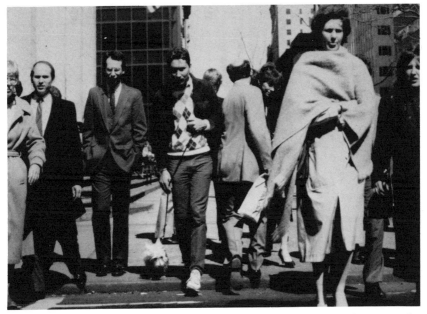

I finally gained enough courage to start training. I even had the dog on the wrong side for heeling. If I can do it, you can too. Take heart city owner!

I learned to compensate for my environment. For instance, one of the first lessons is on heeling, to get the dog to walk calmly and peacefully by your side without lunging or lagging. As part of this lesson most trainers teach turns and to make sure all turns are executed most trainers use a figure-eight pattern, curving around two "stewards" who are standing facing each other about ten feet apart. The stewards give the trainer a point of focus to pattern the figure eight around and they also serve as nifty distractions for the dog, who might stop to lunge at or otherwise relate to them and can then be corrected. Since I was training alone, I needed helpers. I hit upon the idea of using the hookers as stewards. They were just standing around anyway, I figured. I think some of them thought it was quite kinky!

I continued to adjust and began to get clients in all areas of the city. Daily, I saw my clients' concern that life for their dog be the best they could provide. Frankly, I felt a higher level of concern from my new clients than I had felt from people who dropped dogs off at the monastery and just expected the dog to be trained and returned. Here, these clients knew *they had* to adjust to city life, and their dog did too. And they knew that while difficult, it wasn't impossible. *Now I knew that also.* I had learned it for myself. Now I could really help others. My knowledge was internalized, purchased at a great price. With every client I gained in confidence.

That is what I offer you in this book—the confidence that you can move about your city as a happy pair with your best friend, and education that will *heighten* that confidence. That is why I've started with my own story. I'll not ask you to make vows and promises. I'll just ask you to close this book for one minute, close your eyes, take a deep breath, call your dog over to you, give him a big hug and say, "Okay, we're going to do this no matter what." Then, of course, I hope you'll reopen the book and read on. I promise to give you every shred of information I know so that the two of you can move about town as a team.

Relaxed and at home in the city in 1987, I am shown resting during a training session with one of my students. My student is smiling, I'm smiling, the Circle Line tour boat chug-a-lugs behind us on the East River and all is peaceful.

3

Getting (and Getting Over) "The Guilties"

WE HEAR CONSTANTLY about diseases that one can easily contract living in a city in close proximity to many other people. I have a new disease to offer for observation— one that hits urban dwellers who own dogs they must leave alone, for a day, for an hour or in extreme cases of this disease, even for a minute. The disease is called "The Guilties" and it strikes urban dog owners frequently. There is no known cure and several ways to develop the disease.

If you want to get "The Guilties" *quickly* follow this procedure: Walk around town for awhile, strolling past pet shops especially. Go when you are depressed. Let's say your boyfriend just called and told you to shove off. Or perhaps the apartment above you harbors a weirdo who likes to let his bathtub overflow and you've just mopped up gallons of water. Or maybe you just got off the subway (this is an experience, which in some cities is *in itself* enough to prompt severe depression). These are all good times to stop by a pet store, or even a shelter and take a long look at the adorable creatures frolicking about inside—a good time, that is, if you want to catch a good case of "The Guilties." This will be your incubation period for "The Guilties" virus.

Now, get a puppy in your depressed state of mind. Don't think—just impulse-buy or impulse-adopt and get the puppy home *quickly*. If shelter personnel try to ask you any questions (as they well may) about what type of home you can offer this new being, don't answer them directly. Think only of your depression and the healing it needs *pronto* and how this little lovable dog is going to take away all your hurt. Get out of that shop or shelter quickly—with your "fix" under your arm.

For the next two weeks, everything, and I repeat *everything,* that puppy does is going to be forgiven or forgotten. He pooped on your white wool rug? Well, all puppies have accidents. He scratched your hand or bit you a little too hard? Well, all pups scratch and he's just teething. Your incubation period for "The Guilties" still has a way to go—about one week.

Now, if, as so many books advise (and not incorrectly) you took some time off from work or happened to impulse-buy or adopt on a weekend, you will have had one heck of a *glorious* weekend together, romping about, taking your pup out on the town, playing in the park, chasing each other around the apartment and generally spending almost 100 percent of the time together. Of course you will keep your new puppy in bed, tucked under the covers with you overnight. What the heck? Your boyfriend told you to shove off anyway, didn't he? Your incubation period is coming to an end because tomorrow is Monday and you have to go to work. After all, someone has to buy the dog food around here.

Sunday evening you start to feel heavy-of-heart, which is the first sign that "The Guilties" virus will soon become violent. On Monday morning you lay out the ten thousand toys you purchased for Foo-Foo in anticipation of this terrible moment. Maybe that will make your puppy happy. You've fed him people food all night long the evening before because you were munching taco chips anyway (depression does that to a person) and besides that that blue-cheese dip was *great* and he kept begging. You pet and overpet your little friend as you whirl about the apartment getting ready for work. You soothe Foo-Foo at the door, back out of the apartment crying, while Foo-Foo screams in anguish.

At work lunch approaches and you are no longer able to function. You can't stand to think of Foo-Foo alone in that *huge* apartment without your loving attention. Irrationally, you think about calling Foo-Foo on the phone, but you remind yourself (it comes as a jolt) that dogs don't talk. That leaves you only one recourse—you must go home to Foo-Foo— otherwise he will grow up abnormal. He will also hate you. My God—he might even "turn against you" when he gets older, as he harbors the memory of the abandonment this very morning. You cancel your lunch date and spend $12.30 on cab fare to get home to see Foo-Foo for 45 minutes and take him for a walk. You explode into the apartment, after ripping your clothes on the staircase as you galloped up the stairs to redeem your canine captive.

You've got the first-class *"Guilties."* A bad case. Besides, Foo-Foo was sound asleep! He hadn't even *started* writing the letter saying how lonely he was and if you *really* loved him you would be there, and he seemed irritated when you woke him up. You rationalize further. Well, maybe he's just being *coy* — trying not to let on how much I mean to him . . . or maybe he's too *proud* to show anger . . . or maybe he's *so depressed,* like me, that he just *expects* rejection. With a loud, "Oh my gawd!" you sink to your knees and promise Foo-Foo that this will be the last afternoon you will work, ever. You have an extreme case of "The Guilties" — and you need treatment by a trainer. You *can* get over "The Guilties." You have to.

The Cure

Of course the above scenario is exaggerated, but exaggeration, like repetition, is a great teaching tool. I hope you haven't impulse-bought or impulse-adopted a pet, and that you are level-headed enough to know that leaving your dog to go to work or other destinations is inevitable, and acceptable.

Nevertheless, almost every urban owner gets "The Guilties" now and then. Even if you manage to shake the disease in the early stages, it sometimes reoccurs when you feel you are too busy, too preoccupied, too involved in the hectic pace of city life to spend much time with your canine pal.

In some older training texts, the reader got the impression that if you weren't able to offer your dog constant companionship, you weren't "fit" to be a dog owner. As a city dog owner, your life style is very different than the bucolic portrayals found in much of the older dog training literature. All of this makes you more susceptible to a case of "The Guilties."

The first step in getting over "The Guilties" is to realize that you have them. Take a good look at your motivations in originally getting your dog. Were you distraught? Worried? Depressed? Were you looking for something — affection, warmth, love — that you should have been looking for from a member of your own species? I know *I* was guilty of that with my first dog — and I ruined the dog because of the emotional demands I made on her.

The fast pace, noise, dirt, tension and lack of human warmth that is unavoidable in an urban setting can make the warmth and unconditional love of a dog very attractive. But to select a puppy or dog simply to balance the coldness of city life is to set yourself up for potential disaster. The only real reason to procure a pet is a desire to *steward* the animal — to feed and shelter it properly, to care for it, to educate it and, yes, to give and receive affection. But the subtleties of owner motivation in taking in a pet are murky ground. You must take a good look at why you brought this puppy or dog into your life. If you come up with an answer in which the name of the dog could be easily substituted with the name of a past, present or future boyfriend or girlfriend, no wonder you have "The Guilties" — and perhaps problems with your dog. Even if the names turn out to be interchangeable, you can still get over "The Guilties" because, frankly, you *have* to. Why? "The Guilties" can literally *fry your dog's brain* if you persist in having them. How? Because of the subtle body and word cues you send out due to your guilty and stressed emotional state. Some examples:

Overemotional hellos or goodbyes keep dogs on edge, making it harder for them to negotiate staying alone and not giving into chair leg munchies, toilet paper teasing and other forms of destructive chewing. Leave quietly and calmly!

Constantly coming and going in and out of the apartment or home is often *more* worrisome than just leaving, period. Your dog has to face more hellos and goodbyes.

Some dogs need dog walkers and others don't. Again, comings and goings may alleviate guilt for you, but they don't necessarily make it easier on your dog.

What William E. Campbell calls the "whirling dervish" act might cue the dog that you are about to depart and actually spur bad behavior. Don't run around like a banshee when leaving. It will make your dog upset.

Hovering over a puppy or a dog, even if love is the intention, can distress a canine. Sniveling and whining tonalities, even if the English (or whatever language) employed is an attempt to soothe the dog, will backfire as the dog will see and hear you as a littermate—an *unfaithful* one that just comes and goes.

Leaving myriad toys when departing, in an effort to assuage your guilty feelings about leaving, can have a bad effect. The dog might come to see *everything* as a potential chewable item. Three toys are enough.

Loading the dog's food dish up with kibble or leaving excess water might complicate the housetraining process. The extra food and water is left to get rid of "The Guilties" but the ruse will backfire when the dog consumes the rations and leaves "presents" for you all over the house.

These are just a *few* examples of how "The Guilties" can complicate canine life. I'll discuss alternatives to these actions shortly, and throughout this book, but suffice it to say for now that acting out your guilt can often backfire on you and your dog.

In her pioneering book, *The Weekend Dog,* a book that discusses how to choose, raise and train a dog you see only nights and weekends, Dr. Myrna Milani, says, "Without a doubt guilt is the most damaging, unproductive emotion a weekend dog owner can suffer." She adds that "weekend dog owners who tolerate a dominant, demanding pet often do so out of a sense of guilt, not love. And guilt provides the shakiest of all foundations upon which to build a training program or relationship." That makes *two* canine authorities who are telling you to get rid of your "Guilties." I can't help you if you let your "Guilties" get the better of you and influence how you handle your dog.

Guilt over leaving a dog alone or not being able to provide the best care, or what one *perceives* to be the very best care, runs so deep in some owners that they find it near impossible to shake. Fact is, some owners *want* something to feel guilty about, especially if they were trained in childhood to feel guilty. Getting rid of cultural, religious or sociological guilt is *way out* of the scope of this book but I think noting its presence is worthwhile.

I had a client call recently because she dreaded the upcoming Yom Kippur holy day. Why? She wanted to remain at her synagogue for a long period of time and didn't know what to do with her Golden Retriever. She was literally wracked with guilt and it was nearing a day when one should clear his or her mind of all earthly cares so that thoughts and prayers of atonement can be concentrated on. Since this *was* a former client, not unacquainted with my philosophy concerning dogs, and because as an ex-monk I have a deep respect for the sanctity of holy days, I really put my foot down. "You go to synagogue," I said and you put your dog in his crate. "You give him a kiss on the forehead, make sure that he has some water—but do not overwater—and depart." I added, bluntly, "No guilt is allowed." Relieved, she said, "Thanks so much, somehow I knew you would say that. I feel so much better now, free to observe the day." "Say a prayer for your dog trainer," I added. In this case, guilt fell from grace.

Here are some specific tips to help you get over "The Guilties":

Train your dog from the beginning that being left alone is part of life. Never make a big thing out of coming or going. If your dog leaps around, jumps on you, goes crazy and generally goes into an ecstatic state when you return from an errand or work, *don't play into the frenzy.* Don't give in to "The Guilties." Say a simple hello, pet your pet lightly and go about your homecoming routine.

Remember that your dog is *not* your lover—he's your *dog.* Don't dump on a dog what you wouldn't get away with if he were a lover. Overdependency kills any relationship.

Leave a limited amount of water when you are away, unless instructed by your veterinarian that large quantities of water are necessary. Use ice cubes—they melt slowly and can stop your pet from "tanking up" out of nervousness when you leave. Remember, your pet doesn't know that it will have to "hold it" for awhile before you get home to provide access to an acceptable place to urinate.

dog owners who tolerate a dominant, demanding pet often do so out of a sense of guilt, not love. And guilt provides the shakiest of all foundations upon which to build a training program or relationship." That makes *two* canine authorities who are telling you to get rid of your "Guilties." I can't help you if you let your "Guilties" get the better of you and influence how you handle your dog.

Guilt over leaving a dog alone or not being able to provide the best care, or what one *perceives* to be the very best care, runs so deep in some owners that they find it near impossible to shake. Fact is, some owners *want* something to feel guilty about, especially if they were trained in childhood to feel guilty. Getting rid of cultural, religious or sociological guilt is *way out* of the scope of this book but I think noting its presence is worthwhile.

I had a client call recently because she dreaded the upcoming Yom Kippur holy day. Why? She wanted to remain at her synagogue for a long period of time and didn't know what to do with her Golden Retriever. She was literally wracked with guilt and it was nearing a day when one should clear his or her mind of all earthly cares so that thoughts and prayers of atonement can be concentrated on. Since this *was* a former client, not unacquainted with my philosophy concerning dogs, and because as an ex-monk I have a deep respect for the sanctity of holy days, I really put my foot down. "You go to synagogue," I said and you put your dog in his crate. "You give him a kiss on the forehead, make sure that he has some water—but do not overwater—and depart." I added, bluntly, "No guilt is allowed." Relieved, she said, "Thanks so much, somehow I knew you would say that. I feel so much better now, free to observe the day." "Say a prayer for your dog trainer," I added. In this case, guilt fell from grace.

Here are some specific tips to help you get over "The Guilties":

Train your dog from the beginning that being left alone is part of life. Never make a big thing out of coming or going. If your dog leaps around, jumps on you, goes crazy and generally goes into an ecstatic state when you return from an errand or work, *don't play into the frenzy.* Don't give in to "The Guilties." Say a simple hello, pet your pet lightly and go about your homecoming routine.

Remember that your dog is *not* your lover—he's your *dog.* Don't dump on a dog what you wouldn't get away with if he were a lover. Overdependency kills any relationship.

Leave a limited amount of water when you are away, unless instructed by your veterinarian that large quantities of water are necessary. Use ice cubes—they melt slowly and can stop your pet from "tanking up" out of nervousness when you leave. Remember, your pet doesn't know that it will have to "hold it" for awhile before you get home to provide access to an acceptable place to urinate.

One "cure" for "The Guilties" is to plan your day so that you take your dog with you as many places as possible.

But there will be times when you will have to leave your dog at home, so secure the house properly and avoid overemotional hello or goodbye scenes.

One "cure" for "The Guilties" is to plan your day so that you take your dog with you as many places as possible.

But there will be times when you will have to leave your dog at home, so secure the house properly and avoid overemotional hello or goodbye scenes.

Realize that even in the wild mother wolves must leave their young to hunt for food and to take care of their own feeding and elimination needs. There is nothing "unnatural" in leaving your dog alone, nor anything unkind. True, the puppy had its littermates for company, but the mother of a single pup doesn't sit in the den all day starving out of guilt.

Remember that it's the *quality* of your time with your dog that matters, not the *quantity* of time. Train your dog so that it feels leadership from you, and sees that leadership—that *alphastatus*—within the *context of ongoing time.* Your dog will then be less lonely, and you less guilty because you will know that your dog has you in the back of his mind all the time.

Give your pet a massage once or twice a week (*not* every day—that's overloading the circuits). See the full description of canine massage in Chapter 9 of this book. Don't just pet your dog around the head and shoulders. Stop thinking of your dog from the shoulders up. It might help to make an actual list of the areas you know your dog likes to be petted and concentrate on those spots. Massage your dog on the floor and use a carpeted area. Choose a leg and work up and down it. Insert your thumb into your dog's ear a bit and with your thumb and index finger on either side of the ear gently pull out to the tip of the ear. Avoid pinching, pounding and slapping motions, however. If you are a busy city owner and tend to forget to pet your dog—even though you have "The Guilties"— massage forces you to have extended interaction with your pet.

Have your dog sleep in the bedroom with you. This simple action can have deep bonding effects. Remember again—don't overload your dog's circuits—in the bedroom, *off* the bed. The problem with on-bed sleep is that it makes you look too much like a littermate. But *in* the bedroom is fine. I realized the power of in-bedroom sleep for the dog when I wrote the chapter "Where Is Your Dog this Evening?" in *How to Be Your Dog's Best Friend.* I was having some trouble bonding with and getting obedience from an older German Shepherd bitch who had recently been imported from Germany and assigned to my care. Each of the monks took care of one or more of the monastery's breeding dogs and this particular canine immigrant had been my charge. Since she didn't know English, wasn't yet obedience or housetrained and was generally aloof (I think she wanted to go home to Germany), I wasn't too hopeful about her bonding with me. But one night, two weeks into stewarding her, I was reading in my room late at night—much past the scheduled hour for "lights out." I cast a glance toward my little

"Fraulein," who was snuggled against a wall and looking at me strangely—even, it struck me, lovingly. Since I had only known her for two weeks and we were having substantial difficulty communicating, I wondered what might cause such a look of warmth and confidence. As I reflected, I put myself in the dog's place. "This carpet sure is soft," I imagined her reasoning, "and this whole room is full of the scent of this new person in my life. I certainly didn't understand that English word he tried to teach me today, but he's not making any demands on me right now, and he obviously likes me, otherwise he'd never let me sleep in his 'den.' Maybe he's not such a bad guy after all . . . " And with that I wrote that chapter right then and there. But remember that the privilege of being in your bedroom is not license to hold you hostage in it. If your dog runs around too much or attempts to crash-land on the bed, tether him or her to the foot of the bed. If your dog bothers you in the morning with rude messages to "get up!"—in the form of obnoxious licking or pawing at the bed—don't play into the behavior. Issue a curt "NO!" and if necessary tether your dog. If you want to cash in on the bonding effects of in-bedroom sleeping, you must establish certain standards, one of which is your dog gets to be near you but not *on* you. The in-bedroom sleep is *quality time* for your dog, and often turns out to be quantity time, too, since most of us sleep six to eight hours if not more. This simple technique is a wonderful balm for "The Guilties."

Plan out your errands, taking the dog as much as possible. Read the sit-stay portion in the obedience section of this book and get your sit-stay tight before going on errands. This is a great tonic for "The Guilties" because you get to include your dog in your shopping tasks and errands. Sometimes it's necessary to "pace out" errands dogless and mentally note which stores ban dogs and which welcome or at least tolerate them. If your evening errands include visits to the bank, the video shop and the card store, your dog can probably accompany you. If you must also food shop, you may not be able to take the dog along. But grouping errands into "ok-for-dogs" or "not-ok-for dogs" categories can cut down on loneliness for your dog, and on "The Guilties" for you.

Get Over It or Get Out

So you see your dog doesn't need you there every second to hold his paw and whisper sweet nothings in his ear. Your dog is, essentially, not interested in your guilt, and biologically and genetically unacquainted with and *unable* to relate to the emotion. Guilt is a human invention unknown (at least in intensified forms) in most other species. I am not saying dogs are guiltless, nor am I saying that perhaps they cannot experience individual guilt. We need more data before we can determine this. What I am saying is that they are most decidedly *not* interested in *yours.* If an urban dog owner doesn't get over "The Guilties" quickly, the entire relationship can be undermined because the human has introduced an emotion that has no place in the dog's emotional repertoire. The chances for miscommunication and disaster are elevated. I must be blunt with you: *get over "The Guilties" or get out of dog ownership!* You are your dog's *steward,* not its Siamese twin. You *have* to work, you *have* to play and your dog *has* to be alone sometimes. That's the way it is. Period. Dr. Myrna Milani tells guilty owners to recite the famous "serenity prayer." It bears quoting here:

> Lord, grant me the serenity to accept the things I cannot change, the courage to change the things I can, and the wisdom to know the difference.

That is as great a statement about dog-owner guilt—for that matter *any* kind of guilt—as I've read anywhere.

4

Bonding—and a Skeleton in Israel

I T IS POSSIBLE that the first domesticated dogs lived not out in the countryside or on a farm, but in a city or at least a village. It is also possible that dogs infiltrated themselves into our lives for no other reason than love. It appears that we weren't "using" them, or "employing" them to "do" anything until several hundred or even several thousand years after they beguiled us into admitting them into our home. Witness this report from the *New York Times* (January 18, 1980):

Man's Best Friend

Scientists have found a 12,000-year-old human burial in Israel that may shed light on the nature of the early relationship between human beings and dogs, the first animals known to have been domesticated. The left hand of the deceased was placed over the body of a 4- or 5-month old puppy. The two complete skeletons were entombed about 10 inches below a limestone slab.

Since dogs were domesticated (from wolves, at least 14,000 years ago) by hunting and gathering peoples who had no flocks to tend, it has been a mystery whether the animals were used to aid in the hunt, or for food, or as pets. The more "practical" uses seemed most reasonable, since keeping a carnivore would have been costly in a culture dependent upon hunting for its own meat.

"The puppy," the researchers wrote in the Dec. 7 issue of *Nature,* the British scientific journal, "offers proof that an affectionate rather than a gastronomic relationship existed between it and the buried person."

35

The person's pelvis was crushed, making it impossible to determine the sex. He or she was a member of the Natufian culture, hunter-gatherers who built circular dwellings with limestone walls, establishing what may have been the earliest permanently settled villages.

The skeletons were found by Simon J. M. Davis of the Hebrew University in Jerusalem and Francois R. Valla of the *Centre de Recherches Prehistoriques, Francais de Jerusalem.*

What does this fascinating report have to say to us today? First, it seems scientifically certain that people loved dogs 12,000 years ago just as we do today. Secondly, it appears that the equivalents of "urbanites" were the first to keep dogs. That ought to silence the proponents of the "dogs-do-best-in-the-country" school of thought. Thirdly, and most importantly, it seems obvious that the bond between humans and dogs goes very deep. Our historical bond goes back thousands of years, and it continues today. As a city dog steward, you are in touch with the deepest themes in dog "ownership"—you are in touch with a tie that binds. You can identify with the story of the skeleton in Israel. You know about the bond—the "secret" that all dog owners share, and that others often ridicule. Your heart is in the right place.

Meanwhile, there's plenty to learn, plenty to do. If the bond goes deep historically, that same "history" is played out in the life of each individual puppy as it is born, grows up and bonds with humans. The historical evidence is quite clear, so let's turn from the historical perspective to the perspective of the life of the dog itself. Let's take it from the beginning and look at bonding from a buyer's and a breeder's perspective. If you are going to breed or select a puppy that is just right for city life, you must know about bonding.

When we talk about *bonding* in dog-human relationships we think of it, usually, as a one-way street: the puppy or dog bonding, becoming attached to us, the humans. However, anyone who has ever owned a dog (or more correctly, been owned by one) can testify that bonding is definitely a two-way street and sometimes a very busy two-way thoroughfare.

Buyers: Beware of Breeders! Pick a Good One!

Bonding begins with the breeder and continues with the puppy's new owner. The breeder sets the tone of the bonding process since he or she plans the breeding and, hopefully, educates the client on how to foster further bonding. If the breeder doesn't know or care about bonding, the process will suffer. The process usually does suffer during the first three weeks because many breeders feel that there is nothing they can do to foster bonding at this early stage in the pup's life. "They are bonded to their dam then," one breeder told me flatly, "and anything you do to insert yourself in that process is just ruinous." I couldn't disagree more. I am a big fan of reality and the reality of the situation is that the puppy is not going to stay with his mother for very long—he is going to go out into the human world and will need information and education on how to get close to humans. While nothing should be done to disturb the dam's role drastically, such as very early weaning (except in emergencies) or banishing her from the whelping area, the breeder can do several things to make human presence felt—even before the pups open their eyes and gain full control of their senses.

If you are in the market for a puppy, be sure the pup is socialized from day one, and if you are a breeder, use the following techniques to bond the pups with humans during the first three weeks of life:

1. When you weigh the pups, don't just weigh them. Rock them gently on the scale for a few minutes and cuddle them.

2. After weighing, rub the pup's body surface with your fingers, and with your thumb and forefinger gently squeeze between the toes to provide stimulation for this area.

3. Flash a few lights periodically during the second week and talk softly to the pups as you flash—but don't go over one minute.

4. Add a scent-impregnated item such as underwear to the whelping box to bond the pups with you by utilizing their sense of smell, which is operable from birth on.

5. Play a radio in the whelping area, which should be within the *interior* of the household—do *not* use garages or closets as whelping rooms.

6. Be sure the pups are placed on different types of flooring from an early age.

Some breeders give the most rudimentary advice to clients when asked about bonding. "Just play with him" is a common and inept response. In fact, constant play, especially of the tug-of-war variety, can work against bonding in some dominant German Shepherd pups, leading the pup to assume top-dog position. My favorite bonding method is to simply *umbilical cord* the puppy. Here's how it's done. Take a four- or five-foot leash (the thinner the better), preferably leather, and just tie it to your belt loop or waist. Attach the other end to the puppy. Proceed with your day. Sit yourself down in the morning and tell yourself that unless you have to somehow cross a *moat* you will *not* take the pup off the leash and you will not detach it from your body. The one exception would be for short periods to the bathroom. After that, it's right back on the umbilical cord (leash). I have never seen this method fail to produce bonding in a puppy or dog of *any* age or of *any* genetic or environmental background if practiced for four days without interruption. The largest problem usually is the owner who feels funny about the method, or takes the leash off too soon. While I have only my lived experiences with many dogs to substantiate this as an excellent bonding technique, I suspect that on a scientific level it just may be a throwback in the dog or pup's mind or consciousness to the original umbilical cord.

Using this method, you will have two hands free to do necessary chores, drive, write, etc. With the leash attached to your body the resultant feeling on the other end of the leash is quite different than if you were holding it in your hands. For one thing, there is little "give" to the leash— it's come with me or else—and the owner avoids the tendency to tug gently at the pup or older dog trying to "coax" it to come (another instance where a dominant dog or a submissive dog just stands pat and says no). With this method your hands are out of the picture. Most pups just follow along. I have used this method on German Shepherd imports who arrive from a long plane trip and do not know English (or in some cases even German) commands and in some cases with herding dogs who did not really have a personal master and may be several years old. The graciousness of the Shepherd personality and the breed's ardent desire to bond always works for the owner and speeds up the process.

When I said bonding was a two-way street I meant it. The main impediments owners throw up to the development of bonding are their own *personal psychological projections* concerning certain puppies or dogs. See Chapter 5 for more on this. There are very few dogs that do not care to bond with humans. But the human may project his or her own feelings onto the puppy, endowing the puppy with the ability to make value judgments about the owner's personality (or lack of it). "He just doesn't like me" is a complaint breeders often hear from frustrated clients. "He doesn't give me the love I need (or expected or want or crave)" is another common comment. In these cases, the pup may be either submissive or dominant and need more time to bond, and the owner, depressed because the pup is not responding, probably backs off and does nothing to foster bonding. First, the health of the pup needs to be checked and rechecked because sick puppies do not care about bonding because they are ill and involved in themselves. Secondly, the owner has to identify what his or her projections are and how to handle them. Often the breeder can help by suggesting play sessions, umbilical cording the pup, happy feeding times and early training so that the pup gets a chance to work for the owner and experience the bonding that comes from work.

If bonding is a problem the owner must not take it personally because the dog does not mean it that way. All too often the owner does, and backs away from the pup, or trades it in for a new model. If the owner becomes

My favorite bonding method is to simply "umbilical cord" the dog and go about your day. The results are fantastic!

glum over a lack of bonding and does not employ immediate efforts to obtain it, the attuned puppy or dog soon picks up the dour air surrounding the relationship and retreats into his own little world of private play, toys, stress whining and barking and destructive chewing—the owner becomes the last item on the pup's agenda. It is very often not the pup's fault. It is as if the owner and pup were two ships passing in the night.

In the many dogs I have cared for, the one dog I bonded with most deeply was a German Shepherd bitch imported from Germany when she was five years old. She was a working dog, actively herding sheep up to the day she "emigrated." While she took directions in the field from a human shepherd, she was not bonded to him as a pet dog is bonded to an owner. Each night, after she did her job, she was herded into the barn to guard the sheep and slept there. The next morning, it was back to work. She only took time off to have litters. Her name was "Zanta."

When Zanta came to America she had never had a personal master, acted extremely aloof, did not know English, *did* know herding signals and commands but not household commands and, indeed, had never lived in a house. Nor was she housebroken.

Because of my own training with Shepherds I did not take any of her aloofness or lack of bonding personally. I immediately umbilical corded her and continued with that method for seven days. I structured her feedings so that she was empty by bedtime and could sleep in my bedroom. I took her for long, quiet walks (on leash) out into the woods. I began immediate household training with two short, formal sessions. I made up a jingle for her and put it to music and sang it to her several times a day. Because she was pregnant when imported, I whelped her litter, sitting in the whelping box with her in the early hours of the morning sipping tea and singing her jingle to her between whelps.

Within one month Zanta was my shadow. She rarely let me out of her sight. Because I responded gradually, without overresponding to her every affectionate move and made her work for me, she set the pace along with me, not against me. She also became totally open and gracious to all comers. She became my greatest teacher concerning the depth of bonding that can occur between a dog and human. Bonding between dogs and their human caretakers and stewards is a fantastic process, a challenge and finally a blessing.

5

Special Breeds for Special Needs

THERE'S A SAYING, "Different strokes for different folks."
This applies very well to both city people and city dogs. There are different
breeds for different needs, and it might take some homework for you to
figure out which breed is best for you. The following are some general
comments about my favorite city breeds and what I've gleaned about them
during my years as a city trainer.

PURE–BRED OR MIX?

I don't want to fall into a trap many dog writers get stuck in and sing
the glories of pure-breds and imply that mixed-breeds are somehow inferior.
They most definitely are not. In fact, there is some evidence that suggests
that pure-breds are more susceptible to diseases, congenital defects and
personality quirks than mixes. Something called "hybrid vigor" keeps the
moxie up in many mixes. We don't fully understand this phenomenon and
many of the studies that have been done on pure-breds versus mixes
contradict each other, so mixes and pure-breds are probably neck and neck
in terms of their *overall* adaptability to city life.

If you decide on a mix, just apply the same selection criteria presented
earlier. *Be sure* that you do not impulse buy from a pet store or make a
shelter stop without educating yourself with the tips offered earlier. But,

most of all, don't take any of the comments I will now offer on pure-breds as prejudice against mixes.

PICKING A PURE-BRED

The challenge of this chapter is to provide a system for picking a pure-bred. The usual tact is for the writer to take all 130 breeds and say a few words about each or to divide the dogs into the traditional AKC groupings (toy, nonsporting, terriers, working, herding, hounds and sporting) and then make some general comments about each grouping.

This method makes for tedious reading fills up pages that readers just skip over until they come to the breed they want or already have. Instead, I will provide critiques of breeds that from my own experience do well in the city (in other words, my favorites first). I can only offer my *experiences* with given breeds in the city setting, as well as the contrasts I have seen in these breeds when living in suburbia and the country. I hope that this particular prism of experience helps me see breed-adaptability in as clear a way as possible, especially as it relates to trainability in a city setting. For accuracy and for revisions of this book, I welcome comments from breeders and fellow trainers working in *urban* areas.

MY FAVORITE CITY CANINES

The following breeds are my favorites for city life, but they are listed alphabetically, not in order of preference. I have also suggested breed books in some cases, but it is impossible for me to mention each and every book on each and every breed. An excellent comprehensive reference containing complete descriptions and standards for all breeds is *The Complete Dog Book, Official Publication of the American Kennel Club* (Howell Book House).

Akita

The Akita was originally used to hunt bears in Japan. They are large, over 24 inches at the shoulders, possessing with a strong fore-assembly, intelligent, brave and recently touted (especially in New York City) as the perfect city breed. It's not so simple.

Over the last five years my client load has consisted of almost twenty percent Akitas and their owners. This is probably due to a chain of stores that purveyed Akitas only. The dogs were advertised as "an exotic dog from the Orient" and as a "gentle giant" that would provide protection, love and practically any "service" the owner might desire.

Through advertising and intriguing store-front display this chain man-

The Akita, robust Working dog from Japan.

Gilbert

aged to infiltrate Greenwich Village (where the first store was stationed) with Akitas and then opened several other stores. My understanding is that all these outlets are now closed down. The puppies were bred upstate and needless to say puppy aptitude testing and owner interviews were not a concern.

The breed became a "trend" rather than a carefully evaluated breed designed for city life. Suffice it to say that Akitas were, on the whole, abused, not helped by this trend, which lasted from 1982 to 1986—by then the chain had folded or changed its name, much to the relief of Akita fanciers everywhere. The advice to be gleaned from this unfortunate New York episode: If you live in an urban area and see a store offering one breed and touting it in a trendy way, *walk on.*

The greatness of the Akita for city dwelling lies in its amiable attitude toward people and a heavy "cute factor." Of the more than 200 Akitas I have trained over the last five years, no less than twenty were named "Kuma." "Kuma" means "bear" in Japanese and, indeed, this dog does resemble, in the shape of its head, a lovable bear. This attribute convinces many a soul to purchase and keep an Akita. When you have a heavy "cute factor," allow more time for getting around the block. And if you meet another Akita *owner,* with a dog or dogless, allow for an extra half-hour.

The claim that Akitas make excellent city dogs *does* seem to be true. They are a large breed with a strong fore assembly, which can cause problems unless you train them to heel from a early age, but they are not known "forgers" and train quite easily. The breed does not require an extensive amount of exercise, but, daily walks are needed—and I don't mean only for recreation. The walk should be long and steadily paced for your Akita—at least one-half mile a day—and the important aspect is to *keep moving.* The Akita is not a galloping breed and doesn't need the off-leash freedom many of its owners think it does. It is that very off-leash freedom that can lead to problems with your Akita.

Akitas are easily aggravated when they meet other dogs. In fact, the Japanese standard concerning the breed clearly states that the breed is *expected* to be aggressive with other dogs. Needless to say, this propensity might cause problems in a city setting, but it can be lessened and controlled.

First, inquire with your breeder (you *are* buying your Akita from a responsible breeder, aren't you?) as to his or her bloodlines and just how hospitable they are to other dogs. Don't be bashful about this. Say that you read it in the standard or that my book stated that sometimes they are aggressive with other dogs. Then listen carefully. Any reputable Akita breeder will acknowledge the trait and an honest one will tell you whether his or her bloodlines have a propensity toward it. Query your breeder carefully to find an Akita that can acclimate.

Akitas are brave, loyal, steadfast and loving. There is a statue in a Japanese railroad station attesting to the loyalty of one Akita who faithfully met his master's train—even after the master had passed away. Perhaps this orientation to people is a reason for their indifference or at worst agitation toward other dogs. If you own an Akita *you* will be the object of its love and affection.

Teach your Akita to heel early on, otherwise that powerful fore assembly will one day rip your arms out of their sockets. Because of the breed's propensity to fight other dogs, which might not manifest itself until your Akita is thirteen or fourteen months old, it is vitally important that you *socialize* your Akita, on leash, with other dogs. If you walk down the street with your baby Akita and you see another dog, stop and give your dog an "Okay!" (see heeling section) and let your dog know from early childhood on that other dogs share the same turf and are not to be trifled with. Early socialization, Akita breeders tell me, is the way out of Akita aggression toward other dogs. Don't try to solve this breed propensity by rudely dragging your Akita away from other dogs—this will only convince him that he can, indeed, chase other dogs away and will worsen the problem.

All of this is not at all to say that the Akita cannot make a fine urban pet. An adjusted Akita can give the city dweller years of enjoyment and sheer pleasure, for this breed possesses a nobility, poise, grace and loving nature that let it do well in any city.

Bichon Frise

This dog is, in my opinion, neck and neck with the King Charles as the ideal city dog. They are smart, almost erudite, devoted to their owners, spry and brave—a quality not at all unimportant for life in the tougher cities. They are in general not noise-shy, do not spook easily and keep their tails up high and proud as they navigate through smog, noise, construction sites and dirt. That last factor presents one of the only problems.

Bichons are white—at their best glowingly, stunningly white, and because they are a longish breed with rather short legs they tend to act as a scouring brush to city grime. There is a variety of shampoos that can help you keep a Bichon clean, but be sure to check with the breeder and your groomer for specific brand names. If you use a shampoo with the wrong Ph or the wrong combination of cleaning agents you might wind up with an off-white, yellowish Bichon.

Bichons have a heavy "cute factor"—the whiter they are kept the cuter they are. They have beady black eyes that are set just deeply enough into their heads to make hearts swoon. The facial expression is adorable, and it is a dog you can stroll along with confidently. Getting around the block will be your greatest difficulty, as you will be stopped frequently and asked for permission to pet your dog.

This approachability is no small factor for many city owners who look

The Bichon Frise, charming in all ways.

upon their dog as providing access to an otherwise impersonal city. This should not be laughed at or made light of. Selecting a dog with a "cute factor" increases your, and your dog's chances of social interaction. Let's face it, few will stop to cuddle with a Doberman or American Staffordshire Terrier—rightly or wrongly that's the way it is.

The Bichon Frise is a top-flight city dog, full of energy and pep, yet easily calmed. One possible drawback is that its coat will require a professional grooming about once a month, perhaps more frequently.

One myth about this breed is that it is difficult to housebreak (there is a shred of truth here, but just a shred). I do seem to have a great number of calls concerning Bichons who fall off the housetraining wagon or just never got on it. In trying to decipher what's happening, I've decided it is that "cute factor" at work once again—the owners simply give these canine kids too much space too soon and too often. Confinement is absolutely necessary for your Bichon until it has "earned" the house room by room on my seven-day plan, *The Evans Edict for Earning the Environment* (see the sections on housetraining later in this book).

Another aspect of Bichon personality that comes as a shock to new Bichon owners (who may misguidedly think they are the owners of a Toy Poodle) is their *toughness.* A look at the history of this breed will demonstrate clearly why these dogs are so sturdy. This is a breed founded by pirates, probably on the Canary Islands. The dogs fell in and out of favor in Italy, Spain and France—at one point they were reduced to being gutter dogs, and at another to being circus dogs. Look for Bichons in the paintings of Goya. Any breeder who knows genetic selection theory can see what was happening here: to put it bluntly, the dumb, slow Bichons were weeded out. If you have a Bichon make sure you pick up a breed book and read the historical sections—which many readers tend to skip. It will make for fascinating reading about a breed of dogs who are truly "survivors."

The Bichon has gentle manners, is very responsive, trainable and confident. They have a cheerful attitude toward life and do not do well with depressed people. They are also very agile and able to move *quickly* —no small plus in a city environment. This trait is probably inherited from the early Bichons who had to stay out from underneath the hooves of horses or to perform cute tricks in the circus. A Bichon can live up to eighteen years, if you are extremely lucky, and they are perfect as an apartment and city dog.

Three Terriers: The Cairn, the Norfolk and the Norwich

These dogs take high places on my hit parade of best city dogs. All three breeds are closely related, although there is some controversy about who is related to whom and when. From a trainer's point of view, it doesn't really matter. All three are intelligent, adaptable to the city and resilient. All three are easily educated and brave dogs that can deal with stress and are oriented to the earth.

Why is being earth-confident so important for a city dog? It allows the small urban dog (and let's face it small is easier for most folks in most cities) to weave its way through obstacles such as construction zones and deep dips in pavements. Because the terrier is bound to the earth, manhole covers, gratings and creases in concrete or other seeming obstacles don't daunt him. He is at home on any kind of *terra firma* no matter how varied or unpredictable. And you really do need a dog who can, literally, "hold his ground" on city turf.

The Cairn. The Cairn is warm, caring and has a supposedly "weatherproof" coat. In my experience, they tend to be the feistiest of the three we are discussing, prone to sparking other dogs and forging ahead on heel. This instinct can be tempered, as long as you train. You must also teach your Cairn early on that crazed barking is not allowed, and that forging

47

ahead is a no-no. Don't hesitate to use the shake or leash correction methods detailed in this book. Some owners let these problems go, preferring to think that they are just puppy spunkiness. They are not. Sparking other dogs and forging ahead on heel are truly terrier traits, and are easily controlled with training.

The Cairn Terrier, every inch an earth dog.   *Tauskey*

The Cairn has a heavy cute factor. The pricked-out hair around the eyes is adorable and, again, getting around the block without having to stop for passers-by who want to pet might be a problem. That's another reason to teach a good, tight heel early on. When people see a trained dog heeling nicely they are less likely to solicit attention from the dog.

These charmers train well and have a colorful history, fully documented in *The New Complete Cairn Terrier,* a reissue by John T. Marvin (Howell Book House).

Norwich and Norfolk Terriers. These two tykes are as hardy and forthright as the Cairn in some ways, but mellower in temperament. Both

48

have coarse coats and are easily bathed and scrubbable—something to always remember in dealing with a low-to-the-ground city dog. All three breeds are basically "kissing cousins" in terms of overall trainability and tractability. I also find, as kennel names and names of different breeders continually crop up in my behavior case history interviews with my city clients, that perhaps wildness in any of these three terriers had much more to do with bloodlines than with the breed itself. Let me stress this point again: Buy from a breeder who has placed dogs in your city before and tell the breeder *all about* your city life style. If the breeder doesn't seem to care or doesn't seem to listen, find another breeder.

The Norwich Terrier, equally at home in town or country. *Shafer*

Cavalier King Charles Spaniel

The breeders and guardians of this special spaniel breed are fiercely devoted to the preservation, betterment, protection and even isolation of this breed. Former First Lady Nancy Reagan has one. You see it on television all the time, strutting out proudly ahead of her. (That's the First Lady's fault—King Charles can be trained easily to heel properly). Believe it or not, not a few "Cav" breeders quietly murmured when the Reagans acquired a "Cav." They felt it would bring notoriety to the breed and purchases would zoom. That fear was unjustified. There has been no rush by the public to purchase "Cavs," nor do I think my singing the glories of the King Charles will send registrations through the roof now.

Back in 1982, Roger Caras made a prediction in *A Celebration of Dogs* about the Cavalier King Charles. He commented that the then "unrecognized" breed was "a lead-pipe cinch for recognition." The breed was admitted to the American Kennel Club's Miscellaneous Class despite

The Norfolk Terrier, a mother's work never ends.

the objections of some fanciers who were afraid that any degree of recognition (particularly in the United States) would doom the breed and submit it to mass production and the "puppy milling" process. But acceptance into the Miscellaneous Class is hardly the first step to destruction for any breed. The AKC tries to provide a regular method of development that might result in recognition, and inclusion in the Miscellaneous Class is one such stepping-stone.

The situation in Canada and England is different. The dogs may be registered in both countries and are, in fact, fairly common in England and in British-oriented Ontario and British Columbia.

One way of saving something precious is to limit access to it. Access is most often limited via money—precisely, the lack of it. While no figures are available, it is clear to anyone who has worked with dogs that many Cavalier King Charles Spaniels live among the wealthy. In England, distri-

The Cavalier King Charles Spaniel, traveling in the best of circles.

bution of the breed is more stratified and egalitarian, as it is in Canada, but this is only recently so. In the U.S. discreet ads in *Town and Country* and other such journals testify to the exclusivity protectors of the breed wish to preserve.

These extraordinary measures will not stop the breed from finding a home in the hearts of many dog lovers, regardless of economic status. The real challenge for breeders and others concerned with the future of the King Charles is not to guard a well-kept secret, but to actively prepare for the surge in popularity that is sure to come.

What is it that is so special and endearing about this breed? It is not the fact that the rich frequently keep them, because "status buying" only takes a breed so far. Nor is it the breed's size—generally about 13 to 18 pounds (much less standardized than many other small breeds)—because Cavaliers can be found in city and country environments. They are not just "lap dogs." Rather, it is the delightful traits of this breed: pliability, willingness to learn, an attentive stance toward practically everything and everyone, high trainability and low excitability.

The Cavalier King Charles needs a soft touch in training, and they do

51

well if the trainer uses inducive rather than coercive techniques. Shyness can be a problem, but breeders are on the lookout for this, as well as for structural faults. For breeders, the biggest problem is not so much correcting the breed's few faults, but restricting breeding to the persons who will be fully dedicated and knowledgeable.

Cocker Spaniel

The Cocker Spaniel is the most popular breed in America. Its cousin, the English Cocker also has its fans and both dogs make pretty good city pets. Some say the "American" Cocker is no longer the sporting dog it was meant to be, while the English version is, and they are probably right. But since the Cocker won't be asked to hunt in most cities, the reduction in working ability is unimportant to most city owners.

The Cocker Spaniel, enduring American favorite.

The challenge is to find a Cocker with good temperament, and *here* is where the loss of sporting and hunting skills in both breeds may present problems. Generally a Cocker (of either type) that is closer to its hunting roots will be more tractable, trainable and pliable. The name "Cocker" comes from the breed's proficiency with woodcock. Naturally, city pigeons fascinate both breeds—they will attempt to "retrieve" them for you, and you must teach a tight heel and pigeon-proof your dog as described in the obedience section.

The small size of the "American" Cocker Spaniel appeals to many city owners. The grown dog will stand only 14 to 15 inches and weigh only 18 to 23 pounds, while the English Cocker is somewhat larger. These are near perfect size-ranges for many urban dwellers—especially those who prefer a medium-size breed.

The English Cocker is less popular in the U.S. than its cousin, so you will have to look harder for a reputable breeder. Breeders of this breed are interested in having their dogs preserve their hunting skills, so while you may find them highly trainable, you may have trouble finding a breeder who will sell you one for strict city life. If you can honestly promise that you will get the dog out of the city and back into its natural element—the fields and the woods—you can offer a balanced lifestyle that will suit most English Cockers, and their breeders. The "American" Cocker won't care as much about field-and-stream alternatives, as it has been experiencing modifications in breeding since the 1930s. In fact, some English Cocker Spaniel breeders are highly critical of the "American" Cocker Spaniel's modifications and consider the breed frivolous. I don't agree with this. I feel breeds have to change and adapt to changing lifestyles and tastes. While a dog should be close to its roots—as this usually means the dog will have more structural and mental integrity—some changes are for the better. My experiences with both Cockers is that they train well and seem to feel good in the city.

Dachshund

Dachshunds are Teutonic in origin: *dachs* for badgers, *hund* for dog. Most researchers believe that they are the descendants of German dogs bred to follow badgers underground. This was tough work, for a tough dog. They are good for city life. But don't let the cute factor get to you—train early and train hard.

Dachshunds are spry, active, a bit pushy, yet highly trainable. Many call them "sausage dogs" or "hot dogs," but if you see a Dachshund with its belly dragging on the ground, the dog is most probably overweight. Prevent this by exercising your puppy early and often.

A word about the "Doxy" temperament: The official standard says, "He should be clever, lively and courageous to the point of rashness, persevering in his work above and below ground, with all the senses well-developed." If that isn't a description of a city person, I don't know what is. Courage to the point of rashness is a desirable city trait, and the toughness of these dogs will enable you to move through the city with style. Read up on Doxys soon after obtaining one, so as to get the upper hand on your dog as soon as possible.

The English Cocker Spaniel, gentle companion of field and fireside.   C.M. *Cooke*

Dachshunds are constantly taking it on the chin concerning their behavior; they are often accused of being "naughty." There's no doubt about this, says Leni Fiedelmeier in her new guide to the breed, *Dachshunds.* "It is true that Dachshunds are stubborn," she confesses, but promptly provides a good reason: "They have to be. Being the smallest breed used for hunting, Dachshunds must be plucky and independent to do their job. This is the source of their obstinacy. But people pick them because they have irresistible charm . . . and they keep dreaming up new tricks. It is not at all easy to resist a Dachshund's innocent gaze after it has done something naughty or to scold it rather than laugh."

I have often had the urge to laugh rather than correct when dealing with Dachshund students in my professional training work in New York. If professionals often double over in laughter rather than double up on discipline with a Dachshund, just think of what owners must let them get away with. Think also of how many households Dachshunds are controlling and how many owners they have successfully trained!

Fiedelmeier is a strong advocate of early and consistent training for Dachshunds, and her own are beautifully behaved. While hers is a general care book, it emphasizes behavior and training as well. It is also very frank about the idiosyncracies of the breed, instead of just

The Smooth Dachshund, a model of self-assurance.   *Tauskey*

extolling the breed as if there could be nothing wrong with the dog being written about.

Besides the section on training, there are good treatments of raising Dachshunds, proper diet, sickness in the breed, history and grooming. The book opens with a few choice words, asking potential owners to consider their environments before acquiring a Dachshund. One major problem is stairs. "Dachshunds are simply not built for climbing stairs. They have poor . . . 'transmission.' Climbing stairs puts the Dachshund's spine under great strain, which can result in slipped or ruptured disks, often accompanied by partial paralysis." And if you think you will just carry the dog upstairs, think again—the regular size model weighs 20 pounds. You have to bend way over to pick up either size. If you live on the top floor of a walk-up, wake up: You shouldn't have a Dachshund.

German Shepherd Dog

Have you ever closed your eyes and envisioned the perfect dog? If you had the time, desire and expertise to pull it off, could you put in motion a breeding program to produce the dogs? And even if you could, would you dare to think that perhaps your dog someday would become the most popular breed in the world?

It may sound farfetched, but this has already been done. In the early 1900s Captain Max von Stephanitz, a retired German military officer, started his breeding program to produce a versatile herding and working dog. His dogs—the popular German Shepherd Dog—have been faithfully serving mankind ever since.

Most people think of the German Shepherd Dog as an old, venerable breed and are surprised to find it has been around less than a century. Captain von Stephanitz took a long, hard look at the motley herding dogs being used at the European farms of his time and set about incorporating into them the best characteristics of modern stock to produce the German Shepherd Dog we know today. He used Horand von Grafrath, a dog that would appear plain by today's standards, as his prototype. This dog had a strong, workman-like build and was highly intelligent. It was the intelligence bred into these dogs that made them the ideal workers that caught on around the world.

With the signing of the armistice in 1918, American soldiers returned from overseas with tales of the beautiful, intelligent German dogs they had seen. Strongheart and Rin Tin Tin were starring in silent pictures about this time, and suddenly the country went Shepherd crazy!

During the Depression, however, big dogs became a burden, and the popularity of the German Shepherd Dog waned. But as economic times got better, so did the demand for German Shepherds, and soon the breed was climbing the popularity list in America. (They have always been extremely popular in their native land.)

The German Shepherd Dog is first and foremost a working dog. It is used in seeing eye work, search and rescue work, police work, military work, hearing dog work and for many other specialized tasks. "Work" is this dog's middle name, and the German Shepherd handles these jobs without becoming pushy, neurotic or nervous.

German Shepherds seem to have a need to keep busy, probably because of their working heritage, and obedience training is a good outlet for them. Don't try to live with a German Shepherd without giving it early obedience training in a class or with a private trainer (and, please, unless you are a professional handler, skip the attack training altogether).

Health and temperament problems abound in German Shepherds, so it is imperative that you buy your dog from a reputable breeder who will guarantee that the dog won't be extremely aggressive or overly shy. A good

The German Shepherd Dog, loyal servant of mankind

breeder will have his stock screened for hip dysplasia (a congenital malformation of the hip joint prevalent in many large breeds) and guarantee that pups from these breedings should be clear of hip problems. Many dogs can have a degree of dysplasia that never bothers them until old age, if then. Other health problems include panosteitis (a self-limiting bone growth problem that runs its course by age two or three, but is nevertheless painful to the dog), gastrointestinal problems (especially pancreatis) and occasionally epilepsy.

Now that the Shepherd hazards have been presented, I'll tell you frankly that living with a German Shepherd is a unique experience. With full apologies to other breeds, I confess that I believe the relationship that develops between Shepherd and owner is close to my idea of perfection. A German Shepherd will return your love and trust tenfold, maybe more!

One Shepherd comes to mind that typifies many of the traits of the breed. I took care of Zanta during the years I was at New Skete Monastery, which is famous for raising and training German Shepherds and other breeds. Zanta was a West German import who had been working as a herding dog moving sheep to pasture every day and returning her flock to the barn where she and the sheep slept at night. When I got her, she was five years old and had never slept indoors. She did not understand English

57

and was used to running about 21 miles a day during her 12-hour working shift.

When she landed in America, like many immigrants, she was unemployed and didn't speak the language. I spoke to her softly in my broken German (always tagging the English commands onto the German ones) and started her training program. I ran with her on leash and then off. I could not provide sheep for her to herd, so I obedience trained her so she would have a "job." She gave me her full cooperation. She learned English in three weeks, got along with other monastery dogs and became a dog of great pride and dignity. She embodied the most valued traits of any dog, which are so strong in German Shepherds: poise, loyalty and unconditional love.

By selective breeding, the breed has become a talented and loving servant to mankind. German Shepherds are impressive dogs both in character and stature, a natural worker in any environment, including the city. But, some still object: "I don't think German Shepherd Dogs belong in a city and I would prefer never to place one of my puppies in such a setting!" One eminent breeder said this with such finality and seeming authority that I had to retreat. I wanted to tell her about German Shepherd Dogs who live and thrive in Berlin, Stuttgart, Hamburg, Cologne and many other large German cities and how Von Stephanitz himself envisioned the German Shepherd Dog as both a city and country creature, but her mind was made up.

Actually, Shepherds can and do live and thrive in big cities and always have—it just takes twice as much dedication, twice as much training and twice as much enthusiasm.

Your city Shepherd must be taken out at least five times a week and preferably daily for aerobic exercise. By this I mean—yes, you got it—you run with him on a leash for at least one-half to one mile per session with *no stopping.* Barring health problems such as dysplasia or panosteitis, it is essential that the Shepherd get sustained aerobic exercise, on a leash so that the dog is forced to keep trotting. The exercise should be at a trot since this is a trotting breed. This usually means a light jogging pace for most owners. It also means that the owner will have to train the dog to trot *on heel* since running often makes the dog forget itself and lunge, lag or generally act like a hooligan. Often, for city Shepherd owners, getting the dog exercised aerobically is contingent on teaching the dog to heel on trot—but, it has to be done. It is also best to take the interior of a city block to do the sustained running so that traffic lights do not cause you to stop.

Why not just leave the dog out into an enclosed area and let it run, if you can find one in a city? First, if the dog has a brain in its head, it will stop dead in its tracks for at least a few moments when it gets tired. The exercise is then most definitely not sustained. Any good conformation handler will tell you all about the benefits of prolonged, on-leash running or trotting. Letting the dog stop when it wants to is useless in terms of toning and other behavioral benefits. Big city Shepherds need sustained aerobic exercise—and the owner must make a commitment to that. If the owner is too old (or handicapped or too tired or too lazy, etc.) to get the Shepherd out, then a dog walker can be employed—even sustained walking is better than nothing.

The point to remember is you can't expect a herding breed like a Shepherd to graciously accept the confinement entailed in city living without some sort of release. Some may adjust, but most won't. Chewing, overbarking and even aggression are often linked to lack of sustained, exhausting exercise—a point some suburban and country owners of Shepherds might also bear in mind.

The big city owner of a German Shepherd Dog faces serious problems in terms of getting his or her Shepherd socialized. In many large cities, Shepherds are perceived as a threat and are often purchased for precisely that reason by persons who want a measure of security. The ensuing problems are well-known to trainers: the Shepherd overprotects the owner, lunges at everyone on the street, chews up the elevator man, mounts and mauls the doorman, and so on.

The key is early socialization—deliberately inviting all comers to pet and love the baby Shepherd before it grows up and is seen as a menace that nobody will socialize with. Big city owners need to place themselves in the flow of pedestrian traffic and gently keep pressure on the training collar so that the puppy Shepherd is "held" in place and should invite socialization. An excellent technique is the "Round Robin Recall," explained in *How to Be Your Dog's Best Friend.* This procedure helps build discrimination and poise in the Shepherd.

City Shepherds need early and effective obedience training, especially in heeling, the sit-stay (the stay must be absolutely rock-steady) and the down, including a long down (over five minutes—preferably a one-hour down) and an emergency down. Training a really well-behaved city Shepherd would be a challenge for even the finest competition trainers because the training environment is so full of distractions and challenges. But it is not impossible. Early, tight training commencing at age four months is essential. Unfortunately, for many city owners this often entails hiring a private trainer because most city dog training classes still do not accept young dogs. On the other hand, there is a greater chance of finding a KPT (kindergarten puppy training) class in a large city than elsewhere.

The big city Shepherd has to learn to think of himself as a small dog, for spatial dimensions in a big city are often extremely constrained. For instance, most Manhattan stores are very small, and if you want to take your dog in while you make purchases, he or she will have to be trained to literally turn on a dime to get out of certain aisleways, alleys and corridors. Any blind handler or search and rescue trainer can tell you that a good Shepherd, however large, can be taught to curl up, shrink up and otherwise condense space if necessary—they are that talented. If you are in the process of selecting a Shepherd for city life, pick a bitch or a small male, as size can be a difficulty—and any size Shepherd will look enormous in a big city when stacked up against Yorkshire Terriers, Llhasa Apsos and other breeds that predominate on the city streets.

Golden Retriever

"You can't go wrong with a good Golden" is a common statement amongst breeders, obedience trainers, guide dog trainers, TV commercial directors looking for canine models, groomers, boarding kennel proprietors and practically everyone in the dog fancy. Ten years ago the word "good" wouldn't have had to be added as a qualification, but, like every breed that has zoomed in popularity, Goldens have suffered at the hands of inept breeders out to make a fast buck.

No breed that leaps in popularity and in AKC registrations escapes this syndrome. A breed gets popular because it has traits that are desirable. But these traits are there only because they are bred in by good breeders— more accurately, *preserved* in the breed by those who love it. The quick-buck breeders just want to produce something that *looks* like a Golden and sell the dog to an unsuspecting and uneducated buyer. These people are not breeders; they are nothing more than *puppy pimps,* in my opinion. Sad to say, there will always be customers lacking in knowledge who will buy their dogs.

The Golden is certainly not at a point of serious trouble yet, but people who love the breed are concerned. Find, visit and get yourself interviewed by a reputable Golden breeder who has placed dogs in the city in which you live, or at least in a city like it. If you are new to this breed, ask to see the mother and father so that you can get an idea of how large your Golden will be. For some reason (it's probably the soft yellow coat) this breed is not perceived correctly by many first-time owners. They are suddenly shocked when the dog starts to grow in leaps and bounds.

All Goldens really care about is being able to be with their people. This is the reason they train so well. It is not because they are Einsteins. Rather, Goldens are less aloof than the Germanic breeds, such as the German Shepherd, and realize that if they obey commands and submit to training rituals they get to be around the people they love that much more.

This love of people works fully in the city-owner's favor. A Golden does not mind crowds. After all, someone might stop to pet him, and the more people there are the more chances he'll get to cash in. Almost every Golden I've known has one message that they are shouting from the rooftops, or in the case of the city dog screaming from the skyscrapers, and that message is *Love Me!*

Some people take this trait as a sign of weakness and there is a certain amount of "Golden-bashing" that has developed because of the popularity

The Golden Retriever, family friend second to none.

of this breed and its incredible success in the obedience ring. "Of course she got a high score, she has a Golden," is a common remark ring-side at obedience trials. A remark such as that demeans the Golden Retriever breed—as if they fit the "dumb-blond" stereotype type of dogs who will do anything for a quick squeeze. How silly we humans are to bring our culturally induced prejudices into dogs.

So, get your Golden—a *good* Golden, a soft, cuddly, eminently pettable Golden. Socialize early. Park the Golden on a city street in the heel position and just stand there, with a little upward tension on the lead to enforce the sit. Get ready, a crowd is going to gather.

The Maltese

Whether you frequent Park Avenue, Rodeo Drive, the Via Venetto, Regent Street, Bollor Street or the Champs Elysees, if you are walking or carrying a Maltese you have in your possession an international symbol of urban elegance and sophistication. In fact, of all my "favorites" this is the one breed most people do not associate at all with the countryside. If anything, the trite version of a Maltese owner is a blue-haired lady in a mink coat carrying (never walking!) her perfectly groomed Maltese, who of course has cute bows in its hair. Snob appeal is still a factor in Maltese ownership, and Nicholas Cutillo wrote, in his book *The Complete Maltese* (Howell Book House).

> The growth in the number of Maltese in the United States and several other nations over the past few decades has been astounding. There are, therefore, great numbers of newcomers to the Maltese family. These newcomers are charged with the responsibility of keeping the Maltese the same aristocratic little dog he has been for centuries. It would be tragic for the Maltese to go the way of some other breeds which have attained popularity.

The sentiments of the author may sound a bit extreme, but they are right on target. Popularity *is* the downfall of many breeds.

That said, the Maltese *is* the perfect city pet. Maltese do well in apartments, are easily paper-trained if not too much space is granted all at once and depending on the cut you decide upon, easily groomed. I said easily—not quickly. Your biggest decision will be the kind of coat you want your Maltese to wear. If you are the type of owner who cannot or will not devote time to grooming, keep the coat cut short for life. Even then, grooming will be necessary. If you decide to keep the dog in full coat and if you oil the coat, it will attract dirt and dust from the city street. Eye stain can be another problem and here you might be fighting heredity. Nicholas Cutillo says:

> Most authorities agree that heredity plays an important part in the amount of eye staining a dog will have. A heavy stainer is likely to pass on this condition to his or her get.

Like the Yorkie, Maltese suffer from the myth that they are difficult or impossible to housetrain. This just isn't so. In my opinion, it's the "cute factor" at work once again. Owners simply give these cute cuddlers too much space too soon, and then pay the price when the puppy can't figure out the maze of turns it must make to get back to the paper or to the desired area for defecation. You must enforce *The Evans Edict for Earning the Environment*, the seven-day, step-by-step plan outlined in the section on housetraining. And don't cheat! That marvelous Maltese must be in your arms, tied to you with a leash or in the room(s) he or she has earned.

There's nothing like the responsiveness of this breed to challenges— especially city ones. They are rarely sound-shy, don't avoid ground distractions like man-hole covers and have no problem with crowds. They can be

The Maltese, shimmering essence of style.

easily taught a tight heel with *very light* corrections on the training collar. They are a class act all the way, and rate high on my list of potentially perfect city dogs.

Welsh Corgi, Pembroke

I had extensive contact with Pembroke Welsh Corgis during my years at New Skete Monastery, where a consultant to the breeding program for German Shepherd Dogs tried unsuccessfully to "infiltrate" Pembrokes. The consultant claimed that Corgis were "little Shepherds—German Shepherds with their legs cut off."

Now, several of my close friends own Pembrokes, and I receive many for training. This is another low-to-the-ground, tough dog—the type I feel is very fitted for city life. This is the smallest of the herding dogs. The breed originated in Pembrokeshire, Wales, and the Queen of England has several. The "Pem" has a long and honorable history as a cattle herder, guard and companion of Welsh farmers, but will adapt anywhere with proper care (Buckingham Palace is certainly not a farm). An apartment probably won't resemble *either* location, but can still be a good home for a good dog.

The Pembroke Welsh Corgi, fit for a Queen—suited for city life. *Brown*

The Pembroke Welsh Corgi is small in stature only. He has big ideas about himself, just like the Dachshund. He wants activity so don't let the size fool you—four walks a day are going to be necessary, plus an off-leash walk whenever and wherever you can grab one (legally). Early training is a must.

The wonderfully pettable, soft coat requires no more than a weekly brushing to keep it in shape and remove dead hair, and other grooming needs are minimal. Eye contact with this breed is, quite simply, out of this world; they will look at you constantly waiting for instructions or affection.

Be careful about the "Corgi's" back—it is long and "slipped" discs can be a problem. It's not the dog for anyone who lives four flights up in a nonelevator building. They get to be too heavy to carry up or down the many stairs, so that compromise is ruled out. But the tail is docked, which makes this breed fine for buildings with revolving doors!

Poodle

Whether you are looking for a Toy, a Miniature or a Standard Poodle, this dog is truly a dog for all cities. You can choose from three sizes, all adaptable to city life, and you can choose from a rainbow of solid colors, including black, silver, blue, brown, apricot, red, cream and white. You can choose to keep your Poodle in a show trim or you can keep him or her in a pet trim. This breed offers the city owner and city seeker of a perfect pure-bred a wide scope of options.

The Poodle, in this case Miniature puppies, makes the ideal urban companion. *Shafer*

Poodles are easily trained and adapt well to city life. They are usually two steps ahead of their owners. They do not like depressed people so if you are one, go to a psychiatrist, not a Poodle. They have cheerful, sunny dispositions if not neurotically influenced by their owners and like the city and all the distractions. They love a party and they love interaction, the more the better.

Since Poodles are very clean and do not shed they make excellent apartment dogs. The smallest size, the Toy, is a great choice for singles, allergy sufferers and the elderly. The Standard, while my personal favorite, is a heftier dog who needs early training, especially on the "heel" command.

All Poodles, even the smallest, can be yappy watchdogs. You must teach your city Poodle to be quiet and sign off when you say, "That's enough!" Consult the section on overbarking and apply the techniques there. Poodles are self-elected guardians of any household they happen to be ensconced in and will not hesitate to bark their heads off for any reason—and you *must* control this trait.

Whether to keep the Poodle in a show trim or not is a personal decision. I personally prefer the Poodle *au naturel* to the full show trim. But then, I'm not actively involved in the show ring. Whatever trim you prefer, there is a grooming commitment in this breed that you must stick to.

A book I'd recommend is Mackey J. Irick's *The New Poodle* (Howell Book House), which originally appeared in 1951. A book that has been in print for 35 years must have something to say, and indeed this one does. It has some fine writing about the character of the dog:

> The Poodle is a gentleman with all the reserve, dignity and delicacy of feeling the word implies. . . . He makes up his mind about you in his world and very seldom changes his idea about your worth. From that time on, your moods and your commands are his sole concern in life.

Poodle owners will agree that these comments hit the nail on the head. And what about Poodle intelligence?

> We flatter ourselves when we say that Poodles are the most intelligent of all breeds. This is true . . . but the real difference in Poodle intelligence is, I believe, this: Whereas other dogs think in a doggy way, Poodles' brains react in a much more human fashion and one that we humans can better understand. Perhaps their 300 or more years of earnest effort to understand us have given them this quality of mind.

Portuguese Water Dogs

I can hear some readers saying right now, "He's really flipped. Now he's touting for city life a *water* dog." Actually, Portuguese Water Dogs do more than swim. They do, after all, live on land, and besides I'm not suggesting that you take the dog swimming as part of a fitness regimen. I *am* suggesting the "Portie" as a potentially perfect city dog—especially if your city lifestyle includes a second home or niche in the country or if you are the outdoors type.

In Portugal the dog is known as the *Cão de Água*, (pronounced Kown-d-ahgwa), "dog of the water." These seafaring dogs carried messages between ships, ship to shore or vice versa, and sometimes stood watch in the bow, barking warnings of dangers. In his homeland the dog has survived as a courier between fishing boats. The dog is brave—a main attribute for city life—and would not hesitate to dive into the sea to retrieve a broken fishing net or retrieve an object accidentally dropped overboard, including a human being. They are extremely loyal without being aggressive toward others. *You* will be the PWD's captain and your apartment will be the ship. I do not believe that taking away the water changes the responsiveness of the breed, nor its loyalty.

A headline in an April 1965 issue of the *New York Times* sums up the once-tenuous status of this breed on our shores: "Breed Brought Here in 1960 Now Numbers 19." Deyanne Miller was a moving force in saving the breed, which, though still rare, is now well established with a thriving club and newsletter and a cadre of dedicated enthusiasts.

The Portuguese Water Dog. Sturdy companion of sailors past and present. *Ashbey.*

This relatively rare breed has a book of its own, *The Complete Portuguese Water Dog* (Howell). The authors, Kathryn Braund and Deyanne Miller, are pillars of the Portie community, and it is due largely to their determination and the determination of many other lovers of the breed that the magnificent Cão de Água did not vanish from the face of the earth. There are excellent chapters on grooming (including some special techniques for the Portie), feeding, and the delightful Portuguese Water Dog trials. The book is impeccably researched, well written and honest about the dog portrayed. This is a fine book about a fun breed.

These dogs listen to you on their own terms; they aren't stubborn, but they do have a sense of humor. There is a certain naughty streak to this breed, and if you are the type of owner who cannot take a joke, then the Portie is not for you.

Teach your Portie to be quiet from an early age—they like to bark, but it is not an uncorrectable trait. There is little shedding with this breed, making life in an apartment easy. Be sure your Portie gets plenty of exercise each day—four walks is fine—and that, if at all possible, he gets a chance in the water from time to time. Cold doesn't bother the Portuguese Water Dog at all, and he is a fine choice for a northern city. Finally, early training is a *must*. You will most probably not be successful at home but will need to go to class or use a private trainer for a few sessions. These dogs can be tough, but tough dogs belong in tough places—cities.

Get out of town to the beach and if possible let the Portie get back to its element. One outing lasts for weeks, but go as often as you can and obey the leash rules. Just be careful if you heel by a pond with a young Portie. They do not care to "test" the water when they see it—they leap right in until informed through training that every puddle is not for swimming. Once I was training a Portie near the children's boat pond in Central Park. I turned to explain a training technique to the owner and the Portie, sensing my involvement elsewhere took the opportunity to heart. He ripped the leash out of my hand, dove into the pond, "rescued" some kid's plastic boat, dropping it nicely in front of him, and then returned to the heel position, mission completed. Shore to ship, ship to shore!

West Highland White Terrier

Westies are a tough, resilient sort with a good measure of bravery and spunk—traits needed for happy life in town. While the coat is coarse and easily cleaned, the main obvious fault is the care of that white coat.

During his narration of the Westminster dog show, Roger Caras always remarks, "The West Highland White Terrier *likes* people. They demand attention. When you are in a room with a Westie you will constantly be reminded of your good fortune." All Westie lovers reading this book are now nodding their heads.

Is this demanding nature obnoxious, you might ask? No, not if you teach an *early* down-stay. Use the techniques detailed in the obedience section and start teaching the down and stay commands as early as the fourth month. Westies learn quickly at an early age.

Want a cheerful, friendly dog tailor-made for apartment dwelling? This one may be for you. Most terriers, including the Westie, originated in the British Isles. The name "terrier" comes from the Latin *terra* which means, "earth." These "earthy dogs" were bred to go to the ground, scraping and digging if necessary to get to their prey. Apartment dwellers who have low-lying potted plants and procure a puppy may soon find that the plant is de-potted and used to satisfy that Westie love affair with *terra firma*. Obviously, if you bring any terrier into your home, elevate potted plants or get into hanging plants, pronto. While we're on the topic, be careful to check with your veterinarians as to which plants are poisonous to dogs and which are not. The best policy is to arrange living conditions so that your dog and your plants just can't interact.

The West Highland White Terrier, in a class by himself and he knows it.

While underground the Westie would alert the hunter that he had found the prey. Then, the earth could be dug and the prize bagged. The terrier was expected to bark its head off until the prey was discovered. This trait is bred in and your neighbors might not like it, so you must teach your Westie from an early age to be *quiet*. See the section on overbarking and apply the ground rules early.

Finally, although the breed can have a haphazard appearance, there is more to the grooming commitment than just keeping the coat white. The amount of time involved will vary depending on whether you are show-bound or want to keep your Westie as a pet. Westies are strong-boned and make excellent playmates for children, but some must be taught not to nip as puppies. In sum the West Highland White is a fabulous breed for the city.

Whippet

These are great city dogs. Whippets are one of the few Hound breeds that adjust well to city life (not that all hounds can't, but the challenge for, say, a Bloodhound is more pronounced than it is for this breed). If you like a slim dog that can learn to heel well, and can glide through tight city spaces quickly and easily, this may be the dog for you.

Besides, they're stylish—I don't normally endorse status-breeds, but let's face it, these dogs are *elegant*. They are easily trained, not hard to correct on heel, can be carried if necessary and have a short coat that is easily groomed and doesn't get dirty easily. They are not a breed that grabs the attention of many first-time dog owners who are looking for a heavy "cute factor" in a dog.

If you are trying to decide if a Whippet is the breed for you and your city, a good resource is Bo Bengtson's *The Whippet* (David and Charles, Inc.). Bengtson states in his introduction:

> This is not going to be one of those how-to breed books that use valuable space on "general care," which is basically the same in every breed of dog.... What concerns me are matters that pertain to the Whippet: its history, its breed standard, its modern development, its many different uses.

He should have added "its temperament," because he discusses this area brilliantly. Bengtson admits that when he first saw a Whippet, "I decided I would never have a dog like that." He considered them mousy-looking, shivering creatures. But he fell in love with the breed when he spotted an excellent specimen (Ch. Laguna Ligonier) at a show.

The book opens with a chapter on "liking Whippets," then moves into showing and judging, the various Whippet standards (the English standard is quite different from the American), the various jobs that Whippets do (lure-coursing, open-field coursing and racing, to name a few) and a section on the history of the breed.

I, too, used to think of Whippets as skinny neurotics—until I met some and read this book. What more could you ask of a breed than that it win new converts to its side?

Yorkshire Terrier

My client load is now about 20 clients. Five own Yorkshire Terriers. This is typical. I know these tots rather well at this point and like them very much. I see through the "cute factor" that enables them to bamboozle their owners into all sorts of spoiling and permissiveness. While Yorkies *are* cute, they are still, believe it or not, dogs, and potentially great city canines.

The Whippet, not just for the racetrack.   *Shafer*

A look at the breed's history helps one to see through the cute factor quickly. About 100 years ago, Yorkshiremen got together and began breeding a small, game terrier to help keep homes free of rats and even larger forms of rodents and vermin. This is another tough terrier whose ratting instincts can be converted nicely to holding its ground in the big, tough city.

You will have to decide on what kind of cut you are going to keep your Yorkshire in. If you opt for the show style, get ready for a substantial grooming commitment. You will have to oil and wrap the coat and perform all sorts of procedures that may drive you to distraction in a very short period. If you opt for the shorter cut, you will still have to have your dog groomed professionally on a regular basis and keep up the grooming at home. Your reward will be enjoyment of a beautiful dog.

Yappiness can be a problem, and you must teach your city Yorkie that silence is golden. This may be a small dog, but most of them have big ideas about themselves. The bark of these tiny tykes can rattle the rafters—and your nerves. If you don't want fellow tenants beating down your door, teach silence early on.

The Yorkshire Terrier, tiny in stature only.   *Dueben's Studio*

Because of the ratting instinct most Yorkshires are nuts about toys that squeak. They will try to "kill" the toy as soon as it is presented, and a certain amount of this play is perfectly fine. Be sure the squeak toy does not have a "squeaker" that can be detached and ingested. Be careful about tug-of-war games, as *you* will then be perceived as prey.

Be careful about where you purchase this breed. They are commonly presented to attract impulse buyers. In my opinion, you should never impulse buy anything other than an ice cream cone, certainly not a dog. Go to a reliable source.

Also, my apologies to sensitive Yorkshire breeders who will note that one of my photographic models in this book is an oversized Yorkie. I know this rankles some fanciers, as will the dog's tom-boy cut. But Bev Higgin's "Bunde" is literally a bundle of joy and a perfect city dog. His size is an attribute and my advice to Yorkshire breeders is to place your larger, tougher dogs in cities. The smaller models may be lost (or even crushed) in a crowd.

SOME BORDERLINE BREEDS

The following breeds may adapt well to city life, given proper selection and training, but they will require additional indoctrination and care.

Chow Chow

Sigmund Freud had one, as did his daughter, Anna. In fact I trained the late Anna Freud's Chow Chow. There is an old story about Freud and his Chow, whom he used to invite to "sit in" on his analytical sessions. His Chow was trained to go to the door and scratch when it wanted to relieve itself. The Chow rose in the middle of the doctor's session with a certain patient to do just this. Freud, who was bored with the patient's discourse, commented wittily, "I think he's bored with your talk." The patient did not laugh and prattled on. Freud listened, as all good analysts do. The Chow returned, scratching on the door for re-entry, having relieved itself. "I think he's decided to give you another chance," Freud commented, as his patient rattled on.

Chows are, in fact, great at giving people second chances, and their nobility and loyalty are legendary. They do not adapt very well to city life for several reasons.

First, they are notoriously one-mannish and life in a city automatically means interaction with more than one person. Secondly, Chows have deep in-set eyes and their peripheral vision is somewhat impeded. A Chow is best approached within the scope of its vision, which means direct, frontal approaches are best. One cannot always count on that being the case in a city where children will see a dog and run up from behind, or where passers-by will attempt to pet a cuddly Chow. Chows have a heavy "cute factor"—they are bear-like in appearance and the coat is super soft—but it is the Chow's nature to be reserved and discerning with strangers. In this case, the cute factor can backfire on both the dog and the owner.

I'm not saying that a Chow can't crack the city, but if you are in the market for a top-notch city dog, this breed is, in my opinion, borderline.

Giant Breeds

Few will argue that it is difficult to shelter and exercise a Great Dane, Irish Wolfhound, Kuvasz, Great Pyrenees, Mastiff or Bullmastiff in the city. These breeds fall into the borderline category, especially for the first-time urban dog owner or for anyone not able or willing to provide tons of exercise on leash. Remember the key words are *exercise on leash*. That means you are holding the end of the leash and you are running or at least jogging one of these giants. And that means that you do this at least once,

73

preferably twice a day. For a mile. Without stopping. Still with me? If you have this desire to exercise with your dog, it's quite possible that you can have a Great Dane in the city or any of these gentle giants. I have seen many Newfoundlands and Danes who adjust very well to city life as long as they receive their exercise.

Another factor to consider is that these guys have big appetites. Your food bill will be higher than with a dog of a smaller breed, and you will have to cart home larger bags of food, perhaps up the stairs of a walk-up (or at least shell out a nice tip to the delivery boy after each food delivery).

Coursing Hounds

These galloping breeds will need even more than running—they will need a chance to gallop at high speeds, and the direction they take will often be away from you and the sound of your voice. Breeds like the Borzoi (formerly called the Russian Wolfhound), the Greyhound or the Saluki have special needs that you might not be able to fulfill. Think seriously about this aspect with such dogs and when you see the phrase "coursing hound" in a breed description get out your running shoes at the same time you get out your checkbook. That said, I must say that I now have a client with two exquisite Borzoi who are exceptionally placid, like to gallop but will not die or even complain if their owner misses a day—but not several days. It can work, but it is difficult.

The Family of Bull Terriers

No responsible text written for owners of urban dogs can ignore the controversial question of "pit bulls" and their suitability for city life. There are several municipalities that have already specifically banned pit bulls— sometimes without even knowing what one really is.

In fact, that's a tough question because four breeds (and sometimes even the grumpy-faced but super-sweet Bulldog) get drawn into the controversy. The breeds most frequently referred to as "put bulls" are the American pit bull terrier, the American Staffordshire terrier, which are about equal in size, and the smaller Staffordshire Bull terrier. Then there is the round-nosed Bull terrier, sometimes brindle in coloration but usually white; the most popular representative of which is the "Spuds McKenzie" dog on Budweiser commercials. Most agree that this last breed has been gratuitously thrown into the controversy and is really not responsible for the damage and even death that has occurred. Not quite as many professionals feel that the American Staffordshire terrier is innocently enveloped in the controversy simply because it resembles the remaining two breeds. Still others feel that all four breeds, if bred correctly and raised well, will not be aggressive. I agree. The two main problems are (1) there is considerable interbreeding between the different breeds, much of it irresponsible; and (2) the *quality* of the bite delivered by these breeds *is* different from that of other dogs.

Even though these breeds do not lead the list of breeds that bite (German Shepherd dogs have that distinction), when a bite from a member of these breeds is delivered the dog clamps its powerful jaws down and holds on for dear life. The damage done to the animal or person being assaulted then is more serious than that caused by other breeds because the "pit bull" bite is totally uninhibited and the dog attempts to go deep beneath the skin of the victim into muscle. In sheer panic the victim usually attempts to wrestle away from the dog, which makes the dog bite down *harder.* Many of these dogs *like* to wrestle. This distinctive, but dangerous bite-power comes from the pit bull's background as a fighter of other dogs.

As I write, I have spread before me the front pages of three New York City dailies. Recently an off-duty cop was mauled by a pit bull and before that incident there were several injuries or deaths of children and adults. One headline proclaims that Mayor Koch wants the dogs banned. Another shows a snarling pit bull incarcerated at the ASPCA where owners are turning in their pit bulls—even pre-bite—because they are suddenly terrified of them. The legal battle is heating up. See Chapter 8, "Legal Lairs," for advice if you have a dog of this breed (or any breed) who is biting, and what your choices and responsibilities are as a citizen.

For the purposes of this section, let's address whether these dogs make good city pets. On many levels, they do. In general, they have short coats and do not need inordinate amounts of exercise. Despite rumors and newspaper headlines, and even despite the unfortunate incidents that have occurred by dogs who are *abberations* of these breeds, I do not feel they should be banned or that they are not acceptable for city life. They fall into my borderline category, for several reasons.

First, all four of these breeds have extremely powerful fore assemblies and if you do not train a good, tight heel early on, you are going to go for a ride. Secondly, as previously discussed, with the exception of the Bull Terrier and possibly the American Staffordshire Terrier, these dogs are not enamored of other dogs. There is no way you can avoid other dogs in most cities. Thirdly, whether we agree or not, banning pit bulls (that includes, unfortunately, lumping all four breeds together in the wordings of many ordinances) is becoming more frequent. How can you be sure that you will be legally allowed to own one in your town? Check with local authorities and if you hear even a whisper about such a law, seriously consider whether you could move. It might come to that, or you would have to place the dog elsewhere.

DEFINITE NO-NO BREEDS

If you turned to this section first thinking you would find a list of breeds to avoid, or if you are a breeder worried that I will suggest your breed should or should not live in a city, I will have to disappoint you. The fact is, after much reflection, training experience and consultations with other trainers I have to say that there are *no* breeds that should *categorically* not be in the urban environment.

The reasons for this statement are several. First, I have had direct training experience with too many breeds that would seemingly *not* do well in a city—large breeds needing tons of exercise, breeds with a propensity toward aggression, small breeds that can be easily trampled underfoot— and, given the proper care and training, these potential (or actual) "problem dogs" have shaped up nicely.

Just as human beings of all ethnic backgrounds and races inhabit cities, so can almost all dogs. If we start saying this or that breed shouldn't be in an urban environment, what results are owners who start making excuses for bad behavior on the basis of breed and ship the dog off to the suburbs or to the countryside where the bad behavior will most likely simply continue. It is impossible for me to imagine that a dog would have a particular problem with a particular town, although I've heard this as an excuse from clients many times over. "He doesn't like the noise in New York, it makes him shy" or "He Can't take the rain here in Vancouver and won't walk in it" or even "Tippy doesn't like Chicago's wind." Why not try to acclimate the noise-shy New York dog? Why not get the Vancouver dog a raincoat and teach him to heel? *If* it is really true that the Chicago dog can't take the Windy City, then get him a stylish windbreaker. The point is, *don't make excuses.* As trainer Jack Godsil used to say, "Train, don't complain."

Too often these excuses are simply psychological smokescreens for a lack of dedication on the part of the owner to securing training and working on problems. The mythology that the countryside is the "best" environment for dogs is still, unfortunately, quite strong in the public mind. *"All he needs is a good country home."* Yes, and a little education, and if you train the dog, he can probably stay in town, with you, happily ever after. If we start adding breed type to the excuse list, a lot of city dogs are going to be out on the streets or in shelters.

In penning this chapter I realize that it is rife with opinions about favorite city breeds, borderline breeds, and even the opinion that there are no forbidden urban breeds. But at least they are the opinions of a city trainer who consults owners and trains dogs each day—and has seen the progress that can be made.

Much more important and influential than the environment is the *love of the owner,* and this I have seen denied dogs who are having difficulties in town and for whom the "solution" looks like the countryside. Yes, there will be everything in the countryside for that dog, I tell my clients when they bring this up. There will be lush fields where he can leap and play, there will be fresh air and there will be trees and flowers and maybe even a stinky fish to roll in. There will be many pleasures there, *but there won't be you.* There won't be your love and concern. Even if the dog finds a country home complete with a loving owner, that owner will be a secondhand owner and he or she won't be *you. Your* love is more important to your puppy or dog than the fact that he "has" to live in a city. You are the center of that dog's world, and if you could interview him he would tell you he doesn't care if he lives in Vermont or Vancouver, Peoria or Pittsburgh—as long as he can be with *you.* I believe that this desire to please, to bond, to be with you lies in the deepest recesses of your dog's heart. The love in the heart of your dog can enrich yours so much—and the love of others is where enrichment for the heart comes from, not the other way around. (I remember that line from *The Wizard of Oz* when the Wizard is presenting the Tin Man with his long sought-after heart, "And remember, my sentimental friend, that a heart is not judged by how much *you* love, but by how much you are loved by others.") How can you deny your puppy or dog the opportunity to show the love of his heart just because of where you live? See why I say there are no no-no breeds? It would be silly to say that there are, when, just as in human relationships, love can conquer all.

Just remember that when I say "love" here I mean honesty, understanding, compassion, education and training for a being of a species quite different from your own. But whoever said love was easy, or simple?

6

Legal Lairs

Y OU CANNOT OWN A DOG in Peking. It's also illegal in the capital of Iceland and on Roosevelt Island, part of the city of New York. Your city could be next. I'm not kidding, either. Since you're reading this book, you're probably a dog lover and may find it difficult to believe that there are people in this world who do not like dogs and would just as soon legislate them right out of existence—or at least out of town.

Dog owners get upset about proposed legislation that will interfere with what they perceive to be their "right" to own a dog. Let's get one thing clear: dog ownership is not a defined "right," it is a *responsibility*. Nowhere is that responsibility heavier than in an urban area.

Let's begin with a piece of legislation that is probably tucked away in the top drawer of your desk—your lease. Reading mine over, it says that I have no right to have a dog in this studio and if I try to, the landlord can kick me out. Landlords can claim that dogs do damage, create disturbance, soil the hallways and bother tenants who don't like dogs. By not allowing *any* pets at all, the potential problems are nicely avoided. Is it a cruel power-play on the part of the landlords? You bet it is.

Since housing is so short in many cities, many people look for a city apartment and, once they've found one with a reasonable rent, hang on to it for dear life. Most cities have some form of rent control or rent stabilization that keeps the rent from skyrocketing each year. If a tenant leaves an apartment, the landlord is usually free to raise the rent, at least to some degree. You'd think landlords would value stable, rent-paying tenants but such souls are actually a nuisance to many landlords who wish they (and their dogs) would just move out so that they could hike the rent. Landlords will use every ploy they can think of to empty an apartment they want to charge more for, and this is where your pet comes in.

If you have sneaked your pet into your life, ignoring the no-pet clause and just hoping that Larry Landlord will not put up a stink, or if you think you have a wonderful, friendly, open, even loving relationship with Larry Landlord and he gave you a verbal promise that you and Tippy will not be thrown out into the street—you might be in trouble. You should have gotten it in writing, as they say. Because Larry Landlord is going to turn into Scrooge someday and tell you to get rid of that dog or move. (Watch: he'll probably do it on Christmas Day, too.)

Lest my cynicism get you down, here's some constructive advice. It may be possible to get that no-pet clause eliminated from your lease, even if you've been sneaking Tippy in and out of the building for years. If you are presently looking or plan to look for an apartment and want to have a dog, try these tips:

- Be absolutely honest with your landlord. Don't try to hide that Great Dane or, for that matter, that Maltese. Tell the landlord you have a pet and *in the same breath, within the same sentence* offer to pay a security deposit to cover it. Do *not* say, "to cover any damage it may do." Just offer.

- If you have had training for your dog, ask your trainer to give you a letter stating that you have attended class or had private lessons. Have the trainer type, not write, this note on their professional stationery. I do this often for my New York clients and they tell me it helps.

- You may want to ask the landlord if he would like to meet your dog and see firsthand how well-behaved he or she is. But ask. Don't just trot Tippy into the real estate office and expect the red carpet to be rolled out.

- Don't beg or snivel. Present the facts as they are and emphasize that you are a responsible pet owner. Don't try to emotionally sway your landlord. Remember some non-dog persons already consider all dog lovers as *a priori nuts* so emotional appeals will just make you look unstable.

- If the landlord agrees, you must get the clause struck out of the lease itself and initialed by the landlord. Bring the lease along with you so that if the landlord agrees it can be taken care of immediately. After all, the landlord might change his mind later! It's even better to have an actual waiver typed out and ready to sign. For this, you'd have to consult a lawyer in your state for the actual wording.

LOOKING FOR LOOPHOLES

What do you do if you're already ensconced in a building and acquire a pet? Even here, there are measures that can be taken but get ready for a fight. You will need a lawyer and while your case is being fought, you will have to be very careful in what you say (or do) to your landlord, about your rent payments and about the behavior of your dog. Your lawyer can probably use a letter from a trainer as part of an arsenal to build a better defense. Procure one fast.

The lawyer will most look for legal loopholes in the lease, some kind of not-so-careful or inclusive wording that will help your cause. However, you must find a lawyer experienced in such litigation proceedings, so search around via your veterinarian, trainer or local humane society officials. You can also contact The Animal Legal Defense Fund, 205 East 42nd Street, New York, New York 10017.

While I do not deny that problem pets exist—I see them every day—it's obvious that no-pet clauses are simply for the convenience of landlords and often used to force pet owners out of their apartments so that rents can be raised. The only good thing I can say about them is that when threatened with eviction, many dog owners with problem dogs finally *do* decide to deal with the problem behavior once and for all. That's when they call me. It's too bad it has to come to that, and it's too bad it *can* come to that but that's why such laws get passed—or at least one of the reasons. It all keeps coming back to responsible dog ownership.

CRUELTY

Yesterday I saw a homeless woman pushing her shopping cart full of plastic bags containing fabric, beer cans and newspapers saunter along First Avenue. She is a fixture in this neighborhood. She does not beg. She collects soda cans and turns them in for the refund. Then she buys booze and drinks it on the stoop of a vacant building. She has a dog. It is attached to the shopping cart. She feeds it scraps she finds in the street or goes into the corner deli and asks for handouts. They will often give her the butt end of a ham or remnants of roast beef.

She is abusive if you try to give her money or interact with her in any way. She is obviously mentally ill. She lights up only when another dog owner passes with a dog, but she will not talk to the owner, only to the dog. She likes it when her dog relates with another dog. But other times I have seen her strangling her dog, slapping it across the face repeatedly and twice, kicking it. Twice I have reported her to the police. Someday they will take the dog away from her and to a local shelter. Maybe someone will adopt it. Probably not. And it will be euthanized. And so it goes in so many cities and towns.

You *can* report instances of cruelty and you should. But get ready. Most law enforcement agencies attach a very low priority to such calls and even formal, written reports don't get much action. But anti-cruelty laws are on the books and whether they get enforced or not depends on how many calls come in and on how vociferous the callers are when they call. Depending on the enforcement structure in your town, the police might not be the people who handle such cases, but if they don't, they will tell you who does. Follow through. Chances are, somebody else has filed a similar complaint and some cities have a set limit of complaints after which investigation begins, but not before. Your call could be the one that initiates some real action. It's also important to understand the mentality of those who batter dogs.

Battered Dogs

What makes a person hit a dog? Why do some dog owners handle disputes with their dog by chasing the dog through the house, pinning it and pummelling it? What causes a man to press a lit cigarette against his dog's nose? Why does one dog owner handle bad behavior through training and another through abusive force?

A recent issue of *Time* was devoted to "private violence"—child abuse, wife beating and rape. The editors might well have included pet abuse, but at least they mentioned it. They note that once family violence becomes a way of life, there is little family members can do on their own to stop the brawling. Outside help is almost always necessary. Richard Gelles, a sociologist at the University of Rhode Island, maps out the "grim ecology of a violent family": "The husband will beat the wife. The wife may then learn to beat the children. The bigger siblings learn it's O.K. to hit the little ones, and the family pet may be the ultimate recipient of violence."

When it comes to dog abuse, there is, indeed, a "grim ecology" that can often be traced to the way the abusive dog owner saw his or her parents handle the family dog, and the concepts of discipline for dogs the parents taught—not necessarily verbally but usually through example. It's common for veterinarians or trainers to hear, "Because that's the way my mother handled dogs," when they witness abusive handling and question it. But usually, the abuse is private, and kept private deliberately.

Chronic abusers include dog-fight enthusiasts, where elements of sadism are mixed with "sport." Here the abuse is public, yet private—and anyone who would not approve of the proceedings is eliminated from attendance. Porno movies sometimes feature dogs and they are often cajoled into service and then discarded. These are organized instances of abuse, but most abuse takes place on a more individual and subtle level.

Violence against dogs is not reserved for the poor and underclass. And since patterns of handling dogs are often inherited, within a family of four children four potential dog handlers (and abusers, if they have been improperly educated) have been spawned. The problem escalates in this way, and in an area as full of myth as handling dogs, there are few educational efforts that can combat family folklore.

Animal shelter workers can tell you all about dog abuse. They are the sociologists of the dog fancy and know more about this area than most breeders, trainers or even veterinarians who treat the victims of such abuse. One worker commented:

I can spot the dog beaters before they enter the shelter," said one shelter worker in an affluent Southwest Florida city populated by elderly retirees, "and the way I do it is to watch them when they get out of the car to bring the dog into the shelter. Watch when they are *alone* with the dog—or think they are alone and unobserved. They'll yank the leash cruelly, drag the dog to our door, sometimes give the dog one last smack for old times sake. But when they enter the shelter office and close the door behind them, they are sweet as can be—petting the dog, moaning over losing it. "We have to move," they say, but the truth is they beat the dog and the dog won't listen to them.

I asked this worker if these same people sometimes ask for a new dog. "Oh sure, they come back later and say they had a change in moving plans. But if I have the slightest suspicion about someone, we won't make the placement. They just want another dog to abuse. They're locked into a trap. They'd beat kids if they had them, but in our community most of the kids are grown and gone."

Veterinarians, too, often see the victims of abuse. "A client will bring in the dog with a fractured rear leg and say the dog was hit by a car," said one veterinarian, "but radiographically the story doesn't check out. Fractures from cars don't look like that. I feel I have to tactfully confront the client with this and suggest help, and I do this while I still have custody of the dog—they are more dependent on me then and more willing to listen." If a client decides to confess abuse, the veterinarian can then suggest help for placing the dog elsewhere.

The most common type of violence against dogs is hitting the dog for not obeying a command. The most common weapon is the rolled up newspaper, but other objects can be used. In over a decade of training dogs, I've heard some interesting responses when I ask, "Do you discipline your dog for bad behavior and, if so, how?" Objects used to discipline have included belts, horse-training whips, leashes, large wooden spoons, rolling pins, hair brushes, brooms, umbrellas, coat hangers, spatulas, marbles, BBs and even chairs. The fact that the dog can easily develop a fear of any such object seems lost on such souls. "Well, what am I supposed to do?" they reply when criticized. "I don't want to hurt my hand." This is a wonderful juncture, actually, because the client has openly asked for help and is ready for change. I then launch into a description of how a dog learns, how to correct a dog correctly, the difference between correction and punishment and, if truly needed, teach humane, safe discipline techniques like the ones in this book.

Other common types of abuse include chasing the dog around the house when it has stolen an object and then "netting" the dog with a volley-ball or other type of net, or trapping the dog in a corner and then beating it. Unattended children often spend whole afternoons teasing the family pet and invite other children over to participate in the fun. When they have worked the dog up into an aggressive response, they either back off or hit the dog for growling. Among some adolescents and even some dog owners who would classify themselves as adults, getting the dog high on marijuana or giving it alcohol is more common than most of us know. Blowing marijuana smoke into the dog's face ("You have to exhale anyway," one kid told me, "so why waste the smoke?") is easy, as is encouraging a dog to drink sweet wine or other alcoholic beverages. Despite the fact that the dog doesn't like the smoke and hates the taste of the booze, he will "perform" out of love for social interaction.

Abuse is not always so blatant. Subtle forms of violence against dogs are a problem also. Nagging can be a form of abuse. The dog is nagged all day: do this, do that, no, no, no, stop it, stop it—and sooner or later the owner hauls off and hits the dog. Training is the answer, and well-timed and properly delivered obedience commands will stop the vicious nag-hit-console cycle. Even the most abusive owners "make up" with their dogs after beating them. The dog, benign and loyal as he is, accepts the apology and the cycle starts again. All the while the owner knows he or she has a wonderful ace in the hole: the dog *can't talk* and nobody will know about the abuse unless they confess it (usually to a trainer or veterinarian) or someone sees it. Or so they think.

A trained observer *can* detect dog abuse if he or she knows what to look for. First, try to observe anyone you suspect of abuse when they are alone with their dog. Next, engage them in casual conversation about the pet and somehow bring up behavior problems—perhaps even creating a few you have with your own dog. You can ask for advice on the problem and very often the suspect will detail the course of action that should be taken. If the reply indicates physicality that is *not* the result of misinformation or a lack of education, but seems to have violent underpinnings, you have cause for concern. If you hear a dog screaming continually or hear low sustained growls and the laughter of children, you can deduce that some abuse is going on. Since families with a history of private violence among themselves also frequently abuse their dogs, they are prime suspects. Finally, you can ask the children of the family. Engaging a child in casual conversation can expose such problems. If you are a professional trainer or specialist, you should try to include children in your initial behavior case history interview. I always do, and often receive valuable information that I would have to dig hours for if the children were not present. In one case a nine-year-old child piped up with, "Because daddy kicked her," when I asked why the family's Cocker Spaniel was limping. The spontaneity of the reply precluded all pretense, and the father simply looked down at the ground. But we had made a breakthrough, and the Cocker has a happy life now.

Dog trainers and other specialists can often recognize dog abuse just from the tone or "feel" of a discussion with a dog owner. I reported on one such instance in *How to Be Your Dog's Best Friend:*

> The man wanted to know if he could train his dog to the down in response to a cough. The gentleman explained that he wanted "total control" over his dog, and that he didn't want to have to bother giving the dog a command, but thought that an "ahem-type" cough should do the trick. He then demonstrated by clearing his throat suggestively. He never praised the dog physically or verbally. "My family had plenty of dogs," he explained, "and none of them needed to be hugged every two seconds." The children in the family sat rigid throughout the interview, contributing little. The wife contradicted the husband at one point and he shot a silencing glance at her, clearing his throat in the same suggestive manner!

Here is a man who can silence his wife and children just by clearing his throat and wants to extend the practice to his dog. As it turned out in this case, the man was vocally and physically dominant with the dog, and corrected his handling once educated, but in another few months the situation could have easily escalated into abuse.

The dog's reactions are also a clue, especially the eyes. Does the dog hold its head down, with the neck seemingly pushed into the shoulder/withers area? Does the dog cast continual upward glances, and then quickly look down? What happens when you suddenly move to pet the dog on its forehead—does the dog flinch downward? Does the dog hold its tail tucked, even flattened against the inner belly? Be careful, however, for all these reactions can stem from genetic causes and the handling of the dog may be fine.

Discipline for dogs *is* occasionally necessary, and even humane techniques involve some *acting* in order to make an impact on the dog. Dogs with serious behavior problems need structured discipline, and if you see someone correcting their dog, try to ascertain what is *acting* (but with a serious purpose) and what is *abuse*.

If, after investigating the situation, you think you have a solid case of abuse, don't hesitate to call the proper humane officials. You may or may not be able to make an anonymous complaint, depending on how the agency handles abuse reports. The officials will check out your complaint, and often just one interaction with humane officials can shame abusers into seeking proper training or giving up the dog before irreparable damage is done. Remember, the abuser thinks nobody knows, and the dog can't tattle—an interaction with humane officials or the law breaks open the private world of abuse and tells the abuser clearly: "We don't know what your inner problems are, and if you want we can tell you where to get help for them, but we will not have this dog abused."

Finally, remember that all dog owners, technically, have the potential to become dog abusers. There isn't a dog owner on earth who hasn't at some point lost his or her temper with a dog. Many professional trainers meditate for a few minutes before commencing *any* training session, reflecting on what they will or will not do, how they will correct the dog, when they will end the session, etc. If you have a problem that is leading you to strike out at your dog, seek professional training *and* one-to-one counseling. If necessary, board the dog until you feel you can handle the situation. When you witness what you think may be abuse, report it if necessary, but remember too that the owner probably dearly loves the dog, but has a set of inner conflicts that are taken out on the pet. Except for the criminally insane, such owners readily reform with training for the dog and perhaps treatment for themselves. Patience isn't inherited, it's learned, and patience, education and compassion are the keys to reducing the number of battered dogs.

DANGEROUS DOG LAWS

New York is currently embroiled in "pit bull" discussions—whether or not this breed should be banned from the city. The trouble is that nobody can define the "breed" and any enacted legislation doesn't look like it would stand up to court action anyway. So now, because of heavy lobbying by dog trainers, breeders and others, "dangerous dog" laws are getting more attention than breed-specific legislation.

If you think this is just a New York City problem, you are wrong. Sooner or later the subject of dangerous dog legislation will crop up in your city and you'll have to be prepared—especially if you own a breed that is perceived to be "dangerous." While I personally think that "pit bull" dogs and their relations do not do well in a city environment, for reasons having to do with proximity to other dogs and spatial dimensions in urban life, *I do not support any breed-specific legislation.* Such laws are almost always overturned when challenged in court and legislation of this type has an escalating effect. It is too easy to simply add the names of more breeds perceived to be threatening to city citizens to the existing legislation.

Breed-specific legislation penalizes responsible owners of the targeted breeds, and bans are difficult to enforce and costly to taxpayers.

In New York City on October 29, 1987, trainers, breeders, AKC President Ken Marden and scores of others beseiged City Hall to testify against breed-specific legislation. At the meeting, Councilman Maloney stated that she was no longer in favor of breed-specific legislation and would now support a law aimed at all dangerous dogs. But at this writing, the Honorable Edward Koch, mayor of the city of New York, stands resolutely in the way. He is for breed-specific legislation and refuses to be swayed. The hearings are nearly complete and by the time you read this something will have been decided here—or you'll be too involved fighting the same proposed legislation in your city to care. Here is a statement issued by the Society of New York Dog Trainers, which reflects my sentiments exactly:

> Because of the national attention given to the recent wave of dog attacks resulting in fatalities, some communities are proposing legislation to ban specific dog breeds, primarily American Pit Bull Terriers, American Staffordshire Terriers, Bull Terriers and those breeds (and mixed breeds) that appear to be similar in type.
>
> The Society of New York Dog Trainers does not believe that breed-specific legislation will afford the community complete protection from dog attacks. Rather, we believe a nondiscriminatory "dangerous dog law" is more logical and will serve the entire community far more effectively.
>
> As a group of professionals dealing with dogs and dog behavior every day of our lives, we would like to make you aware of a large portion of the population's love for their companion animals. It is estimated that 50 million American families live with one or more dogs. The companion animal has entered society with full "member-of-the-family" status, enriching the lives of millions of people with their loving devotion, their ability to ward off loneliness while adding a touch of nature and a great deal of pleasure to the millions of devoted dog lovers.
>
> We believe the current rise in dog attacks has been caused by human irresponsibility and ignorance, animal abuse, dog fighting involvement, neighborhood gangs promoting "macho-status" and drug-related activities. Banning one or more breeds will not protect the public from dog attacks. As professionals involved with dog behavior, the members of the Society of New York Dog Trainers support the concept of a nondiscriminatory "dangerous dog law" and would like to suggest as a model law, Senate Bill No. 5301 recently enacted by the state of Washington. It is our conviction that this law is logical, enforceable and effective.

The Washington state law is indeed a well-devised, consise piece of legislation. Dogs that are defined as dangerous are restricted to enclosed yards under, essentially, pain of death; dogs that are potentially dangerous are also targeted. The one problem with the law is that it doesn't address the problem of what to do to prevent a "potentially dangerous" dog from biting. Any city thinking of tightening up dangerous dog legislation should apply the law of the land to *all* dogs, but find a way to target the dogs who *might* bite soon. There should be a provision that allows citizens to report a *potentially* dangerous dog before it hurts someone. In New York, a dog that bites someone is reported to the Bureau of Animal Affairs. All that needs to be done is to expand this provision to allow citizens to report animals that they perceive to be dangerous. The bureau can then notify the owners (if known) and, as it does with dogs who have already bitten someone, let them know the consequences of *existing* laws. Owners with potentially dangerous dogs might then be motivated to seek out training so that their dog doesn't progress to biting seriously. Behaviors that could be reported are snapping, lunging, growling, snarling, baring teeth, being encouraged to bite by owners and chasing people. Even if the owner decided to do nothing and lets the dog continue to engage in such behaviors, notification by the authorities, even if repeated and ignored, could be used effectively in court to get the owner fined and the dog impounded and humanely destroyed. Either way, responsible dog owners would still gain, as would the public.

STOOP TO CONQUER!

I rhapsodized about New York's "pick up or pay up" law in *The Evans Guide for Housetraining Your Dog.* Maybe I rejoiced too soon. Recent signs are that there is considerable backsliding on the law, which at first was a success. The canine waste law here is nine years old, and while still basically obeyed, it is ailing.

Cleaning up after your dog is probably the law of the land in your city and, in my opinion, if it's not, it should be. Pedestrians should not have to hurdle heaps left by your dog, and enactment of strict laws makes for better public attitudes toward dogs in general. If you are a dog lover I advise you to agitate and demand that your public officials enact and enforce canine waste disposal laws. Don't wait for the antidog forces to agitate for such a law—beat them to the punch and do it yourself. Believe me, the benefits to dogs all over your city will be immeasurable.

You can try to cheat, I suppose, but the price might be high. In New York, the fine is now $100 and in Toronto it is $1,000! That's a heavy price to pay for cheating on the law and picking up is really easier than paying up. A good method appeared in the *Cornell Animal Health Newsletter,* complete with diagram:

Cleaning up your dog's act is the law in a growing number of communities, as well it should be. Owners who refuse to clean up after their pets are the major cause of much antidog sentiment—and that is as it should be too. The reasons are not just aesthetic: the Centers for Disease Control estimate that from 10 to 30 percent of public playgrounds and parks are contaminated with *Toxocara canis* eggs, the eggs of the common dog roundworm found in the feces of infected dogs.

There has been a proliferation of utensils to help you comply with the new clean-up laws, but many of them have limitations that discourage use. Some are so cumbersome they distract from the pleasure of a walk or a jog with the dog. Even those that are compact enough to carry easily present a different sort of problem: how to clean the tool for carrying it home, and when home and where to store it?

The solution to these problems is actually very simple and even more convenient than the rolled-up newspapers one often sees. A few lightweight, medium sized plastic bags take up no space in a pocket or handbag and can be effectively used by anyone who can bend over.

The technique is equally simple, as the illustrations show. Simply slip the bag over one hand (like pulling on a thumbless mitten). With your hand thus protected pick up after the dog. With the other hand, turn the bag inside out, enclosing the collected material and removing the bag from your hand in one simple, sanitary motion. The top of the bag can be tied shut or closed with a twist-style strip. If it is necessary to carry the bag for some distance, remember to come equipped with a paper bag as well, into which you can drop the plastic. Practice might make perfect, but not on Rover's time. Try it out at home on an orange or clump of potting soil.

Commissioner Howard Stern, in charge of the parks of New York City, has deduced that "you can legislate cleanliness." He's also been liberal enough to let dogs go off leash—although owners must clean up—before 8:00 A.M. in Carl Schurz Park. Dog owners should respect such liberality, but don't expect it in every town.

The worst abuse of the canine waste law I've ever seen was when I witnessed a domestic in full maid uniform pick up after her dog (actually, her employer's dog) and then ceremoniously deposit the waste in a Post Office mail drop box! Another incident involved a man who was walking his Maltese on Park Avenue. I observed with great satisfaction as the man stooped to scoop his pet's refuse into a plastic bag. Now, here was a person who really respected the law, I thought. But then the man threw it into the gutter.

Neighbors who want dog owners to pick up or pay up often can't supervise every dog in the area, and are reduced to ploys that make it difficult for canines to defecate, urinate, squirt, anoint or otherwise defile their efforts at gardening or conservation. Dog owners should respect such efforts and if you train your dog using my "Either-Or" heeling methods you will be able to control your canine's eliminations. The way to teach your dog respect for signs that warn dogs away is to teach a strict heel and allow the dog only occasional "Okays" to eliminate. See the section on heeling for more on this.

Most cities start off with a "nice" approach to the problem of canine waste. This is an old sign in New York. It said "please." Nobody obeyed the law.

So the city got tough. The sign is self-explanatory. Compliance now runs at about 85–90%. I wonder why . . .

Toronto has signs that circumvent Canada's bilingual problem with absolutely clear drawings. The fine for breaking the law here? Try a cool $1000. Canadians like cleanliness. Of course you can choose to cheat and ignore the law and watch signs like this one on the right go up all over town.

For those of you sick and tired of irresponsible dog owners allowing their dogs to urinate or defecate on your plants, trees or shrubs, here is some defensive advice. An inexpensive way to dress up a tree pit is with wildflowers. Wildflowers resist urine and feces better than some domesticated varieties. They are tough. Plus, some wildflowers such as asters, wild petunias, chicory, black eyed susans, sunflowers and spotted knapweed send out a smell to dogs that says, "keep away." Once established, these wild flowers will carry on year after year since they self-seed. In New York, seeds are available at the New York Botanical Gardens or at most florists and can be planted in the summer or fall. Other cities will have seeds available at similar outlets. Fight back with flowers and force dog owners to pick up or pay up!

Remember, as of August 1, 1985, more than 2,000 New Yorkers had been ticketed under the New York City Canine Waste Law. Pick up or pay up!

PLAY GROUPS

If you think the $100 fine in New York for failing to clean up after your dog is a stiff regulation, you'll probably be disappointed to find out that letting your dog run off leash costs $50. The concept of play groups is controversial, and I don't want to advise you to break your community's laws. On the other hand, plenty of cheating goes on and in Manhattan early morning and evening play groups are quite common in city parks.

Owners get together and let their dogs off leash to romp around and play. The dogs love it, and it vents off a lot of steam for many of them and gives them a kind of exercise and socialization that just can't be approximated on leash. There are some play groups in Manhattan that are more than a decade old, and the members swear that no leash law is going to stop them.

In some cities officials have made quiet, off-the-record compromises with this reality. For example, it was recently revealed that Commissioner Howard Stern had quietly issued orders that off-leash dogs under reasonable control not be ticketed before 8:00 A.M. But the policy is subject to change, and it probably will if irresponsible dog owners get into the act. The hint here is you may want to join an *early morning* play group to avoid a fine. You'll also be less of a bother to nondog persons.

In my opinion, a better place for a play group is a nook or cranny such as the kind I suggest in the chapter on training spaces. If you can find an area that is not being used by anybody else when you get there you might be able to stake your claim, have your play group and get out without too much trouble. Another solution, especially for evening play groups, is to meet at a school playground. These are often enclosed and the children will be at home. *Never* let your city dog run free around strange children

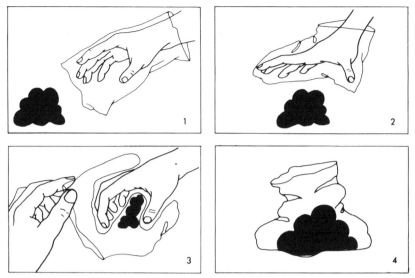

A simple way to clean up after your dog: 1. Slip bag over hand. 2. Pick up refuse. 3. With other hand, turn bag inside out. 4. Deposit waste.

Courtesy of the *Cornell Animal Health Newsletter*

Only a heartless dog owner would ignore such a sign. But some will, and city gardeners should know that some types of wildflowers and ivys repel dogs and last longer.

92

and *never* allow any aggression with any other dogs. It's a good idea to simply let your dog drag his leash so that you can get the dog if trouble starts. An alternative is to put a short "tab" leash on the dog.

Careful supervision is a *must.* Some city owners actually find play groups *more* stressful than keeping their dogs on leash because they are not sure of their dog's behavior or the behavior of the other dogs in the group. If this is your feeling, I'd advise against play groups. Your dog will pick up on your tension, decode it as indicating danger and may fight or flee. Carefully weigh the advantages and disadvantages to your dog (and to your pocketbook) before joining any play group.

DOGS IN RESTAURANTS?

Right now, forget it. You might be able to dine with your dog along in the outdoor portion of many restaurants but if you try to come inside with your pooch you won't get a table. Every American and Canadian city presently has health code regulations that prevent access to pets in restaurants. The situation doesn't look like it is going to change.

The claim that dogs present a "health hazard" in restaurants doesn't really hold up to scrutiny. In most European countries dogs are freely admitted into food stores and restaurants and present no health hazard. It's clear that the restaurant regulations have more to do with *cultural* differences regarding the "place" of the dog in the social fabric than with public health.

There is an effort afoot in New York City called PAW (Pet Access to the World) spearheaded by Victoria Newhouse, Pat Buckley, actress Glenn Close, Brooke Astor, several veterinarians and humane society officials and trainers like myself to obtain permission to have dogs in restaurants. We've enlisted the cooperation of several top restaurants such as Bellini, The Four Seasons, Cafe des Artistes and others and have petitioned the commissioner of health to give us a trial run at such establishments with our dogs. Nothing is settled as of this writing.

As Mrs. Newhouse states, "We are trying to make the current prohibition against animals in all restaurants slightly less strict. One of our main arguments is that many older people, and single people of all ages, would feel safer going out at night if they had the protection of their dog, not to mention the purely pleasurable aspect of having the company of one's pet during one of the day's few moments of relaxation. In sum, we feel that the lives of many people would be enhanced if we achieve our aims." Mrs. Newhouse adds that rather than change the law to force all restaurants to accept dogs, "We propose a relaxation, rather than radical change, in our city's mores. A simple adjustment of present rulings so that they might be interpreted at the discretion of individual establishments would make life easier and fuller for a great many people."

City play groups are a fine idea
if they are safe for the dogs
involved and do not disturb
others.

Dogs in restaurants? Well, not yet, unless you're dining *al fresco*. But in some cities there are restaurants that allow dogs inside too, as they are in most of Europe.

94

Travel in Europe has proven to me that the idea is workable. Upon observing dogs in Europe in restaurants with their owners, it is clear that there are some unwritten rules that are followed that should also be observed in North America if laws are liberalized. They are:

- Never feed your dog from the table.

- Do not hold the dog in your lap; place the dog on the floor and, of course, keep the dog on leash.

- Do not let the dog move around. An excellent method, if your dog does not know the down-stay, is simply to *sit* on the leash. The dog will then feel the dead weight of your body and settle down. Measure out only as much lead as your dog needs in order to lie at your side. You can do this by simply shoving the dog down for a second and adjusting the length of the leash. If you give the dog too much leash the dog will cavort around, may try to jump up on the chair or table and will disturb other diners. Correct the dog by snapping the leash down hard if this happens.

The whole point is to enjoy the *quiet* companionship of your dog as you dine. If you are granted this privilege in your city, it must not be abused. Most guide dogs snuggle under a table out of sight and out of mind to all else in the restaurant. Train your dog in the same way. Your dog must be fully housetrained if he is to visit restaurants and if you have the slightest doubt about this, leave him home.

Do not make it a practice to feed your dog from the table at home, otherwise he will attempt to get food while in the restaurant. Consistency is essential. Taking something home for your dog, however, after you are done dining, is perfectly acceptable. That's why it's called a "doggie bag." Remember though, no chicken bones, no overly greasy foods and no chocolate. Chocolate can be toxic to dogs. Supervise all bone-gnawing so that the bone does not splinter.

RESOURCES

If you need help finding out about laws dealing with vicious dogs, dog fighting, "pit bulls," interstate transport of dogs, or ordinances limiting the number of dogs per household, direct requests for information to:

American Dog Owners Association
1920 Route #9
Castleton, NY 12033
(513) 477-8469

For information dealing with anticruelty, abandonment or euthanasia laws, contact the headquarters of one of the national humane associations:

American Anti-Vivisection Society
1903 Chestnut St.
Philadelphia, PA 19103
(215) 887-0816

American Humane Association
5351 S. Roslyn St.
Englewood, CO 80111
(303) 779-1400

American Society for the Prevention of Cruelty to Animals
441 E. 92nd St.
New York, NY 10028
(212) 876-7711

Animal Protection Institute of America
P.O. Box 22505
Sacramento, CA 95810
(916) 422-1921

Friends of Animals
11 W. 60th St.
New York, NY 10023
(212) 247-8121

Humane Society of the United States
2100 L. St., N.W.
Washington, DC 20037
(202) 452-1100

Royal Society for the Prevention of Cruelty to Animals
The Causeway
Horsham, Sussex
England

7

Care, Concern, Comfort

I WILL START WITH THE standard disclaimer you've no doubt read at the beginning of most books solely devoted to canine care: *The statements here are in no way a substitute for the care provided by a veterinarian. If your pet is ill, take it to a veterinarian immediately.* Yet, it never ceases to amaze me how many times I hear the statement, "Oh I don't have a vet," when I ask a client who is caring for their pet's health. Another variation on this theme is the city/country owner who has a veterinarian in the country but no veterinarian in the city—as if the dog is supposed to get sick only in one location. The worst attitude is the owner who simply reads books and tries to apply home remedies because he or she is too cheap to pay a professional. Or too poor. I can sympathize with poverty, but not with penny pinching. In most large cities there are sources where you can get your pet treated for low fees. Check into this if cost is a problem for you, but don't try to treat your dog medically from books.

PICKING A VETERINARIAN

The cardinal rule of making wise real estate purchases might also apply to the selection of your veterinarian: *location, location, location!* While suburban or rural owners might be able to easily get to their chosen veterinarian, regardless of the location, it may not be so simple for city owners. We have these little inconveniences that confront us, two, three, even four times a day. They are called *"rushes"* or "rush hours." Residents

Choose a veterinarian who explains procedures carefully and keeps in touch with you about your pet's health. Dr. Lewis Berman is pictured answering calls at Park East Animal Hospital in New York.

Dr. Sally Haddock, author of *The Making of a Woman Vet*, is a caring practitioner, and excellent communicator—you want that in your veterinarian.
Dona Ann McAdams

98

with cars can become effectively immobilized during a rush, and many city owners don't own cars.

Mass transit really doesn't make the situation any better because in most cities pets, even sick ones, are not allowed aboard buses or subways. Hailing a cab during the rush hours in some cities is next to impossible—especially with a pet (moreso with a sick one you may be carrying or dragging on a leash).

For this reason, and because you can never predict or schedule when your pet may become ill, I always advise my New York clients to find the most talented, most compassionate veterinarian near them—and preferably one that offers a 24-hour care service. Then, if worse comes to worst, you could *carry* your dog to the veterinarian, by yourself or with others. That way, if you were stuck in the rush hour traffic and couldn't use your car (*if* you had one), couldn't hail a cab and couldn't use the bus or subway, you could still get help fast. Sometimes a city will have an animal ambulance service, but don't bet on it.

Even with the location limitation in many cities, you will still have quite a few practitioners to choose from. Some clients will make the choice along some pretty rudimentary lines. One will be the sex of the veterinarian. Some people prefer to have their pet treated by a woman and some prefer a man. That's understandable, although I'd think competence and qualifications should overide such concern. But if you have a strong feeling about this, you should follow it, because the lines of communication between *you* and your veterinarian will have to be absolutely open and honest. Remember the patient is this case can't speak for himself or herself, so the two of you—you and your veterinarian—will have to do a lot of discussing in order to arrive at a diagnosis.

You must always find out about the veterinarian's qualifications. This is not at all inappropriate, especially in these days of consumer awareness. Ask the receptionist over the phone what school the doctor graduated from, what his or her specialty is and how many dogs of your particular breed he or she has treated and is treating. This is especially important if you own one of the rare breeds.

There are many breed-specific conditions, and new ones crop up every day. There are some specialists who, for instance, consider the German Shepherd Dog and the Chinese Shar-pei (just to mention two breeds) walking health hazards. I don't fully agree but I do know that these breeds, and many others, have their share of *potential* health problems. You should have a veterinarian who knows the possible problems in *your* breed. Sometimes you will be really lucky and be able to use the same veterinarian your breeder uses. A concerned breeder will have already shared information with the veterinarian about breed-specific problems. Also, that veterinarian will be on the lookout, by watching professional journals and in conversations with colleagues, for any new problems in your breed simply because he or she will *need* the information. Some problems can be minimized by preventive care, so if the veterinarian knows in advance that your breed is susceptible, to, say, bloat, he or she can advise you to feed lightly and frequently and not to overexercise your dog right after eating. Or if your breed is prone to hip dysplasia, your veterinarian can advise you on the importance of keeping your dog slim, well exercised and muscled.

Most importantly, do you feel comfortable talking with the veterinarian? I like a veterinarian who is open and friendly, who really seems to like animals and who keeps a clean office and hires staff that reflect the practitioner's own taste and style. While evaluating the *staff* may not seem like a relevant criterion for selecting a veterinarian, I believe it is because the staff is the support system for the veterinarian.

Because I lecture so frequently to veterinary groups, I am well aware of the inner working of veterinary practices. There is sometimes a veneer of calmness and even recollection at some veterinary offices, especially if the waiting room is sufficiently far from the exam rooms and other treatment spaces. In the waiting room, everything seems quiet as clients snuggle with their pets or leaf through magazines waiting for their turn with the doctor. But meanwhile, behind the reception desk, chaos might be breaking loose as the receptionist scurries to answer the phone, stuff charts in pockets and take in or release patients. The technician is chasing a Great Dane around the bathtub and Dr. Smith is overscheduled.

While this type of situation is rare, it does happen, so snoop out the staff. Put down that magazine and look around. What is the demeanor of the receptionist? Is the receptionist doubling as a technician? That's okay, and it is quite common, but if the receptionist is *tripling* as receptionist, technician and all-around clean-up kennel worker, that's a heavy work load. It *can* be done if a practice is just starting and is rather small in scope, but this isn't usually the case in city practices.

As for the doctor, I find if he or she hires good staff they are usually solid-gold persons themselves. I like a veterinarian who gives me some credit for understanding health matters and does not make fun of me when my limited clinical and surgical knowledge breaks down and procedures need to be explained. I do not need, or for that matter *want,* to know every aspect of a given procedure, but I appreciate knowing what will happen to my dog—especially if I have to leave him at the clinic for any reason. Nor am I going to be a neurotic father and call every two minutes, bothering the staff, to see how my little poopsy is doing. Unless it is a matter of life or death, I'll trust my doctor and his staff, and I'll call once a day. I'd really be pleased if someone on the staff called *me* to give me a report and that is exactly what many of the caring clinics do if a patient must remain overnight.

Finally, while it is perfectly okay to shop around for the right veterinarian for you, but don't play one off the other. Second evaluations and

Snoop out the staff! Are they caring, concerned individuals? A good veterinarian hires a good staff.
Courtesy of *Park East Animal Hospital*

As if fleas aren't bad enough, city owners have to watch out for rats also —and the poisons that kill them. Be on the lookout for such warning signs.

second opinions are sometimes necessary but in my opinion you should *always* tell your present veterinarian who formerly treated the animal and, frankly, if you are on the rebound for a second opinion. Don't be afraid, the veterinarian will understand perfectly—but don't say rude things about the former veterinarian and put the present doctor in the uncomfortable position of having to field such remarks. Most probably the second doctor won't respond with a comment anyway.

Check with your city veterinary association for a referral. If a veterinarian is a member of the association, that probably means that he or she is interested in consulting with other practitioners and keeping up on the latest techniques. Veterinarians who go it alone soon fall out of touch with current techniques. The name of the city veterinary association will most probably begin with your city's name and then "Veterinary Medical Association." Ask the secretary for the best veterinarian near you.

VETERINARY COLLEGE HOSPITALS AND CITY ANIMAL HOSPITALS

There are as many veterinary specialties today as there are in human medicine—neurology, ophthalmology, cardiology, oncology, nutrition and behavior are a few. Each requires hours of study, board examinations and certification.

If your dog has a special problem, you might be referred to a veterinary college hospital or a city animal hospital. These hospitals have access to the latest in medical techniques, and because of the large number of veterinarians on staff your pet's condition will be the subject of consultations and examinations between doctors. Experimental procedures will be available there that are available at most regular clinics. Treatments and cures for various ailments are often pioneered by institutions like the Cornell Veterinary Medical Center, the Animal Medical Center in New York or Angell Memorial Animal Hospital in Boston.

What about selecting a large animal hospital as the *regular* place for treatment for your dog? There are several aspects to consider. First, location—remember our rule. Secondly, how important is it to you to have *one* doctor that you see every time you come for care? That can't always be guaranteed at a large animal hospital where doctors rotate and others are interning and will leave to go to their own practices. Some clients feel that the "personal touch" is lost at the larger animal hospitals, and occasionally the waiting time can be long. But in an evening or late-night emergency, especially on a weekend or holiday, many city owners are thankful that their town is host to such a hospital. So make it a point to see if your city has one or if a college or university near you has a veterinary hospital. The hospital can serve as a backup to your regular veterinarian.

Three final points. Don't refer to your veterinarian (at least not in conversation with him or her) as a "vet"; this rankles some veterinarians. House calls? You'll be lucky if you find a doctor who makes them, but some veterinarians do operate this way. You might have to pay more for such a service. Finally, whether your veterinarian sports DVM or VMD after his or her name makes no difference. The University of Pennsylvania awards its veterinary degrees using the Latin title, "Veterinariae Medicinae Doctor," while other schools award the degree in English as "Doctor of Veterinary Medicine." If you see VMD you will know that your doctor attended the University of Pennsylvania veterinary school—a fine school indeed, as are the others. I prefer the Latin, but that's just my monastic background creeping up on me.

STARTING OFF RIGHT

As soon as you get your puppy, take it to the veterinarian. Take along the shot record the breeder gave you as well as a fresh stool sample. Be sure that you take along the breeder's name and phone number so that if the veterinarian can't decipher his or her handwriting a call can be placed to find out which shots have been given and when. There are various regimens for vaccinations and your veterinarian's protocol might be different from the breeder's, so it is very important that the doctor know what has been done to date.

You can get your pet vaccinated against the five canine diseases (distemper, hepatitis, parainfluenza, leptospirosis and parvovirus) in one simple shot. Some city veterinarians will also suggest a vaccination against a newer virus, coronavirus. *Do exactly what your doctor says.* Regular rabies shots are also important, even for the city dog. Rabies isn't passed from dog to dog, so your dog would have to be bitten by a rabid animal like a raccoon or a skunk, and that's hardly likely in town where these animals are not common. But do you expect to live your whole life in the city? Of course not, and if you take your city dog to the country he will be that much more likely to chase such animals simply because he is fascinated by them. One might be rabid. It only takes one bite from the wrong animal, so be sure to have your dog vaccinated against rabies as well.

Be especially careful about parvovirus and coronavirus. These viruses are spread via feces, but your dog doesn't have to go tromping through defecation to pick up either virus. Most city veterinarians suggest three or four vaccinations, which may delay when you can take your dog out for walks on the streets. If your doctor tells you to keep your dog inside until the third of fourth "parvo" shot, *do what he or she says.* You might talk to rural or suburban owners who will say that they could take their pup out sooner, but they don't live in the city where many other possibly parvoinfested dogs walk the streets. Don't risk it! While some dogs can be saved if they contract this dreadful virus, it is often fatal. Many die, even with immediate, top-notch care. For this reason I will not accept for training a dog who has not had four vaccinations against parvovirus. It is not safe to take the dog out onto the street. Sometimes I'll suggest that new puppies come into the household at a later age—*if* they are being properly socialized— rather than at the traditional time of placement, six to eight weeks of age. City owners who procure pups at that age face the prospect of keeping the pet indoors for possibly two months. If the pup is being properly socialized (not just kenneled) at the breeders, later placement is a possibility and the pup will only need perhaps one more parvovirus shot before taking to the streets safely.

Everything you will read in other books will drum into your head that the optimum time for placement of a puppy is six to eight weeks of age. Scientific studies bear this out. The best bonding is obtained if the pup is placed in the new home at that time. However, this theory was formulated pre-parvovirus and the reality of parvovirus changes the situation for many city owners who may not be able to keep their new pup cooped up in an apartment until all the necessary parvovirus shots are completed. So later placement is often desirable. Meanwhile, let's hope a cure for parvovirus is soon discovered so that our pups can hit the city streets sooner.

DIET

After vaccinations, your central concern will be what to feed your puppy. I am convinced that puppies need a high-quality, meat-meal based ration with a fiber substance like bran, beet pulp or corn cobs that will help them to maintain sphincter control and learn that cleanliness is next to godliness. City owners have easy access to the specialty foods that I prefer, since they are usually sold only in pet stores and pet stores proliferate in cities.

Canned Food Conundrum

Canned foods are not a good *sole* ration for your dog. First, they are 50 to 78 percent water. Look on the label. The ingredients on American pet foods are listed, by law, according to what predominates in the can or bag. In Canada, the first three or four ingredients must be listed according to what makes up the food. The first or second ingredient you will see on the label of a canned food is water. Water has many benefits but here it is simply filler. You are paying meat prices for water, which is silly on an economic level. There are nutritional problems as well if you feed canned food as the sole ration to your dog. Any extra water inside of a young puppy might complicate the house training process, and the greasiness of some canned foods make them the equivalent a laxative for dogs.

These foods are loaded with sodium nitrite, which is a color enhancer that keeps the food bright red or at least muddy brown so that, you, the consumer, are not turned off when you open the can. Most specialists agree that dogs see the world like we see black-and-white TV, so the coloring is strictly for consumer appeal, and may be harmful to your dog. High levels of sodium nitrite have been correlated with behavior problems, especially oral ones such as overbarking and pica (ingesting glass, metal and other objects dogs don't usually eat). One recent study showed that perhaps dogs can see the color red. Even if this is true, I doubt that they use whatever ability they have to see red to make value judgments on their canned food!

Worse than sodium nitrite is iron oxide, which is not just a color enhancer but a color *stabilizer*. It makes absolutely sure that the canned food will be reddish. It is nondigestible and irritates the lumen (lining) of the intestine as it passes through the dog's system. When eliminated it is concentrated and can leave a deep stain on your carpet.

Use canned foods only in moderation. I recommend only two to three teaspoons in each meal. If you are having any housetraining difficulties, eliminate canned foods completely, along with coat supplements, people food, B or C vitamins and anything else you're tossing in that food dish until the dog cleans up his act.

Semimoist Solutions

The semi-moist foods pet foods are soft to the touch, usually colored bright red or yellow and come in easy-open packages. The shape and coloring of the nuggets are supposed to suggest meat or cheese—but you know better, don't you? The coloring has nothing to do with either of those food stuffs and is simply a dye—and possibly harmful behaviorally.

Even worse, semimoist foods are chock full of sugar. The second or third ingredient will be sugar. The label may not say "sugar"; instead it will say "sucrose" or "high corn syrup." That means *sugar*. Sugar is addictive, sugar can cause bulges and sugar can cause near hyperactivity in many dogs.

Use these foods sparingly—never more than one-quarter of the ration. If you want my most rigid advice, don't use them at all. If you decide to switch from semimoist to another food, get ready for some missed meals and a battle from your dog. These are the hardest rations to switch dogs from—it's probably that sugar high—and you should mix the semimoist food with your new food half and half and then cut down gradually.

Dry Food Dilemmas

Non-fixed-formula dry foods are another group of foods to be familiar with. They are the big brand name dry foods. In the pet food industry a non-fixed-formula food is one that is made from stored ingredients that are usually bought in bulk on the commodities market at, of course, the cheapest market price. The main ingredient—or at least one of the main ingredients—will be soy, wheat feed flower, wheat middlings or corn gluten. Since all vegetables have a layer around them that hinders their biological value, these protein sources provide inferior protein to the dog. Depending on the food, there may also be problems with quality control. Ingredients that are stored too long, exposed to light or not properly ventilated will suffer a loss in nutritional value.

The biggest problem with non-fixed-formula foods is that the dog simply can't eat enough of the food to get the promised percentages of protein, fat and carbohydrates. A simple look at the labels of many non-fixed-formula foods will substantiate this fact. Let's say you have a 70 lb. German Shepherd bitch. You look at the label of "Palpo" dry dog food to see what size category she fits into. You find out, not much to your surprise, that she is considered a "big" dog. The size categories are usually three simple choices: little dog, medium dog or big dog.

Once you've settled on a size, you look in column B and find the amount this "big" dog is supposed to eat. It is going to say to feed her anywhere from eight to ten cups a day. You are then going to laugh. Of course your dog doesn't eat that much. Even if you fed her four times a day she wouldn't eat that much. Even if you fed her four times a day and laced it with *filet mignon* she wouldn't eat that much. So, you decide (wrongly) that she just doesn't have that big of an appetite, or that the manufacturer is overshooting in the estimate or, worse yet, that this discrepancy is good news for you because now you won't have to buy as much of this food.

It's not so simple. Truth-in-advertising laws require the pet food manufacturer to present labels that do not lie and that add up in relation to each other. The fact is you are caught in a classic consumer crunch. You can't get enough into your animal to get what they are promising you and the pet food company hopes you won't sense that something is wrong. While there *is* an occasional dog who will eat the required amount and thus get the promised nutrients, this is rare.

For city owners feeding non-fixed-formula foods, the sheer amount the dog has to eat, or be bribed to eat, makes for mountains of feces, sometimes loose ones. This complicates the housetraining task and necessitates many walks for elimination. If you live on the twentieth floor and have elevators that take forever to arrive you know that non-fixed-formula pet food manufacturers didn't have *you* in mind when they concocted their food. It is precisely for this reason that many city owners use a specialty food that contains a fiber substance like beet pulp, bran or corn cobs. These "bind up" the stool and make for easier housetraining and fewer walks. These are the first reasons city owners turn to fixed-formula foods. Remember, city owners have to clean up their dog's stools. The smaller and firmer the stool, the happier we are. What many city owners don't, at first, realize is that in choosing a specialty food they are also making a decision that will often have positive ramifications on the overall health of their pet.

Fixed-Formula Dry Foods—"Specialty Foods"

These foods have "weird" names—names that are not recognizable to some rural and suburban dwellers and instantly recognizable to many city owners who prize these foods as they would an elixir. These foods cut stool volume in half, enabling city owners to obey the laws and pick up instead of pay up. These foods contain meat-meal protein, fiber substances and proper amino acid counts that help our dogs maintain sphincter control when the elevator takes forever to come. These foods also come in smaller bags so we city owners can tote them home easily if we don't have a car or if we live in a fifth-floor walk-up.

More often than not the dog *can* eat the prescribed amount of food and thus get the promised nutrients when you feed a specialty food. Stool volume is lower and generally the stools are firmer. Quality control is usually better in a specialty food as it undergoes careful ingredient selection, checks on the ingredients as they arrive at the plant and testing of the food as it is being made. Samples of each batch are kept at the plant so that if there are consumer complaints about a certain batch, the plant batch can be checked against the complaint batch to see what went wrong in the distribution cycle. You most probably will have to buy these foods at a pet store or from your veterinarian.

It's in the Bag

Take a careful look at the bag your dog's food comes in and become your own "quality control" inspector. If the manufacturer has a real awareness of quality control you will find a multilayered package with an inner lining of food grade plastic. Of course you can't rip open the bag before you've bought it, but you can ask the sales clerk, or get the company's number off the bag and call and check before you buy. Remember, you want "food grade plastic" not just wax paper. This is especially important for urbanites.

The inner lining stops moisture from migrating into or out of the pellets themselves and keeps aroma in the bag. I've had owners complain that specialty foods "stink." Well perhaps they do, but that aroma is important to your dog. Simply folding the bag tight after each opening will stop the "problem." I personally haven't found any specialty food aromas offensive. The inner lining also prevents insects from entering the bag and contaminating the food. This is no small concern for city owners. The reality of roaches is something that surprised me when I came to New York. The best buildings have roaches. They love apartments of all shapes and sizes and in all areas. Within the apartment they seek out warm, moist places like the areas around sinks or bathtub—or the warm, moist environment of a dog food bag. Within the bag there is an added treat for the roach, food! So that extra-tough bag is important. If you have any feeling that the bag isn't strong enough, double bag the food when you get it home by putting the bag inside a plastic garbage bag and using a twist tie to seal the top of the bag.

Measure and Memorize

It is extremely important to *measure* specialty foods. Consult the label and weigh your dog. Turn to the absolute impartiality of the measuring cup and parcel out the correct amount until you have memorized what it looks like in the bowl. Remember, with specialty foods, *measure and then memorize*. If you are switching from a non–fixed-formula food, measuring is especially important, because you will probably be feeding much less of the new food than you were of the old. You might be surprised and even feel guilty about the smaller amount in the bowl. Don't worry. All the nutrients *are* there and you're not "cheating" your dog. More is not better.

If you have a growing puppy, weigh your pup every week and match the weight to the amount dictated on the appropriate panel on the package. A simple way to weigh your dog is to simply weigh yourself, mark down the weight and then cup your arms under your puppy or dog and remount the scale. Subtract your weight from the number that registers when you carry the dog and the difference is how much your dog weighs.

Where to Feed

There are many New Yorkers who avoid Grand Central Station, especially at rush hours, because they feel pressured and stressed in that environment. Yet, many city owners feed their dogs using a Grand Central Station method that is stressful for the dog that is eating. The owner places the food down in the middle of traffic, often in the kitchen, and then members of the family strut around while the dog bolts his food. I think this is a terrible way for a dog to eat.

If you were to get down on the dog's level and watch his eyes you would see them flitting up defensively as he eats. Sometimes the dog will snarl at somebody nearby. The humans don't think much of such displays until little Timmy Toddler one day gets a little too close to that food dish and WHOMP! Fido takes a hunk out of Timmy Toddler. This scenario is so familiar to trainers we could have set it to music a long time ago.

The fact is, the dog is a pack animal that instinctively guards its food. This fact should be appreciated, and the dog not aggravated. Feed your dog alone in a room unoccupied by people or in his crate. If you feed this way, it is also less likely that the dog will run off and have an accident, simply because his space is restricted.

When to Feed

When do the majority of American dogs eat? 5:30 P.M., I'm willing to bet. Why? "Because that's when I get home from work," is a common answer or, worse yet, "Because that's when my mother fed the dog." The fact that the dog's stomach is empty all day doesn't seem to dawn on the owner who is experiencing problems with a dog who has chair leg munchies, overbarks or howls. There is a center in your dog's brain called the hypothalamus. Dogs are like children in some respects and this is one of them. If the hypothalamus acts up, the dog does too. The hypothalamus controls appetite and temperature. It is very sensitive. It should be kept satisfied. Content. Even placid. Here's how.

Feed your dog *twice* a day, if possible, giving half the total ration at each meal. I often suggest an early morning, early afternoon feeding schedule. This keeps the hypothalamus satisfied and keeps food in the dog's stomach during its waking hours. Feeding two meals a day has a calming, resting effect on many dogs and may help in solving behavior problems. If you are not home for the early afternoon feeding, you can feed when you do get home but wait at least ten minutes. You don't want your dog to be conditioned to expect food immediately upon your return at a set hour. The down-side of such a pattern is that, on the night the subway breaks down or the bus stalls and you're late, you may find him ripping the house apart because he wants something to eat.

If you are having a housetraining problem, simply feed one-quarter of the ration in the morning and three-quarters at night. Don't leave too much water or the dog will tank up and not be able to hold for any length of time. A good solution is to leave ice cubes. These melt slowly and "ration" out the amount of water the housesoiler can drink at one time and may help in preventing urination from overdrinking.

How to Feed

Never free-feed your dog—that is, leave food out all the time, unless told to do so by your veterinarian. It is a bad idea biochemically and behaviorally. Biochemically you'll simply force your dog's gut to work harder as digestion in the dog properly begins in the mouth with secretion of saliva. A dog only works up saliva if he eats quickly because he knows the food will be taken away.

Behaviorally, free-feeding can backfire especially in the area of housetraining. If you leave the food down all day and your dog snacks at will there is more of a chance that the food will come *out* all day—all over your home or apartment. If you free-feed you will also have to walk your dog more often and your dog will produce smaller stools more frequently. You will thus find it harder to figure out which walks are really necessary and which you could eliminate because the dog is producing stools (albeit small ones) at each and every walk. Free-feeding will doom you to a life on the streets. Further, placing the food down and then taking it up makes you look alpha and highlights your leadership qualities in a very subtle way. This is eliminated with free-feeding.

Simply place the food down and leave the dog alone in a room or in his crate with his food for ten to fifteen minutes. Time yourself if you have to. Then, return and pick up the food even if the dog has not finished. Say nothing. If you do, you may be engaging in a faulty paralanguage, informing the dog that something is wrong with the food by whining at him or her to finish it. When littermates are in trouble—the mother is away or she refuses to nurse—they huddle together and they whine. Often owners will huddle over (or even with) their dogs and whine to get the dog to eat. Of course in English (or whatever language is being used) the owners are saying things like: "C'mon, eat up, it's okaaaay, eeeat it aaalll up, now . . . " or "That's my boy, oooohh, yum yum, eeeat it aaallll up." The tone is so whiny and whimpering that the dog will decode the owner as a littermate—and refuse to eat. The dog will reason, "Something must be wrong with this food, otherwise why would my owner be whining? I'd better not eat it."

What does the distraught owner do? He or she picks up the food and ceremoniously dumps it into the garbage pail, perhaps cursing the dog for not eating. This is another disturbing and confusing tonality switch from the dog's point of view. The owner deposits the food in the *bad place.* It's the place that, whenever the dog goes near it the owner says "Get outta there!" The dog reasons, "Never go there. It's bad to go there. Bad things go there." And this is where, in full sight of the dog, the owner is pitching the food that was just whined and driveled over. The dog sits there and thinks, "I was right not to eat that horrible food. First, my master whined about it and now he's throwing it away in the 'bad' place!" This makes the dog even more determined not to eat the food the next time so as not to upset you into whining and hasten the moment when you will throw the terrible concoction in the trash. Never let your dog see you throw food away, and say *nothing* when you offer or take away the food. That's the best policy; otherwise food games begin and food confusion takes over.

Finally, don't add anything to the dog's food once you have placed the ration down. If you do, the dog will simply wait for you to add something

110

before chowing down. Remember, if your veterinarian advises against set feedings and suggests free feeding for health reasons then his or her advice supercedes what you have read here.

City owners have a great stake in feeding correctly. Because of our social setting many of us do not have access to a backyard and cannot enjoy the convenience of slipping Rover out for a romp or for elimination or installing a dog door. Because elimination is the final step in the digestive process, and because what goes in one end inevitably comes out the other, we must carefully monitor how, when and what we feed.

Fleas

City owners often think of fleas as a country-owner concern, until their dog gets a case of them, often after frolicking in the countryside. Flea infestation is a problem for the city dog and city owner as well.

The worst aspect of fleas is their remarkable tenacity. They will hang on forever and hatch forever. Dog owners often make the mistake of thinking that because fleas have been eliminated on the family mutt, the problem is over. Not necessarily so. They could still be hopping around the house or lying dormant as eggs waiting to hatch. For this reason, the flea-ridden dog must be doctored, and the house bombed at the same time.

If fleas are overruning your house and hound, take the dog to your veterinarian to be dipped in a professional potion and boarded overnight. Meanwhile, de-flea your house with flea foggers and spend the night in a motel if necessary. Close all windows, set off a strong fogger in each room, and open closets and crannies so the fumes can pervade every corner. After returning, vacuum everything with an extra-powerful machine, and immediately dispose of the contents of the vacuum away from the house. If you don't the suctioned fleas will simply crawl back down the vacuum chute and infiltrate the house again. The eggs will love the dark environment of the vacuum bag, giving you a whole new batch to battle later.

Adding Proban Cythioate (available from veterinarians) to your dog's food may also help.

Be extremely careful about the concoctions you use to de-flea your dog. Never put a flea collar on a puppy, and check *all* aerosal and powder treatments with your veterinarian *before* using them. At least one such product has been implicated in dog deaths and other products will probably come under examination soon. Be careful.

MASSAGE

One of the first mentions of canine massage for behavioral reasons was in *How to Be Your Dog's Best Friend,* published in 1978. Before that

111

time, discussions of massage centered mostly on its use for luxations or other medical problems. The idea that an owner could spend time massaging a pet to deepen their relationship and cement bonding was considered silly, even "fruity." When the monks' book was translated into German, the publishers in that country attempted to drop the chapter on massage, complaining that Germans would think it was weird. Since I was in charge of the affairs concerning the book, I went to the abbot. He said to tell the German publishers to keep the book intact, massage chapter and all. I've never gotten any letters from Germany complaining about that chapter, but I have received plenty of comments complimenting the section.

The fact is, every culture that admits dogs and cats into households teaches its members to pet (or not pet) in a certain way. The Germans, for instance, might offer a more reserved type of petting, while the Italians are very physical with their dogs, as they are with each other. Americans and Canadians fall someplace between the two mentioned cultures.

For the city owner, canine massage can be a blessing. It is a way of offering quality time to your dog, especially if you live a busy life. Dogs love a more extended type of body contact, especially at the end of a day, and your massage can be of great help in getting your dog to calm down once you get home. It also helps you enjoy your dog.

First, stop thinking about your dog as a creature with only a head and shoulders. There's a body there, too, and it is there for the petting. I'm willing to bet that there are parts of your dog's body that you've touched and that elicited a pleasurable response from your dog. Right? Touch those spots during canine massage. Make a list of the areas of your dog's body where body contact is a "high." Then list the areas that your dog does *not* like touched. Begin your first massage with the areas of the body on your first list and include one—just one—area from the second list. Do not massage the genitals. Dogs do not like to be manipulated in those areas, and I even advise breeders, who occasionally *have* to touch genitalia, not to overdo it and to be sensitive.

Sit your dog. Take a paw and massage each indentation between the toes gently, praising as you massage. Now, take the other leg and do the same. Many dogs will smile as you do this. They will wonder what you are doing and will be enjoying it at the same time.

Step around in front of your dog. Cup the dog's face in your hands and massage the area between the eyes. This is a very sensitive spot in canine anatomy. Tap it *lightly* twice and then just massage it with your index finger. Ever wonder why Hindu women wear a black dot in that spot? It's because it is a meditation point, a *chakra* point, and it is on dogs, too. Now, gently massage the eyelids of your dog—gently now—and work your way down to the muzzle. *Never* pull your dog's whiskers, as this will be the equivalent of a terrorist hijacking a television station. Those whiskers are your dog's antennae to the outer world and must be respected.

The urge to touch, pet and massage a dog runs deep in the human soul. Just look at these dogless children "petting" the statue of "Balto" in New York's Central Park. It is the one statue in the park that has never been vandalized.

To begin massage, select a paw and gently rub the area between the toes, working inward. Just look at that Collie smile!

Then, put your dog on a down and massage his side and neck.

114

Your dog will quickly communicate what he likes and dislikes. If the dog wants to get up and play, let him. Don't force the massage. A good time for city owners to massage is after a long walk, when the dog is tired and when all is calm. The "inguinal area"—the groin (not the genitals)—is especially sensitive. Dogs tell each other, "It's okay," by nudging this area upwards with their noses. You've probably seen this transpire between your dog and other dogs on the streets. That's their handshake. So massage this area too so that your pet will see that contact here is to be accepted. This is an especially appropriate area to massage for dog fighters.

For the busy city owner massage has several benefits. First, it is a way of forcing yourself to examine your pet's body, which will quickly alert you to any health problems. Secondly, it is *quality time* that doesn't take much time in actuality. While your dog might be a little uncomfortable at first, it will be abundantly clear to him or her that this is special. The dog will think: "This is my time, and my owner is doing this for me!"

Finally, if your dog is sensitive to city noises, such as a shy dog who freaks out at the sounds of garbage trucks unloading, jackhammers hammering away or sirens wailing, a ten-minute massage *before* you take your dog out will work as a "set-up" (see problem section) to "proof" your dog against such distractions. This can be of great help, as can one afterwards.

SILENCE IS GOLDEN

I learned a lot about silence in the monastery, and what it can do for humans and dogs. When I migrated to the city, I found silence hard to come by, and the noise stressful. I'm sure many dogs find noise pollution stressful. Yet, there are ways that you can provide your dog, and yourself, with silent times even in the setting of the city.

Brother Thomas once said, "Learning the value of silence is learning to listen to, rather than screaming at, reality: listen to a dog until you discover what is needed instead of imposing yourself in the name of training." But how can one listen if the city blocks out all sound? The solution is to find the secret, silent places in your city and make it a habit to take your dog there.

The park will be the first place to head, and of course the deeper into the park you go, the more silence you will find. Churches are another often overlooked silent spots and you don't have to be of the denomination to enjoy the silence. After all, your dog is nondenominational, isn't he? I've slipped into Saint Patrick's Cathedral many times with a student dog in tow and never been questioned. A client of mine takes her obedience-trained Mastiff to the local library. Still others have found the rooftops of their buildings to be a haven of silence and peace. Remember, in some cities the solution to seeking silence is to go either in or up. Go deep into the park or get up on a higher floor and the roar of the city recedes.

Dogs love silence, so include your city dog in the quieter times of your life.

Dogs love silence! Think of the world of wolves. It is a very quiet world, except for some occasional group choral singing and howling. The woods are, as Frost said, "silent, dark and deep" and you do have a promise to keep to your dog. That promise is to let your dog get back to its roots by taking the dog to silent places as often as possible. Breaking that promise, or never making it, can result in a hyperactive pet that is terrorized by the city and lives a noise-filled, stressed life. The end result is often behavior difficulties.

I find that owners who live such noisy lives themselves often have problem dogs. When a call inquiring about training is left on my answering machine I usually try to return the call within a day and will try a return call once in the morning and once at night. If I receive an answering machine each time I know the owner has a busy schedule and that the dog is alone. This is not a productive kind of silence. On the other hand, if a caller places a call to me and I hear a television in the background, a stereo blaring or other commotion that tells me something about where silence is ranked in that owner's priorities. If you are the type of person who is conspicuously noisy and hyperactive, no wonder your dog is stressed. The solution is silence. Seek it out, and include your dog in your silent times.

NEUTERING

I am a strong advocate of spaying or neutering every dog not being used for breeding purposes. Further, the only reason a dog should be bred is if he or she is a superior specimen of their breed, and knowledgeable people have told you this.

Why am I so "strict" in my opinion? Just open up your daily newspaper and look at the ads for unwanted pets. Go down to your local shelter—better yet, *volunteer* some of your time—and observe the endless, sad parade of pets brought in because they are unwanted. I always tell owners who want to breed their dogs because they want to watch the "miracle of birth" to first go down to the local shelter and watch the "miracle of euthanasia." Over 14 million dogs and cats are destroyed each year at shelters. Fourteen million! Some shelters don't report accurately, either, sometimes for fear that if the public knew what was really going on, donations might slip. Actually, that should be a reason for the public to give *more* money to shelters but the public doesn't think that way because the public doesn't understand the overall problem of pet overpopulation. Instead, owners tend to get all wound up in their little poopsy and their desire to make poopsy a parent. Chances are your dog has little or nothing to offer to the betterment of his or her breed, and there's no compelling reason to breed the dog. Owners often forget that terrible complications can arise from breeding. If you have a female, she could die giving birth. Infections, behavioral problems and a wealth of other difficulties can crop up once you enter the breeding game, which is best left to full- or part-time professionals.

Furthermore, the city environment is no place to whelp a litter. It can be done, but it is difficult. By the time the pups reach four weeks of age, depending on the breed and the size of the litter, they can raise quite a racket. The neighbors will complain. Clean up chores at this point can occupy the large part of a day along with feedings and caring for possibly sick pups. Veterinary care skyrockets, especially if a Caesarean is needed or other special care. You will not make any money, believe me, even if you don't count your labor as a business expense. You'll probably break even or lose.

Neutering has definite behavioral advantages in dogs, especially if it is done before puberty is over. In my opinion it is always indicated in the case of aggression, regardless of the age of the animal. Consult with your veterinarian about the best time to neuter your individual pet. In some towns, reduced-fee clinics are available to keep your costs down. Spaying and neutering are important operations and anesthesia is required, but both operations are routine and there is little risk involved. Neutering costs less than a spay operation, usually. Discuss with your veterinarian the health and behavior benefits from neutering.

Most importantly, try to remove your own psychological projections about neutering from the decision-making process and approach this rationally. I've had many male clients instantly cross their legs when I bring up the idea of having their male dog neutered. The operation will not make your dog fat, unless you overfeed and underexercise him. Nor will it quell protection potential or deaden the dog's spirit. It will prevent prostate cancer and some other infections, and will keep the dog on an even keel behaviorally, assuming proper training is also provided. Sit down with your veterinarian and rationally discuss the process.

CATS AND DOGS TOGETHER–CITY STYLE

Before you think of this section as a "problem piece," you should know that, contrary to popular rumor, dogs and cats usually get along famously. I know plenty of clients who leave their cat and dog together unattended for hours with no problems. So, don't worry if you plan to have both or have one species and want to get the other. It usually works out.

Trying to keep both a cat and a dog in a city apartment does, for some owners, present problems. I've been in apartments where the decor had been so modified that the apartment looked like a barracks. Gates are put up to keep the dog in one room and the cat in another. The dog tries to dive-bomb over the gate and the cat stands at the gate hissing at the dog.

Meanwhile the owner is screaming at both and the neighbors upstairs are stomping on the floor and screaming about the noise.

This war zone situation can be prevented or at least a truce called between the two parties with some effort on your part. Whether your two pets can live together in peace has a lot to do with how each of them see *you,* so if you are not perceived as the leader by both of them, you're in for trouble. If you don't think you're perceived as alpha by your dog, be sure to get into the role soon by using the techniques in this book. Practice *eye contact* especially so that you can warn the dog out of a cat chase before it commences. Eye contact can be increased with your cat too, although you will have to pretty much lock eyes with the cat when it feels the urge, since eye contact sessions can't be staged as with dogs. Get your cat's eye and issue a low warning phrase *before* hissing and back arching begin. Most owners know their cat's eyes better than they know their dog's eyes. They are experienced in reading the cat's moods in its eyes. You will probably be able to tell when the cat is getting that glazed, "hard" look in the eyes that signals aggression. Issue your warning *now.* Try to stop the look before violence escalates. Having a squirt gun or spray bottle around the house really helps and a well-timed shot in the face coupled with that warning phrase can work wonders. In *City Cat,* Roz Riddle suggests isolation as a disciplinary technique.

> I would recommend putting the cat in the bathroom to cure all big discipli-nary problems. A cat banished to the bathroom will cry and cry piteously. He'll also tear up all the toilet paper into tiny pieces so take it out ahead of time. When the cat is locked in the bathroom give him something with your scent on it for him to curl up in and derive comfort from.

She adds that yelling at cats literally goes in one ear and out the other, so gentle scolding is the key. I have advised this technique to clients and asked them to discipline the dog using the shakedown and immediately "bathroom" the cat at the first sign of a fight. Then, open the bathroom door after ten minutes. Do not pet either animal during this time. Issue advance warnings to both with eye contact and see what develops. If there is renewed aggression repeat the procedure immediately. Do not physically discipline the cat. The isolation has a greater effect.

If this ruse doesn't produce peace, then you might have to let the cat and dog "work it out" under your direct supervision. Put a short "tab" leash on the dog and get that squirt bottle ready for action. Sometimes the bathroom discipline will backfire (especially if the hatred between the two pets is deep and long-standing) because the dog will perceive that it "chased the cat away." So, experiment with both cures.

I do not suggest declawing your cat unless the hostilities cannot be worked out in any other way. Declawing is painful, and many cat specialists advise against it. Declawing will deprive your cat of the climbing ability it may need to get away from ferocious Fido. It's a last resort.

I'm often asked if one particular breed of cat gets along better with dogs. I haven't seen this to be so, although I have noticed a *slight* propensity in Siamese cats to be more possessive of their owners and sometimes more resentful of dogs. Meanwhile, Abyssinians often do quite well with dogs. They are extremely alert and practically take to the air at a moment's notice. For this reason they often avoid unpleasant encounters with a dog simply because they are so quick to exit at the first sign of trouble. One drawback: unlike most cats many "Abys" *like* water, so the squirt-gun discipline method might not work. But the bathroom one probably will.

Some dogs are absolutely fascinated with kitty litter and with cat food. If the litterbox has feces in it, so much the better. They will delight in throwing the litter and its contents all over the bathroom and house, thus depriving the kitty of its toilet. I've seen dogs who guard the litterbox to keep the cat from eliminating. This territoriality forces the cat to have an accident and often get a squirt from the squirt gun. The dog watches gleefully.

The solution is to place the litter box up on a shelf or on the back of the toilet and let the cat know the new location by placing the cat in the box several times a day. Another possibility is to purchase an *enclosed* litter box with an entrance hole small enough to keep the dog out and still allow the cat entry.

Once I had as a student a German Shepherd Dog who was highly enamored of kitty litter and feces. This dog enjoyed litter more than her own food. Everything my client and I tried to break the habit failed, so I suggested an enclosed litter box. The client bought one at a pet store. Unlike many models, it was made of seamless molded plastic, all in one piece. One day while the owner was at work the German Shepherd somehow got her head stuck in the hole of the box. The client came home and the dog was crashing around the apartment trying to knock the box off her head. The client tried to pull it off, but couldn't wedge it free, even after putting vaseline around the edges and on the dog's fur and pulling like mad. She had to walk the dog through the streets of New York like this to the Fire Department where special equipment was used to safely detach the box. In all the commotion my client hadn't given a thought to the where-abouts of the cat. Guess what? You got it—the cat was *in the box!* And, thankfully, safe. The Shepherd loved the kitty as much as its litter. By the way, no one batted an eyelash or even looked twice at this dog walking on leash with a litter box stuck on its head. That's New Yorkers for you.

GROOMING

It is outside the scope of this book to give tips on grooming different breeds. There is a vast selection of breed books available and almost all of them contain definitive grooming sections, whether you intend to keep your pet in show coat or pet coat. It is best if you find out what kind of grooming commitment you will have to make to your dog *before* you actually procure that puppy. Otherwise, you might be in for a shock when you find that your Shih Tzu sheds or your German Shepherd germinates enough hair to stuff a pillow or a couch. The following is a guide with estimates for various breeds.

Minimal Grooming (15 minutes, once per week): Border Terrier; Pointers; Chesapeake Bay, Labrador, Curly-Coated and Flat-Coated Retrievers; Bullmastiff; Wirehaired Pointing Griffon.

Average Grooming (20 minutes, twice per week): Brussels Griffon; Manchester Toy, Australian and Cairn Terriers, Brittany, Field, Clumber, Welsh, Springer and Sussex Spaniels; most shorthaired hounds; Miniature Pinscher; French and English Bulldogs; Chihuahua; Boxer; Saluki; Boston Terrier; Weimaraner; Pug; Papillon; Great Dane; Mastiff; Akita; Doberman; Bernese Mountain Dog; smooth-coated Collie; Rottweiler; Siberian Husky; Schipperke; Cardigan and Pembroke Welsh Corgis.

More Grooming (30 minutes, twice per week): West Highland, Lakeland, Welsh, Sealyham, Yorkshire, Irish, Norwich, Norfolk, Dandie Dinmont and Bedlington Terriers; English Toy Spaniel; Affenpinscher; Bouvier des Flandres; Alaskan Malamute; English Springer Spaniel; Shetland Sheepdog; Great Pyrenees; Kuvasz; Newfoundland; Samoyed; Pomeranian.

Breeds That Shed Heavily Year Round: Dalmation; German Shepherd; Pomeranian; St. Bernard; Siberian Husky; Alaskan Malamute; Belgian Tervuren; Curly-Coated Retriever; Newfoundland; Samoyed.

After surveying these breeds and time estimates, many a city owner will opt to secure the services of a good groomer. I think this a very good idea. A professional groomer will save you literally hours of time untangling knots of hair, bathing your dog and then drying out your clothes after hectic baths, and feeling guilty that you are not doing a sufficient job in keeping up with the grooming. Sure, a groomer costs money, but if you budget a once-a-month grooming, and keep up minimal grooming between professional groomings, you'll be surprised how cost-effective it is.

To find a good groomer, ask your veterinarian for a referral. Then visit the grooming parlor and meet the groomer. Apply the same standards you would for selecting a good boarding kennel (see section on this) and

121

have the groomer meet your dog. Be sure that the groomer is *behaviorally oriented* and knows how to discipline a dog humanely so that tranquilizers do not have to be used or inhumane techniques applied. The best shops will have a grooming room that is open for public inspection and where you can watch dogs being groomed. Remember, it is illegal for a groomer to administer prescription medications to a dog, and while tranquilizing unruly dogs is rare, it does happen. Most behaviorally oriented groomers can calm a dog and get the grooming accomplished without them. If in doubt, ask.

Be sure to ask what *your* duties will be between professional groomings. Purchase the tools that are necessary to keep your pet in reasonably good shape between groomings. You simply cannot leave all the grooming to the groomer and expect your dog to look or feel good. There are some city groomers who will simply refuse to groom a dog that is severely matted or tangled. Instead they will demand that the matted hair be cut off and a new coat allowed to grow in. And they are absolutely right. This is not laziness on the part of the groomer, just an appreciation of reality. But your groomer need never suggest this if you keep up minimal grooming between shop visits.

Most cities have groomers who work out of the shop and in your own home. If your dog is more comfortable being groomed this way, go for it. The groomer will bring the necessary implements and will probably use your kitchen sink or bathtub for a bath, so be sure to have those areas ready for use when the groomer arrives. This service is usually more expensive but can be great for the older dog, or the older owner.

I personally prefer that city owners take their pets to the groomer and have the grooming done in the shop. The best system (and the one most professional shop-owners require) is to leave your pet off at the groomer's in the morning and pick the dog up at night. Some overprotective owners don't like this system and insist on waiting until the dog is groomed and then taking it immediately home. These owners are passing up several fringe benefits by doing this.

First, if the dog stays all day, it is easier for the groomer to schedule the dog into the working day and provide full attention to that one dog. Secondly, your dog gets socialized—which is especially important for the shy dog—because hanging around the shop waiting to be groomed the dog will meet other dogs and people. Shop stay-over grooming also gets your dog ready to be boarded, because, even if left for only a few hours, your dog will note your absence and, most importantly, the fact that you *came back.* This is very reassuring for the dog and makes future longer boarding stays much more endurable and even fun. The dog knows that sooner or later you'll return, so he might as well enjoy himself. After all, you always come to get him at the groomers and then you take him home and make a bug fuss over him because he looks so good. What could be more comforting? Finally, shop stay-over grooming gives you a free day without having to pay a boarding bill. I have one client who goes upstate to ski areas or to the beach on her dog's grooming days. "I take Sparky in at 7:00 A.M." she said, "and beat it out of town just as the morning rush is coming *in*. I get to Hunter Mountain ski area by ten, ski, have a fabulous lunch and drive back into the city just as the mad rush is coming *out*. My side of the road is clear, so it's smooth sailing. I pick up Sparky at 7:00 P.M. He's had a nice day and so have I. He was occupied and not pining away for me at home or housesoiling, and I've got a groomed dog and no board bill!"

WINTER WORRIES

Some words of warning about street salt during the winter. It can do damage to your pet's paws, so be sure to clean your dog's paws off if you've walked through strewn salt. In fact, it's better to dip your dog's paws in water if possible or, if you have a smaller dog, use the spray attachment on the kitchen sink to wash out salt rather than wiping the paws. Sometimes wiping will actually rub the salt *into* the cracks between the dog's toes, making the situation worse, especially if your dog has a paw cut. If you follow the heeling methods prescribed in the obedience section you will be able to more effectively skirt strewn salt.

YOUR OLDER CITY DOG

If you think of aging as a sad development, an "event" that can be postponed, a "trial" better not suffered through, you really should not be a dog owner. If that strikes you as a blunt statement, just remember that, unless you are quite old yourself, you will probably outlive your dog. That means, in most cases, you will watch your pet get old. Surprisingly, very little is said about the phenomenon in most of the existing dog literature.

First, it helps to realize just how long you can expect your pet to live. Owners often hear erroneous figures, sometimes based on "estimates" from lay owners or owners who had exceptionally long-lived dogs. It is better to ask your veterinarian or breeder for an estimate and go from there. Here are some guidelines:

Average Lifespans of Some Popular Dog Breeds

Cocker Spaniel	14–15 years
Poodle	10–14 years
Labrador Retriever	10–12 years
German Shepherd	12 years
Golden Retriever	10–13 years
Doberman Pinscher	10–13 years

Beagle	12-15 years
Chow Chow	12 years
Miniature Schnauzer	12-13 years
Shetland Sheep Dogs	14-15 years

I personally think that some of these figures are quite high. I have seen many German Shepherd Dogs, for instance, who are "old" at eight years of age—by that I mean they have lost partial or total sight, walk more slowly, may have lost hearing—but they are still looking forward to each new day and definitely not candidates for euthanasia. The point is, don't get hung up on estimates and then feel cheated if your dog didn't live as long as it was "meant to live." Each is an individual and statistics are just statistics.

Your older city dog might have a problem with slowness and here you have to be considerate. Don't force the dog to walk fast but don't succumb to the temptation to take the older dog off the lead and just let him or her saunter along. You may think your older dog is street-wise but some older dogs wander into traffic without much notice and if your dog is losing his hearing, he will not hear you shout out a warning.

Watch out when crossing lights. In some cities the time limit pedestrians are granted before the traffic light turns green can be as short as one minute! That's the case at some intersections in New York before the warning flashes begin saying "Don't Walk." If you or your dog are elderly and you don't think you can make it across that broad avenue, don't risk it; wait for the next light. Most cities, especially Canadian towns, are more generous in their timings, providing two or more minutes for street crossing. My rule of thumb is: Balk if the sign says "don't walk," especially if you have an older dog in tow.

Irritability and incontinence are two problems owners of older city dogs have to endure. I do not believe in justifying the irritability of an older dog—it should be disciplined. Of course, the dog is disturbed by failing senses and he might be more liable to act aggressively when he hears sharp sounds or is touched rudely. The old adage, "Let sleeping dogs lie" is never more true than when applied to the older dog. Instruct children to leave the older dog alone and provide a spot—possibly a crate with the door left open—where the oldster can go and retreat. Usually I suggest that if a dog is in the way, the alpha owner should tell the dog to move. After all, you are the pack leader and you should have the right to tell lower members of the pack to get out of the way. But with an older dog, this isn't an iron-clad rule. Sometimes it will be better to simply step over the dog or walk around him. Use your judgment.

On the other hand, overt aggression should *never* be tolerated, nor should a lack of obedience training. You *can* teach an old dog new tricks and often an obedience course can engage the mind of an older dog and give him or her a new lease on life. Don't make excuses for your older dog's biting behavior or lack of manners. Enroll in a class or hire a private trainer and teach your older dog that he, too, can be a civilized city canine.

If you have a problem with incontinence, you must have your older dog checked by your veterinarian at once. Dribbling is a problem with older dogs and lapses in housetraining are common. There are medications that can help, so check with your veterinarian. In fact, I always suggest that any older city dog go to the veterinarian every three months for a checkup. Often the veterinarian will detect problems during the checkup that the owner missed at home. Be sure to write down what you want to say to your pet's doctor before coming to the office. This simple practice makes it possible for you to remember everything that is on your mind concerning your pet's health and will alleviate any nagging doubts you might have when leaving the office that you forgot to mention this or that. Remember, your dog cannot speak for himself and since the patient cannot communicate directly with the doctor, you must intercede.

Older dogs still need exercise, and even though some joint stiffening is inevitable, walks are usually in order. The body regenerates itself through exercise so don't just let your dog mope around the house because of stiff joints. Check with your veterinarian about the proper amount of exercise and then get out and provide it. Remember, your older dog might not want to go to his play group anymore or romp around with other dogs in the park. Younger, more playful and robust dogs might be more of a bother than a joy, so don't push your older dog to play with others.

Just how old, in human years, is your dog? The "old school" of thought estimated a dog's age to be the equivalent of seven years for every one year of the dog's age. Other specialists have disagreed, noting that because of the speed with which dogs pass through puberty, the first year makes them 21 years old, in human terms. Then instead of seven years for each year of the dog's life, they add just four. I tend to agree here, but really, who knows? We don't know how dogs experience time, although I personally feel it must fly by for them, since they live shorter lives than we do. Even Einstein couldn't figure out the concept of time—in fact, he gave up his studies on the matter because he found them overwhelming. So who are we to dictate how dogs experience time when one of our greatest minds couldn't even figure it out? Enjoy your dog for the time you have together. Treasure your time together because the best of times is always now.

8

The Training Turn

BEFORE I TELL YOU HOW, when and where to seek out city training it might be good for me to give you a brief overview of how training techniques have changed during the last 15 years. I find that many of my city clients are quite aware that dog training still involves a great amount of bunk and folklore. City clients are often well-read, urbane and acquainted with trends in human psychology. For instance, many of my clients know that child "training" and education have changed dramatically over the last two decades and they vaguely suspect that perhaps similar "turns" have occurred in pet care and training. They are absolutely right, and to help you understand what has happened in dog training, and to help you pick a top city trainer, I'll give you the following survey.

Over the last decade and a half, training has taken a definite turn—if not a complete turn-around—for the better. Let me preface my remarks by saying that I have been professionally involved with training dogs for the last 18 years. Fifteen years ago, a major book on dog training advised taking the head of a dog that digs in the backyard and plunging it into the holes that have been dug—after filling the holes with water! Today, few training texts would advocate such a "correction."

Fifteen years ago, a trainer would advise a client to take his or her unhousebroken dog's nose and rub it in feces to teach the dog not to house soil. We know now that this method teaches a dog to eat its own stools. I often think a generation of dogs turned to stool eating as a result of such misinformation and also acquired all the problems associated with that bad habit: worms, intestinal tract disorders and bad breath. We now know that it is important for a dog to look at the misplaced stool, but we certainly don't want to shove the dog's nose into it!

Dog care and training are where child care and training were 100 years ago, before Dr. Spock, Anna Freud and child psychology, before any decent enlightenment in that whole area. Back then, human parents expecting a baby (or even those with one) used to go to park benches and "consult" with other expectant or not-so-expectant parents on just what constituted proper child care and training. Another solution was to call up Mom and ask her what she did. The result was the perpetuation of a long list of folklorish "cures," "techniques" and "punishments." Today, many dog owners still follow this haphazard pattern. But, there are glimmers of hope in the overall dour situation—beacon lights in the form of books and seminars by trainers who truly know dogs and are against the "park-bench" system of finding out about them.

The struggle over the past 15 years has centered basically on the differences and benefits to dog and owner between inducive or coercive training techniques. All training involves force, but it is the degree of force that has been hotly debated among dog trainers and behaviorists. It is worthwhile to note that often our perceptions and justifications color the disagreements over methods, not to mention our ideas of status, ego, money and pride. The result is that the dogs have often gotten lost in the crush.

When people think of training a dog, they often think in two restricted patterns of thought—housetraining and obedience training. The idea that training is an ongoing concept in a dog's life, indeed a way of life with the dog, wasn't mentioned until 1978 in *How to Be Your Dog's Best Friend.* But if the monks were the first to point it out, other trainers already knew this to be true and were steadily getting away from the basic commands formula in their classes and texts. Few dog owners came to classes to train their dogs for the ring, but even ten years ago all they could secure for their animals from a class was ring-type training. This seemed to ensure that the dog would obey in the obedience ring but still be naughty at home. It was a schizophrenic situation. The dog learned certain exercises in the class that had little or no bearing on what it was expected to do or not do at home. For example, a dog would learn a three- to five-minute down in a class (a required skill when showing the dog in the ring); at home during a 30-minute dinner it would rest in the down for three or five minutes and then raise hell the rest of the time, while people tried to eat. From the dog's point of view, it had been trained for a three-minute or five-minute down—so what's the problem?

The problem was, precisely, that it takes most people longer than three minutes to eat. Obedience classes back then (and, unfortunately, some even today) actually engaged in an unintentional form of "antitraining" in which dogs were taught that they only had to be good for a certain length of time and then they could do whatever they pleased. Child psychiatrists talked about "boundaries" and "setting limits for the child" and "teaching the child not to act out" and "teaching the child longevity in training," but seemingly none of this had dawned on dog trainers—most of whom had children themselves but applied one standard of behavior to them and another, usually colored with forceful or not-forceful-enough folklore, to their dogs.

Dog training as a science and art traces its start to Joseph Allen and Col. Konrad Most, two gentlemen who lived in pre-World War I Germany and used basically inducive techniques (detailed in the classic, *Training Dogs*, by Col. Konrad Most).

When the war came, and messenger and attack dogs had to be trained in a big hurry to meet wartime pressures, coercive techniques started to creep into the obedience training ritual. It is a fact that many coercive techniques get the job done faster than inducive techniques, which often take only a few seconds or minutes longer. Coercive methods, meanwhile, played into a very American mentality during and after the two world wars, especially when they were given sanction by professional trainers who got their original experience in dogs—guess where—in the military. The fact that dogs are not little machines or robots geared to respond solely to human whims was again lost in the crush. It's worth noting, however, that a military man, Col. Most, can be called the originator of obedience training as we know it today, and he used mostly inducive techniques.

Today there are regional differences in how dogs are trained, depending on the area of the country and the influences operable there. I travel widely, teaching seminars on canine behavior and nutrition. In one part of the country, I'll see techniques that should have been banned along with public hangings, but in another area I'll see quite advanced methods that are humane and reasonable.

A certain oral tradition is still very much operable in dog training circles, and trainers tend to inherit good or bad techniques from the trainers who trained them. One of the most interesting and heartening trends in the "training turn" is the small, but influential number of trainers who specialize in teaching seminars to other trainers, that is, trainers who train trainers.

Finally, as the dog training game becomes more diversified, many trainers are offering more personalized services in the form of dog owner counseling. This is one-on-one training between a trainer and a client, usually in the client's home and it usually includes a lengthy interview of the owner and evaluation of the dog before training even commences. In my book, *The Evans Guide for Counseling Dog Owners* (Howell Book House, 1985), I detail the techniques used in this fast-rising subsection of training. I firmly believe that discerning owners will seek out more one-on-one services in the future, as they come to see that for many dogs it is a more effective way of training than class-style training. This type of training is especially effective for city dogs and owners. In this type of training, the owner is seen as an integral part of the dog's life, not just a nuisance that the trainer has to deal with. The "Just-get-out-of-the-way-and-let-me-train-your-dog" attitude is giving way to an approach that takes the owner and the dog into full consideration—not just as a "team" to learn set exercises that may only be usable in the obedience ring, but as two parties that have an ongoing relationship that must be balanced and healthy if such exercises are to be mastered and if problem behavior is to be corrected.

The focus of a good trainer should always be on the quality of the relationship between dog and "master" or, if you prefer (I do), the dog and its "best friend." The "training turn" during the last 15 years has been from quantity to quality—from coercive and even inhumane techniques to more inducive, humane methods that fully respect dog and owner.

Just as child care and child psychology have changed over the last century, dog training is moving out of darkness into more light—light that I hope will more fully illuminate what dogs are and can be for us, and what we are and can be for them.

9

The New York Example

IF YOU ARE ONE of those persons who categorically rejects the idea that dogs can live healthily and happily in large cities, this isn't the book for you. If, on the other hand, you believe that dogs can tolerate and even enjoy life in a huge metropolis, if the particular city tolerates and enjoys them, then read on.

Training texts abound that will describe in detail how to train your dog to deal with city stress and dangers. Many of these tracts are written by theorists who envision what life must be like for the city dog, but actually write their books while ensconced in a country retreat. What many authors see in their mind's eye isn't the stark reality. There is a great gap in this area of canine studies.

I will not talk about what makes it easier for dogs to tolerate city life, but rather about what makes a city tolerate, enjoy and even love its dogs. In this way, you may discover some techniques to employ in getting your own town to be more hospitable to our best friends.

I look at the subject through the prism of my experience as a trainer in New York City. This is a city of dog lovers. The ASPCA has almost 300,000 dogs registered and licensed, and estimates of the true dog population run as high as 1.5 to 2 million! This, in a city with a population density similar to Tokyo, with twice-daily traffic-jams, a city of tiny, narrow shops, littered sidewalks, constant construction noise, pollution, rats, stink, roaches, fast-thinking pigeons and even faster-thinking humans. In short, New York would not be expected to be the *least* bit tolerant or welcoming to its canine population. With the exception of perhaps Paris, in no other city has the dog so infiltrated the fabric of human social life. Why do some cities, often the most unlikely ones, welcome dogs so successfully and others don't?

First, the pace of life in a given city has a lot to do with this. New Yorkers are fabled for their cynicism and even rudeness. Outsiders find us terribly blunt and always in a hurry. We extend this treatment, I'm afraid, to each other. But one part of life that is very important to New Yorkers is our dogs and how they are treated and where they are allowed to go. In short, New Yorkers are *pushy* and because of that we often secure rights for our dogs that they would never enjoy elsewhere. For examples, on any spring or summer evening all along Columbus Avenue on the Upper West Side, thousands of dogs will nestle underneath the tables of the sidewalk cafes. Dogs are not allowed in restaurants, of course (a peculiar American custom, supposedly stemming from health concerns but rare in Europe or any other part of the world). On Columbus Avenue not only the outdoor tables harbor dogs, but many of the indoor-outdoor zones, and if questioned many New Yorkers will just get up and leave with Fido in tow—there's always another more hospitable restaurant three steps away.

"I'd never question the presence of a well-behaved dog," one restaurant proprietor said. "Word would get around and I'd lose tons of business." What about the law? "Well, I like to think I make the laws in my restaurant," he added, "and half the time you don't even notice the dogs. They lend a certain ambiance, I think, and the cops won't cause me trouble, especially when they should be out chasing dope dealers and subway killers." A victory for New York dogs, if only by default, who for the most part can join Parisian Poodles at their master's and mistress's tables (on the floor, of course).

In fact, many victories you can help your dogs to score in big cities will be by-default victories. Dogs are also technically banned from delicatessens and other shops that serve food, but it is rare that a dog owner with a dog on leash will be asked to leave. In fact, it's almost a New York custom for deli help, butcher-shop operators and doormen to give dogs tidbits. I've stopped at different churches and seen dogs on down-stays between the pews. At my laundry, dog owners have started a play group for their dogs, with the permission of the Chinese owner, who brings his Shar-Pei. The dogs are allowed to romp on Tuesday evening only (at which time we fill the laundromat) and the play extends to the spin-dry cycle, but during drying and folding, all must lie down. We even have a waiting list of three dogs and owners (who, I presume, have a lot of dirty laundry piling up).

New York is glutted with Yuppies and Guppies (gay Yuppies) who often are childless but may own one, two or three dogs. Whatever the reason, these dogs are "family" and that perception seems to encourage the New Yorkers to at least *try* to take their dogs to a variety of places. Storekeepers seem to realize that if they make a stink (usually unfounded) they will simply lose business, and, if they are dog lovers themselves, they seem to instinctively realize that the alternative for a New York dog owner is to simply leave the dog at hime. Also, when New Yorkers shop, they don't dawdle. The customer is in and out of a store quickly, and so is the dog. This leaves less time for the store owner or fellow customers to get their hackles up, even if they wanted to.

Many New York dog owners take ownership of a pet very seriously. The passage during the 1970s of the "Canine Waste Law," which levies a fine of $100 on owners who do not clean up after their dogs, was laughed at by people in other cities, but toughened New Yorkers have by and large obeyed the law. Nobody quite knows why. Dog owner's compliance with this ruling seemed to make the nondog-owning public more accepting of the presence of dogs—especially when they didn't have to sidestep dog waste. Public sympathy for the law is high, and so is public observation of it. New Yorkers will often berate someone they see running away from a deposited stool. "Where were you born? A barn?" I heard one Park Avenue woman scream at an offender recently, and then she bellowed, "Police!"

Many New Yorkers have small dogs that can be picked up when on the street or entering a store. Many times the presence of the dog isn't even noticed. Many New Yorkers also hide their "portable" dogs in specially designed sacks to transport them on the bus or subway. It is permissible to take a dog on the subway in a crate and, once on the train, many will hold the pet on their lap. Fellow straphangers are usually transfixed by the presence of a dog—it is one time when it is safe to make eye contact with another living being on the New York subway!

Within Central Park and other smaller parks throughout the city, informal and sometimes highly organized dog groups meet each evening. Central Park has, at the present time, at least four recognizable "Dog Hills." Dog owners seem to gravitate to the rolling regions of the park, perhaps because the elderly and children don't frequent those areas. Here, in frank disobedience to the city-wide leash law (which states that the dog must be on leash at *all* times) dog owners can let their pets run free. Most leave a six-foot leash on their pets, and many use 20-foot leashes that can be snatched up quickly if a park ranger or the police appear. "I walk almost an hour each way to get here to give Kenzo (her Akita) twenty minutes of full freedom. I'm responsible about it. We want an enclosed area for our dogs, and we'll get it."

One area affecting canine freedom that has not kept pace with other strides in New York concerns dogs in apartments, especially co-ops and rentals. While condo owners can usually set their own terms concerning the presence of pets in a given building, co-op and rental tenants are almost always forbidden to have pets. Almost all standard leases in New York prohibit pets other than birds or goldfish. "If you have a leash, no lease" seems to be the rule on paper, but in practice it is widely ignored. But if a

133

landlord wants to co-op a building or evict older tenants he or she will often seize upon the pet clause, often forcing tenants to sacrifice a beloved pet. Nevertheless, many New York tenants have fought back and the legal decision usually goes their way. Progress is being made as landlords learn that a dog can act as a built-in burglar alarm, protecting all units in a complex from robbery. Then, too, many landlords are dog owners themselves and live in apartments with "illegal" dogs themselves.

Using the New York model, what steps can be taken in other locations to improve the chances of our dogs living as freely and healthily as possible? I'd suggest the following:

1. Enact and *enforce* a canine waste law. Levy a heavy fine on offenders and publicize the law effectively. Don't forget to teach citizens *how* to clean up. Make sure the law *works*. New York's fine is $100. Toronto's is $1,000!

2. Enact and enforce a leash law. At the same time, seek to provide enclosed areas that are available to the dogs under human supervision so that owners aren't forced to "cheat."

3. Encourage training in your community. Support local obedience courses by city subsidy and/or advertisement. Focus on control exercises such as a 30-minute down-stay, instead of training geared only to the ring.

4. Form informal play groups. Lack of exercise is a major problem for city dogs and affects their behavior in many ways. Start with a friend, a set meeting spot (preferably enclosed) and the dogs on leash (dragging them). Always monitor activities.

5. When entering an area (store, park, lobby, etc.) where you are not sure if you are welcome with a dog, *ask*. Then proceed. Say clearly, "May I come in with my dog—he's trained," because saying that can make all the difference in the world.

6. Be *pushy* (while being courteous). It's your dog—he's your friend, and while rules are rules and you shouldn't take a rebuff as a personal rejection, sometimes pushiness pays off. And once you've proved that your dog is a pleasure and not a nuisance, you've proved it.

7. Finally, don't expect favors for unruly dogs. If your dog is not obedience trained, or if that obedience training is not *tight* and truly applies in *all* situations, you have no rights to claim for your dog. Train, train and retrain and *then* stake your claims!

10

Seeking City Training: The Many Aspects

FOR A CITY DWELLER, there are many ways—in fact, in some cities a bewildering wealth of options—to get your dog educated. You can attend obedience classes. These may be privately sponsored or run for profit. You can hire a private trainer or you can try to do it yourself with the aid of this and perhaps other books. A fourth option, one that because of zoning and spatial requirements is increasingly hard to find in town, is to send the dog to a kennel for training.

DOING IT BY THE BOOK

I find that even for wealthier city dwellers trying to do it by oneself with the aid of a book is still a very popular method. I think it is workable, but it has some drawbacks. It's a fair enough option for someone living in the wilds who, for geographic or financial considerations, just can't get into town, but as an urban dweller you have the advantage of being able to select from a wide variety of services—including dog training ones. Why not take advantage of that fact?

The problem with doing it solo with a book (or for that matter tapes or even a video) is that somewhere along the line you might need a 3-D demonstration from a professional on exactly what to do in training. Even more importantly, you may value *personal* help, a personal touch. No

135

matter how hard I, or any other author try to be painstakingly complete in our advice, the fact is that there is no one there to help you personally.

If you want to train your dog this way, go to a pet store or library and select three training books. Check a pet store first; they are often a better source of dog books than regular book stores.

If you think you are going to train your dog with one hand holding an open book and one holding the leash you are going to find that it will not work. Instead, read at least two books cover to cover before you begin. The books will necessarily cover much of the same information but the repetition is good as a self-teaching discipline, and you'll notice some differences between trainers from which you can pick and choose. If the books say that picking and choosing is a no-no, and that *this* author-trainer's method is the *only* method of training and must be followed to the letter, in my opinion, don't use the book.

The third book can be read while you are actually training. Save the best for last. Evaluate each beforehand by reading the author's bio, the table of contents and perhaps a chapter here or there. Believe me, the investment in three books is a good one, as is using the above method before beginning training. Otherwise, you can become an avid collector of dog books, always searching for that *one* book that will give you all the answers. The truth is, the books are simply *guides;* the answers come from you and your dog in your training together. Ultimately, the answers even come from within the dog itself, with some prompting from you. J. Allen Boone mentions this phenomenon in his book, *Kinship with All Life.* He visited a certain Mohave Dan, a desert hermit known to be contemplative of dogs and man. He asked the sage to help him understand the inner meaning of his dog. The hermit considered the request for a few moments and then said, "There's facts about dogs, and there's opinions about them. The dogs have the facts, and the humans have the opinions. If you want facts about a dog, always get them straight from the dog. If you want opinions get them from humans."

You are bound to see errors and inconsistencies in any book. If you decide to train this way, take some reflective breaks in your reading, call your dog over and ask him for the facts, now that you've read the opinions. By the way, when I said that training a dog this way is not my first choice in terms of methods of training, I didn't mean to imply that I'm not proud of you if you do decide to train by books. You've taken that first step, and it could be all you need.

SENDING YOUR DOG AWAY TO SCHOOL

I *had* to train dogs this way for eleven years. The rules of the monastery didn't allow me to go to client's homes. Clients would bring their dogs to the monastery, drop them off (after a complete interview as to their needs and desires in training) and then return to see the dog's training and receive training and counseling themselves. Hundreds of dogs took their "vow of obedience" at the monastery while I was head trainer there and returned home, I like to believe, born-again saints. Well, I *like* to believe that.

The all-important component that is missing in this method of training is steady interaction between trainer and client. The owner will only touch base with the trainer twice using this method of training and that may or may not be enough. This method of training appeals to people who just want a problem dog to "shape up or ship out" and think that shipping the dog off will alleviate all problems. It also appeals to people who are used to paying for services (top dollar if necessary) and receiving quality work in return. However, training a dog is not like getting a television fixed, a VCR hooked up, a dishwasher repaired or even a child tutored. No matter what the trainer does with your dog while the dog is away, ultimately *you* are the one who is going to have to give the orders once the dog returns, *you* are the one who will have to discipline if necessary, *you* are the one the dog must see as leader and alpha—not the trainer at the training kennel.

Training a dog and having him listen to you is probably the one thing in this world that you have to do for yourself and by yourself. You can pay someone else to perform all the above-mentioned services, but *you* must train your dog. That said, there are some instances when this method of training could be useful:

- If you are going on a long trip and need to board your dog for an extended amount of time. You might as well have the dog educated while you are away, rather than have him sit around waiting to be fed. I always suggest a training/boarding combination for any stay at a boarding kennel over three weeks, even if the dog has been previously trained. Just ask for a "refresher" course. I feel this lessens the inevitable stress of long-term boarding, occupies the dog, gives the dog something to look forward to and provides benefits for you. Hopefully, however, with the aid of this book, you'll be able to take your dog traveling—even to cities.

- If you have a situation with your dog involving extreme aggression in which you or others are in physical danger and the dog must be removed from the premises immediately. If matters are this bad, a boarding stay might be absolutely necessary just for a cooling-off period and to buy some time to start training in the home.

- If you are *truly* too busy to train the dog in any other way. I used to say simplistically, "Why then, have a dog?" But since coming to New York and witnessing the lifestyles of busy executives, power-brokers, stars and stockbrokers, I now realize that sometimes a career can go into a zoom phase and it is a matter of taking what action there is while the action is hot. City living has taught me the complexity of life—it's just not as simple as saying, "Well, perhaps you shouldn't have a dog." Yet I hear such dogmatic statements from trainers all the time.

The following are some guidelines as to what to watch for and watch *out* for when evaluating a potential training kennel. You must, repeat *must* resolve to allot some phone time and/or visiting time into this all-important task. Your investigative work will have a payback in a pleasant stay for your dog accompanied by top-flight training. Remember, you are not going to be there to monitor what is done with (and possibly *to*) your dog. But asking key questions can save you and Fido a lot of trouble.

Look for a kennel that belongs to the American Boarding Kennels Association (ABKA) and that is run by a Certified Kennel Operator (CKO). This means that the kennel belongs to a professional organization and the CKO is a degree earned by the proprietor by passing a vigorous test about canine care and training. Sometimes kennels will include this information in their ads, sometimes they will not. Ask.

The first place to check is not the phone book but with your veterinarian. Ask him or her for a referral, but be sure to mention that you are looking for a boarding/kennel *combination* not just a boarding kennel. Some kennels do not offer a training service.

If you find a good kennel that has this service, ask the trainer (request to speak to him or her directly) what method of training is used, how many lessons a day the dog will receive, how long each lesson is and what specific words the dog will learn. Trainers are busy people, so don't expect the trainer to give you a 20-minute speech on his or her philosophy of dog training, how specific exercises are taught, etc. But from their remarks you should get a good idea of how they teach dogs. Let the trainer volunteer the information that you will be *interviewed* when you bring your dog to the kennel. If after some conversation they do not mention this, ask, "Do you interview your clients to find out about the dog and their needs in training?" or ask, "Do you take a behavior case history?" If the trainer is flabbergasted or puzzled (sadly, some still are) you should excuse yourself politely, breathe a sigh of relief and hang up.

When you arrive at the sterling training kennel you've found, whip out your list of problems, complaints, etc. concerning your surly brat and hand it to the trainer. *Don't* write a three-page essay. If possible, type the list. The trainer will appreciate receiving it. I always did. Sometimes the list contained problems I could alleviate during the dog's stay, other times the problems had to be worked out at home, but at least I could counsel the owner and prescribe a follow-up trainer who would visit. Don't try to make your dog look good because you are sad to be leaving him or because you want the trainer to think the dog is already a saint. If the trainer doesn't know about past, present or potential problems, he or she can't help you—and most trainers have an ardent desire to help their clients.

Be sure, *absolutely positive,* that the trainer who interviewed you will be the trainer you will work with when you return to pick up your dog. Otherwise there will be an information gap. Insist on this. Preferably that same trainer will be the person who works daily with the dog on his lessons. I realize that because of staffing, that's not always possible, but it is the ideal.

Ascertain whether you can return to the kennel for follow-up sessions if the training lags or you have later troubles.

Follow all the kennel's rules concerning innoculations, records, etc. Inquire in advance so that you are not disappointed later.

- Do not let your dog see signs of an upcoming trip (suitcases flung open, toiletrys case stocked, travel documents displayed). They are very sensitive to signs of departure and will rebel. The dog may or may not know he's going to serve a term at Sunnyside Reform School for Dogs, but he does know you're going someplace and that maybe he isn't. I know one Dalmatian who consumed his owner's passport and airline ticket on the morning of her trip as she was showering. The Gucci travel bags he left alone. The France-bound woman was able to save a scrap of the ticket, which luckily had part of the ticket number on it. She rushed the dog to the veterinarian, who determined everything was okay healthwise (paper is paper). She then hurried to the airport, showed the ticket scrap and had the ticket reissued. She gave a note from the veterinarian stating what had happened to the passport officials, who reissued the passport. She then went home, drove the Dalmatian to the training kennel for his stay, got interviewed, added "eats passports and airline tickets" to her list of problems she wanted the trainer to know about and headed for the airport. She made the afternoon flight to France. Score? Human: 1, Dalmatian: 0.

Finally, don't say a big teary goodbye to your dog at the kennel. It will *not* make it easier on the dog, it will make it harder. I ran a boarding kennel for eleven years and believe me, the dogs who pined away for their owners, refused food, whined, moaned and mourned were the dogs who were coddled, cuddled and cried over and put on edge by a guilty owner. Fact is, most dogs adjust well to boarding and your goodbye should be short and sweet, affectionate but not overbearing. Remember the importance of paralanguage and how dogs read our sounds. Whining tonalities, regardless of the love you are trying to communicate to your dog, will backfire on you. The dog will read your tonality as a stress signal deducing that, indeed, *something is wrong with this terrible place, otherwise why would my owner be whining?* If the kennel permits it, take a blanket or a favorite toy for your dog to remember you by, and a supply of the dog's food if the kennel doesn't serve what you feed.

OBEDIENCE CLASSES

Urban dwellers are often blessed with a large number of obedience classes being offered by private individuals, humane organizations and dog clubs. The problem is often not how to find a class but how to determine which one is best. More on selecting a class later. First let's examine the nature of classes.

By virtue of the fact that obedience classes are *classes* you cannot expect a lot of personal attention. Try to find a small class of ten or less dogs. In deciding whether this is the training method that is right for you and your dog look not just at your bank account but at yourself. In general, classes are a cheaper method of training than sending the dog to a kennel or hiring a private in-home trainer, but money should not be the only consideration. In fact there are some instances in which a dog and owner should *never* enroll in a class. They are as follows:

- If your dog is aggressive *do not* go to obedience class. *Do not.* You are endangering the instructor, the other students and dogs in the class and yourself. You need private, in-home training, pronto.

- If you are the type of person who has a short fuse and is easily agitated if not able to ask a question or get the information you need immediately, you don't belong in class. Private training is the method for you.

- If you know that you probably will have to skip more than one class, don't start. Barring illness, or weather problems (in which case the class will probably be cancelled and rescheduled anyway), don't start what you can't finish or do correctly. The class will simply continue without you.

The advantages of classes, besides the cost, are the chance to social-ize with other dogs and owners, the discipline of being in a set place at a set

140

time to concentrate on training and the excellent preparation this is for further obedience work in the ring if you are so inclined.

The disadvantages already alluded to include lack of personal attention, noisiness, occasionally overloaded classes and disturbances by another dog who might be even more unruly than yours. Two other disadvantages that I have rarely heard mentioned are the length of some courses and the inapplicability of what is taught in some classes to the home situation.

If you are searching for a class, you are going to find a wide range of timeframes for the course. You will be told that one course is six weeks long, another eight and still another 12 weeks. What's going on here? Some instructors gauge their courses so that the dog is taught one word at a time and no more. They may feel that they have to pitch the course to the lowest common denominator of canine (and human) intelligence. This accounts for the ten- to 12-week syndrome. I feel ten or 12 weeks is way too long for the busy city owner, who will find it very difficult to commit to a class that long. But this is the extreme. As you "shop" for a class you'll find that they usually run anywhere from six to 12 weeks long. Below six is probably too short.

A further complaint that I hear voiced frequently, especially when clients come to me for private training after trying a class, is that even after just one session they figured out that the class was oriented to dogs going into the obedience ring. "They teach a three-minute down in this class," one client said to me, "but I need a longer down because I'm a scriptwriter and cannot be bothered while I'm typing. What they were going to teach didn't address my needs, so I quit." I can understand the woman's feelings. A good basic class should teach heel, sit, stay, come, down and a *long down* similar to the one outlined in the obedience section of this book. If the instructor insists on teaching ornamental exercises like the "finish" (a maneuver meant for those who are ring-bound), you are probably in the wrong class. Ask about the specific exercises.

TRACKING DOWN A CLASS

Ask your veterinarian for a referral. He or she is probably aware of classes offered in the area. You might also try calling your local humane organization and inquiring. Still another method is to contact a local obedience club. I've had clients who located top-notch classes simply by observing a well-trained dog on the street, politely stopping the owner and asking where the dog was trained. While this might sound strange, urban dwellers with dogs know what I'm talking about. Many owners will stop and chat. If you try this, be sure to bring along a piece of paper and a pencil so you can jot down the name of the class or trainer.

You should make an initial visit to the training school or class and ask to "sit in" on one session. Be sure to make an appointment beforehand. This viewing should reveal a lot to you. Here are some things to look for:

- What is the general atmosphere—orderly or chaotic? What is the class size? If it is over 20, it is too big. If it is over ten, is there an assistant to the instructor? You don't want to be in a class where you'll be lost in a crowd.

- What is the demeanor of the instructor? Can you hear him or her? Are the instructions clear? Does the instructor explain *and* demonstrate or just explain techniques and hope that the students get it? Does he or she give the handlers confidence, encouraging them, inspiring them? Is the instructor funny? Would you *enjoy* listening to him or her for however many weeks the course takes? Obedience work is not pure fun. It is work for you and your dog, but it doesn't have to be drudgery. Place yourself in the class from your sideline vantage point: How do you feel about the instructor?

- How does the instructor relate to the dogs? Does he touch them? Does she praise enthusiastically? Do the dogs look bored? Does the instructor allow distracting behavior on the part of any dog to go unchecked? You want to be in an orderly class that is as calm as possible so that you can concentrate on succeeding in your training.

- While you should not fly off the handle if you see an instructor physically correct an unruly dog, be on the lookout for any signs of inhumane treatment of the dogs.

- Definite no-no's are hanging a dog, kicking a dog, insulting clients, refusing to answer questions, making fun of a handler or a dog, cutting the class short. If you see any of these problems, don't join, and if you are in such a class, quit.

- Do you like the location? Remember, if the class is held in a public park—as many city classes are—you will be prey to the elements and possibly to several cancellations from weather. You also will have to put up with dogs who are not enrolled in the class wandering onto the training field. This might be a good distraction later but you will not appreciate it in the beginning. There will also be gawkers watching the class. This might make you uncomfortable. If the class is indoors what is the flooring? Matting is a must. And, if the class is indoors, does the instructor, at some point during the course, "take it to the streets" so that the training is perfected outside where the *real* distractions are? Ask about this.

Good luck in your search for a class. If you find a good one you will look forward to it each week. Besides getting your dog trained and socialized, all sorts of things can happen in an obedience class. Often owners will form play groups as a result of meeting in class. Hang around after class and chat. Meet your fellow students. You all have a built-in topic for conversation in your dogs.

PRIVATE TRAINING

Ten years ago the idea of having a private dog trainer was cause for laughter. Today, private training is widely accepted, especially in urban areas where this form of training is common and competes in the marketplace with boarding/training schools and classes. While I have run occasional classes during my career, private training occupies most of my time with clients, and so I know this method of training most intimately. Having personally tried or taught all four forms of training, I feel private, in-home training is the best type of training for most owners. The downside is that it is usually the most expensive. The expense comes from the investment of the trainer's time, your direct, personal access to him or her and the fact that in many cases the trainer or specialist comes to you. You are paying for information, travel time, lesson time, possibly equipment, and personal attention, which you should get.

The trainer will probably begin by taking a behavior case history, collecting basic data about your dog and yourself, and zeroing in on problem areas. If you employ a private trainer and he or she does not make an effort to do this, I'd worry. So it is better to ask on the phone how you will be interviewed. Write out a list of concerns so that you will be sure to mention everything once the trainer starts to query you.

Many clients prefer private training because they do not like the hectic atmosphere in some classes. They find class too distracting and need a one-on-one tutorial approach. This is perfectly understandable, but be sure that the private trainer, you and your dog hit the streets during your lessons so that the dog learns to obey there as well. The biggest problem with private training is that it can become too insular—just you, your dog and the trainer holed up in an apartment or in a far away corner of the park. Be sure to work around other dogs and in the flow of human traffic. In New York this is never difficult. We have pedestrian traffic-jams here and dogs are everywhere. In other, more spread-out cities, it might mean loading the dog up and driving to a park you know dogs frequent so that Fido *really* learns to come when called when distracted with other dogs, so that Munchkin *really* learns not to pick up garbage. Ask your private trainer about *where* you will train.

Another great advantage to this method is that you can shuffle appointments to fit your schedule and you are not locked in to a set time every week, as in a class. Many professionals with irregular schedules appreciate this scheduling service and most private trainers will work at night and on weekends. Expect your private trainer to be prompt, since this is part of what you are paying for, but be realistic, too. Because of subway or traffic delays, especially during rush hours, some delays are inevitable.

For a referral, ask your veterinarian, call your local humane organization or query friends. Your last resort should be the yellow pages. If you wind up there, look for ads that stress love, compassion and understanding. The ad should stress that the trainer offers a *service* ("We help *you* to train your dog") rather than a *product* ("Trained dogs delivered pronto"). Watch out for that terrible word "guarantee." You'll find it in many ads and in my opinion it is inaccurate and unrealistic. Since there are three parties involved—you, the trainer and your dog—I fail to see how the trainer can "guarantee" the performance of all three.

Be careful to select a trainer who actually trains dogs and does not just counsel owners; you want both. I know some of you might be wondering how one could be involved in dog education and *not* train but believe me, especially in cities, there are plenty of "experts" who will diagnose your dog's problems but will not know how to train them out. Unless the problem is very complex, you probably don't need diagnoses; you already know all too much about the unpleasant things your dog does. Don't be afraid to ask up front exactly what will be taught, and, without expecting a blow-by-blow description of the course, what training methods are used. If all you hear is vague academic talk about "behavior modification" or "shaping techniques," you've probably found a counselor, not a trainer.

If you really luck out, you are going to find a private trainer who will be able to combine all the best aspects of all the methods of training mentioned. If he or she is heaven sent, you will also get along well and maybe even become friends. At the least you will feel that you have a hotline to call for help throughout the training period and possibly long after.

You might also be surprised at the overall cost. While private training usually is more expensive, often when you add up lost business time to make a scheduled class with an unwavering time slot, gas and driving time and other factors it just about evens out moneywise. Remember there are some problems for which a private trainer is absolutely indicated and necessary, such as severe aggression, so you may have no choice. You could request time payments, or even take out a small loan in order to get the training you need. The investment will be worth it.

EVALUATING THE TRAINER

No matter which method of training you ultimately choose, there will be a trainer involved. How do you evaluate trainer credentials? It's not easy. There is no licensing in our field, so technically, anyone is free to hang out a shingle saying "dog trainer *par excellance.*" There are advocates of licensing, but actualization of any regulations is probably some time off. In the meantime, the following are some tips.

Find out which veterinarians the trainer works with. If you were referred by your own veterinarian, chances are this trainer has a decent track record. No practitioner will remain affiliated, however loosely, with a trainer who consistently turns in bad results. Many veterinarians expect the trainer to report on the dog's progress so that the information can be entered in the patient's permanent record. This is wise because many health and behavior concerns overlap. Further, clients will immediately report poor work to the referring veterinarian, another insurance policy for you against poor trainers. This is why I advise you to ask your veterinarian for referrals for training and boarding services.

Does the trainer work with humane organizations on referral or in another capacity? This is another good gauge of reliability. No humane organization will associate itself with a trainer who uses inhumane methods or does consistently poor work.

Query extensively on the phone. "Buyer beware" are the watch words here and you have a right to ask questions, even many questions. You could put it this way on the phone or in person, "Mr. Smith I am aware that there is no licensing for people in your field. Forgive me, but I don't know your qualifications well and I wondered if you'd mind if I ask you some questions?" I think that's a perfectly fair question.

Be careful of trainers who trumpet the *number* of dogs they've trained (the *owners* trained the dogs anyway) or who overstress the number of years they have been training. Numbers of dogs and years don't necessarily mean a lot.

Has the trainer published? If so, get the titles and sources for the books or articles. You can then look them up and get to know the trainer a bit via writings beforehand. Sometimes just the titles of the works will be reassuring.

What professional organizations does the trainer belong to? Membership in NADOI (National Association of Dog Obedience Instructors) means that the person has been teaching classes a certain number of years and is nicely qualified for it. Membership in DWAA (Dog Writer's Association of America) means that this person writes professionally or semiprofessionally about dogs for publication. Be very careful about anyone who says they "belong" to the American Kennel Club. The AKC is a registry body for pure-bred dogs. Individuals do not "join."

145

Has the trainer earned AKC titles with the dogs he or she has trained? Have others trained by this trainer gone on to earn such titles? Even though most people do not wish to enter the obedience ring with their dogs to win titles, another way of checking out the effectiveness of the trainer is by the number of his or her students who *have* gone on to such glory. Remember, though, many trainers are far too busy with their own work, humane work and other activities to be in the ring.

Has the trainer worked with dogs of your breed? This is an important question for the consumer to ask because it will reveal the trainer's knowledge of and experience with your breed and also often brings out comments from the trainer that might prejudice his approach. Watch out for statements like, "Oh yeah, I've trained hundreds of Dobes, they're all aggressive," or "Poodles? Impossible to housebreak—no wonder you're having trouble. . . . " These silly statements show that the trainer is living in a world of doggie folklore. Each dog and each situation is unique.

Finally, does the trainer demonstrate *caring* for you, for your dog and about your situation when you speak? This is very important. You don't want a hard, macho approach or a brittle, uncaring trainer. Learning is stressful enough; you want someone who will make you feel comfortable and yet is organized, efficient and dedicated to dogs and their owners.

Good luck in searching out the trainer and training method that is best for you. Urban dwellers are blessed with a variety of teachers and courses to choose from. And *bravo* to you for seeking out training. You've already taken the first step—you bought this book, now continue your efforts to educate your dog to be a civilized city canine.

Spend some time tracking down a good class. Look for small class size, a friendly yet efficient instructor and an orderly atmosphere that encourages learning. Courtesy of *Citydog Obedience School*, New York.

Eye contact is an essential element of your relationship with your dog. Do you have your dog's eye? Practice daily!

11

Training for City Control and Manners

"All I want him to do is come when called!"
"All I want him to do is stop pulling on the lead!"
All I want him to do is to stop chewing my things!"
All I want is a housebroken dog!"
"All I want is for him to lie down and leave me alone!"

IN FIFTEEN YEARS as a professional dog trainer I've heard so many "All I want . . ." statements that I could have put them all to music a long time ago. Trouble is, the song would be so repetitious nobody could stand to hear it. Besides, the protestations on the part of owners that they really only want one or two simple things from their pets usually just aren't true. The facts are, we demand a lot from out dogs—we ask them to be companions, friends, servants, protectors— but if they botch up even once, they're in trouble! What we really mean when we say "All I really want" is that we don't necessarily want to put a lot of effort into training our dogs, and yet they are supposed to provide all of the functions mentioned above without education. Pretty poor tradeoff in the eyes of most dogs. It is like sending a 12 year old into the operating room to perform heart surgery. Would *you* want to be at the other end of the scalpel? Similarly, would *you* want to be on the other end of the leash with a person who hasn't even taught you words you need to know? I'd bet not.

The first resolution I'd ask of you as you begin this section on training is to put this book down, go find your dog, give him or her a hug for me, and promise your pet that you are going to put some *effort* into training. Go ahead, do it.

That hug will probably do more for you than for your now probably pretty bewildered pet. I asked you to do it because promises to pets are not easily broken and training your dog to be controllable and mannerly is a promise, and in fact a gift you give to your dog. It is, actually, a *re-giving* of a gift made to your dog by the first authority figure in its life—the dog's mother.

A IS FOR ALPHA, B IS FOR BITCH

In every wolf pack there is an alpha or leader wolf. This wolf (sometimes a male, sometimes a female) established order in the pack and keeps all pack members on friendly terms. Your dog's immediate ancestors were wolves. Domesticating dogs has not cancelled this ardent need to lead or be led. You've *got* to be your dog's leader—no ifs ands or buts about it! Your dog is genetically programmed to accept leadership, or, in its absence, attempt to lead the pack himself.

The bitch keeps order in a litter of domestic dogs in a similar fashion to the way an alpha-wolf runs the pack in the wild—through low growls, eye contact and, if necessary, shake and swat physicality. The more you mimic a brood bitch in her disciplinary and love techniques, the faster your puppy or dog will become a dream dog, a civilized city canine.

THE EYES HAVE IT

The bitch stares down an offending puppy with eyes of steel if the puppy is fighting too much with a littermate, overbarking, even nursing for too long. This icy stare is often accompanied by a low growl: *Grrrrrrrrrr.* The message for you here is to reprimand by making eye contact and using a low tone of voice. Don't really growl—your dog is well aware that you are of a different species. But make your disciplinary sentence sound low, and emphasize a few choice words. A good phrase is, "Okay, Tippy, that will be *enough* of that." Pronounce the "f" sound on "enough" clearly. Drag it out a bit. Know why? When bitches reprimand puppies they will often begin with a low Grrrrr-type growl and cap off the growl with that same "ffff" sound, as in, *"Grrrrrrrrrruffff!"* Got the idea?

LEADER OR LITTERMATE

Littermates—the puppy's brothers and sisters—talk to each other very differently. They communicate in whines, whimpers or yelps, usually high-pitched in tonality. Remember, your dog learned all his communication skills back in the litter, before he ever entered human society. He will forever go back to what he learned there. And the two main points that were abundantly clear by the time he left his litter were these: "The alpha figures in my life will use low tonalities when they reprimand me or ask for eye contact. I have to listen to them. If I don't, they get physical with me. But the equals in my life, my peers, will talk more like my littermates. They'll whine. They don't have to be listened to.

Even if your dog was an orphan puppy, this is still all genetically programmed. Watch out for whining! Your tone of voice can produce the exact opposite of the good behavior you seek. You can be saying something of the utmost gravity in English (or any other language) but if you sound like you're whining, you'll be demoted to littermate status—and not listened to, probably ignored.

UP THE EYE CONTACT

Don't assume you have eye contact with your dog because he looks at you lovingly when you haul out the treat box. You want that eye exchange at the precise moments when your dog wants to look right through you, like when you call him and he stares at you as if he's never seen you before in his life, like when you tell him to get his mouth off the cable TV wire and he looks at you like you're out of your mind. Practice formally to up the eye contact.

Put a leash on your dog, sit the dog in front of you and keep a little upward pressure on the lead to keep the dog seated. Now, touch the dog's muzzle with your index finger and immediately bring your finger up to your eyes. Talk to the dog in your lowest tone as you do this: "Tippy, watch me up here I want your attention." Get those shoulders back; make the dog look up at *you*, not vice versa. You're looking for a three- to five-second "lock" of eyes. The dog will look up expectantly, even somewhat bewildered, with an expression of "What do you want?" Your unstated answer is, "Well, I don't happen to want *anything* right now, but this is formal practice in preparation for times when I *will* want you to do or *not* to do something." Practice formal eye contact twice a day, just for a *few seconds,* until you feel it overflowing into your normal dealings with your dog.

LET'S GET PHYSICAL

Hopefully all you will ever need to correct your dog will be eye contact and a low tone of voice. But if you need to get tougher, which you will if your dog is experiencing any of the behavior problems listed toward the end of this section, it's best to stick to your policy of mimicking the

151

bitch. The mother would grab her puppies by the scruff of the neck and give a sharp shake. You should invert the procedure and grab from underneath the dog's neck, elevate the dog and shake. It's often easier to shove the dog into the sit position so that the center of gravity will be in the dog's rump and ease your elevating the dog.

Another location for disciplining your dog is under the chin. With the fingers of your hand tightly closed, give a smart swat under the chin. Again, stop your dog first—don't try to swat a moving target. Your dog needs to wear a collar at all times so that you can get the dog quickly and some problem dogs need to wear a short leash attached to the collar at all times to facilitate discipline. Remember, as good as the shake and swat techniques are, as bitch-like as they are, they are worthless if you cannot get your dog quickly. Put a collar on your dog pronto and attach a short leash if you are enduring wild chase scenes.

PRAISE

Nothing succeeds like success and when your dog is successful you want him to know you are pleased, so verbal and physical praise is absolutely essential. I never use food in any phase of training. I consider it bribery, not praise. The bitch never used treats for training so why should we? However, food training is somewhat popular in the United States and Canada and if you do use it I would simply say be sure to phase it out quickly.

I prefer positive praise in clipped, constructive tonalities. When you praise, don't go overboard and slip into high-pitched littermate tonalities. Remember, the ongoing question your dog poses to himself every minute of every day is, "Is this a leader or a littermate?" To me, praise is more a way of life with your dog, a quiet and loving communication, rather than a champagne party simply because the dog performed a recall correctly. To sum up my idea of praise, let me put it this way: I might spend an hour giving my dog a massage while we watch TV together, but if he completed a thirty-minute down-stay, I would release him with an "Okay!" and a two- or three-second "dutch-rub" on the top of his head and a resounding "Good boy!" Act as if you *expect* good behavior and obedience to commands— even in the teaching phase of the commands—and make your praise reflect that attitude of expectation. I know I differ from many trainers here, but I feel that prolonged praise for simple exercises delays the training process, lessens the owner's alpha status in some cases and in many cases effectively switches the dog out of the work mode and into a play mode, which makes learning words more difficult.

The Shakedown: an effective discipline technique that mimics what "mom" would have done to a naughty puppy.

Save the swat under the chin for more serious canine crimes such as aggression. Never overdo discipline.

IN THE BEGINNING: THE WORD

You had to learn words and meanings as a kid, and you have to teach your dog words now. And don't start with the "But all I want . . . " song—remember, you promised to put some effort into training! *Every* dog must know the six basic words in order to live a happy life on this planet. *Every* dog. The words are: heel, sit, stay, come, down and no. I include in the word "down" the concept of a long down, which is the most powerful and most important exercise of all. But first things first. Let's start teaching words. The first is the most important word, "No!" There's a way to say it and a way *not* to say it.

HOW TO SAY "NO" TO YOUR DOG

"Are there any questions?" I asked my seminar group. We had been discussing discipline techniques. A thin woman with an even thinner voice got up and whined, "Is it harder to teach physical discipline techniques or verbal discipline techniques?" Without a second's pause I answered, "Verbal discipline is hardest for dog owners to master. Most people just don't know how to say "no" to their dogs," and I secretly added to myself, "and you're probably one of them."

I really didn't have anything against the lady, and it wasn't her fault she had been born with a strained, reedy voice, but I had to be frank with my seminar group. It was also apparent that the lady in question was having a considerable amount of trouble controlling her St. Bernard, who alternately pawed and pushed her during the seminar and finally pummelled her when she sat down after asking the $64,000 question. Her response was to whimper "No, no-no-no-no-noooo," and wrestle the dog into a down. By the time I stopped looking their way, both in order to answer another question and in order not to break out laughing, the dog's rear end was hiked up about four feet into the air and his front paws were spliced out in a spread-eagle fashion. This was definitely a compromise "down."

After a decade of counseling dog owners, I've come to recognize the verbally ungifted when they make the initial contact over the phone to set up an appointment. If we could insert a small recording into this book to illustrate what I mean, I could convey the undesired voice tonality clearly, but then again, it is not a record you would want to listen to more than once.

The vocally unskilled talk too softly, and when they address the dog, everything they say is posed as a question, either by syntax or by inflection. For instance, the down command, which should be given as "down" or as "lie down," is instead delivered as "How about a down?" or just "Down?" But the dog was not trained with these kind of vocalistics in obedience class unless the instructor was just plain irresponsible.

Most teachers will at least attempt to correct the handler who is

154

verbally ineffective ("Tell him, don't ask him" is a common reprimand) but because of the structure of many classes, the instructor can't spend enough time drilling the person into more effective voice control. So, the owner toughens up the voice for class, or risks another public reproach, but continues to talk to the dog ineffectively at home. This is the wrong kind of training—unintentional training. The dog learns that doing what you're told only applies to class (after all, the owner sounds like they mean it there but doesn't sound that way at home). Then, the instructor hears, "He's fine in class or when *you* work with him, but he's terrible at home," and proceeds to run the student through the physical paces once more in an effort to see what's wrong. This may be the wrong approach. Even if the owner is lacking in skill in executing certain physical training techniques, the real problem is often the voice.

The word "no" is a concrete example. Many handlers whine the word. The long "o" in the word seems to almost encourage this response. The owner can plant his or her tongue firmly on the roof of the mouth, press it there for a second and thereby launch into a sustained nasal, whiny "o" sound. To the dog it sounds like an invitation to play. In some cultures, softly cooed "oooh" sounds are used to entertain and animate both children and dogs. This is especially true in some Slavic cultures. Americans say, "coochie, coochie, *cooo*" to entertain babies. And the dog owner's "no" becomes a similar "noooh" all too easily and all too often.

To remedy the abuse of this all-important word, which is so central to the understanding the dog must have of what his pack-leader wants, I've developed two responses. For the chronics, who will never learn to say the word correctly and in a way that the dog understands, I just forbid them to use it at all. I note that the Germans, for instance, say "Phooey!" to stop bad behavior in its tracks. You don't *have* to use "no."

A second solution is to suggest that the owner always say "nope" instead of "no" in the hope that the added "p" sound will short-circuit any whining. It often does, because it's harder to coo "ooh" when you've already stopped yourself with a "p." Try it.

But even if you say "no" correctly, it often isn't enough. We all remember our mothers using our full names when they wanted our undivided attention: "Michael Richard Evans, *NO,* stop that right now," and of course I did. It's the same working principle with dogs. Your warning phrase should include the dog's name, the word "no" (said, of course, correctly) and a short phrase. Usually it's best to add the dog's name in the middle or even last, so as not to confuse the dog's recall training with discipline. Since many owners simply do not know what phrase to use, I've included some examples. Try these on Fido:

"No, Fido, stop that—I mean it."
"*No*—that's enough, Fido—you know how you are."

"*No,* don't even *think* of it Fido."
"Hey! *No,* I don't want to see it Fido."

Shoot your voice up, not into a shriek, and firmly deliver the first section of the reprimand. Then, for the extension, drop your voice in both volume *and* pitch. This seals the warning into the dog's mind. You mean it. Further action will be forthcoming if this warning is not obeyed. The dog had better think it over.

Many times it is necessary for women (especially if they own large working breeds) to dramatically lower their voices, even to the point where they think such affectation is humorous. All sexism aside, the fact is that many of these breeds were originally developed *by* men *for* men—as working, serving employees. In many breeds, there were already generations of genetic selection based at least partially on the ability of the dog to respond to verbal commands—commands usually issued by a man. Later, when women began to handle the dogs in the field or in the home, it quickly became apparent that the dogs needed a firm verbal style if they were to understand and obey commands. This does not mean that screaming or shouting was common. The key to obedience is hardly ever upping the volume but rather perfecting inflection, tone and pitch from the dog's point of view.

Another interesting phenomenon concerning verbal patterns with dogs: Why is it that our voices almost automatically go up in pitch, become lighter in tone and we start talking baby talk when we meet a dog of the Toy Group? If you meet a German Shepherd, Doberman or Bulldog, you might express verbal praise, but if you meet a Yorkie or a Maltese, you talk to it as if it were an infant—and you might reprimand it in a totally ineffective way. It's probably the smallness of these breeds, the appeal to our protective instincts (which is quite unconscious on the part of the dog) and the overall "cuteness" quotient that encourages this. Yet, a Yorkie being reprimanded is no different, in many ways, than a Great Dane being reprimanded. The vocal quality of the correction should be the same. I'd be the first to admit I suffer from this curious affliction—at seminars or in a class setting I'll be talking to a Mastiff as if he were Sylvester Stallone and immediately turn to the Pekingese and talk as if I was being introduced to newly born Prince William of England. Sex or age has nothing to do with the response—both Mastiff and Pekingese could be the same age and male. I'll have to work on it!

We shouldn't underestimate the importance of talking to our dogs correctly, especially when we have to say no to them. It's not just a matter of getting the dog to do what we want when we want it done. It's also a matter of not hopelessly confusing the dog by our own vocal lacks, of not unintentionally training the dog to ignore us and of not nagging the dog into further disobedience and even manipulation. If this article spurs you to reevaluate your own verbal patterns, the next step would be to tape yourself talking to your dog and play the tape, casting yourself as the dog. If you're not listening to yourself, you're in trouble. If you crack up listening to yourself on tape, chances are your dog has been laughing at you (versus laughing with you, which he should do) for years. The next step? Get thee to a trainer who knows how to talk to dogs. Learning how to say no could be one of the nicest things you do for your dog. Now, on to other "nice" words—words that can liberate your dog for city life.

TEACHING CONTEXT/CITY CONTEXT

In this section I'll first explain how to teach a word, giving just the mechanics and a few flourishes. Then I'll give you tips on just how to *use* that word in a city context. Remember, teaching your dog words will be useless unless those words are really usable in *real life* situations. Please, don't assume that your dog knows a command if he only does it some of the time. For instance, if your dog sits and stays while you fix his morning meal or when you offer a treat but disobeys the same command when you issue it to stop him from jumping on friends visiting the apartment—I'm sorry to inform you but your dog *doesn't know the sit-stay.*

I mention this misperception on the part of the dog owners at this precise juncture because it is one of the most common reasons that dog training doesn't "take" with some dogs. Their misguided owners think the dog already "knows" certain words when the dog just *doesn't.* In my years of training the most common song I've heard, after the "All I want him to do" number is, "Oh, he knows how to sit." At which point the owner says "sit" and the dog does it. How wonderful. But two minutes ago this same dog was literally scaling my body as if it were Mount Everest and the same owner was running toward us screeching "Sit! Sit!" I'm supposed to believe this dog "knows" the sit. The scratches on my body inform me otherwise. Don't delude yourself about which words your dog knows. A good exercise is to think of the *worst* possible moment you could ask your dog to obey a certain word and then level with yourself: Would your dog perform? If you have the slightest doubt about a given word, you must not skip the section teaching the word and teaching the city context for that word. You must read it and practice that section. Don't cheat. You'll only cheat yourself and your dog.

When you first introduce a word, teach it in a *quiet* place, perhaps your living room, and then graduate to the city context training. If you can't practice at home try to find a nook or cranny where city distractions are minimal. Then you can practice in more hectic areas. You can then legitimately correct your dog strongly and be able to say, "Look, Fido, it's not as if we've never studied this word before." The dog will see that words

157

apply at all times and in all places, the parlor or the Plaza, the living room or the Loop.

When you come to the city context portion for each exercise you will find numerous references to "proofing." What is proofing? Let Diane Bauman, author of *Beyond Basic Dog Training* (Howell Book House) explain: "Proofing is a term used to describe a technique of testing a dog's understanding of an exercise. Proofing clarifies concepts while strengthening the dog's concentration and confidence." In other words, proofing means getting that word into the dog's head *good* and *tight,* testing the word, polishing it up, getting your dog to resist distractions and obey the command word each time, every time. By the way, while Ms. Bauman is writing for those showing in the obedience ring, her book can aid city owners as well. After all, what type of training goes *Beyond Basic Dog Training* more than training a civilized city canine? Frankly the distractions to effective training I've encountered in Manhattan make the much more predictable distractions that occur at show sites look rather frivolous. This only indicates the necessity of proofing every word against the craziness of the city that much more important.

Let's begin with heeling, our effort to produce an angelic dog walking calmly, peacefully by your side without pulling, lunging, lagging or dragging you across 57th Street into oncoming traffic.

EQUIPMENT

Be sure to use a metal collar with pounded flat links. The links should be pounded flat, not rounded, so that the collar will have good, clean action and deliver a correction quickly. Run your hand across the links before you purchase the collar. Are they flat? Make your hand into a fist and pass the collar over your fist onto your wrist. Give it a snap. Does it deliver a correction and then release promptly? If so, buy it. If not, look around for a collar that gives a correction with a connection. Nylon collars are also acceptable, but they tend to stretch with continued pulling.

Pinch (prong) collars are, in my opinion, usually unnecessary. Used by angry owners who do not have timing to deliver corrections correctly (which is usually the case, otherwise why would the owner be forced to use a prong collar?) they can inflict pain and even puncture the dog's neck. There are some rare cases where these type of collars are in order, especially if you are slight of build and own a dog with an extremely powerful fore-assembly, but if you invest in a good quality metal collar with pounded, flat links and keep that collar up *high* around the dog's neck, your corrections will most definitely get through.

What about harnesses? Many city owners use such contraptions and I've seen rhinestone and even diamond-studded ones. The fact is, it is almost impossible to get a dog to heel tightly using a harness. The sheer force the dog can exert on the leash, plus the nonspecificity of the corrective tug that is delivered to the harness, hinders proper heeling. Once in a great while there will be a dog with a trachea problem (or a propensity for such problems) that will dictate use of a harness and nothing else. But this is not often the case and unless your veterinarian has specifically instructed you to use a harness, I would prefer that you use a training collar. You will notice that I do not use the stupid term "choke chain." Properly used, there is no "choking" involved.

The most frequent error owners make in outfitting their dogs is to select a collar that is far too high for the dog. It's best to measure your dog's neck and select a collar that is no more than three to four inches oversize when it is pulled tight on the dog's neck. With most breeds, this means that the collar will be snug when you put it over the dog's neck and somewhat tight to remove. Always manipulate the dog's ears under the collar before putting it on or off—don't just tug, tug, tug. Your dog will only resist and you will falsely conclude that you need a larger collar. I've seen collars on Yorkshire Terriers that were more appropriate for Great Danes, and collars on Great Danes that would be more appropriate for Shetland ponies.

There's a right and a wrong way to put on the collar. The best way to learn is to simply duplicate with your body and your dog the photograph that accompanies this chapter. Stand with your dog at your left side. Slip on the collar. When hung in front of the dog's face it will look like the letter "P" turned sideways. Be sure the bulging part of the "P" faces downward.

You also need a good, strong leash. I prefer a leather leash with braided construction. Leather does not slip through your hands as easily as nylon or cotton-webbed leashes. The braided construction serves as an assurance that the leash will not break since there are no sewn parts to fray or give way accidentally. This means you can give quality corrections without the fear that your leash will break.

Remember, proper equipment will be essential in teaching heeling. You will need a *tight* heel. In New York City at the most congested intersection, 47th and 5th Avenue, 12,000 pedestrians pass in an hour. Chicago and Toronto clock in 4,000 to 6,000 pedestrians an hour. San Francisco and Seattle have lower counts but nevertheless, you'll want your dog well trained to avoid the crush.

HEELING

Do your walks with your dog resemble the chariot scene in *Ben Hur?* If they do you need to teach your dog to heel. It's a somewhat funny word to many people and they feel uncomfortable saying it to a dog because they've never said it before. In fact, most trainers don't know why we use

I prefer a metal collar made of pounded-flat links for good, clean action in correcting the dog. Nylon "snap-around" collars are fine, too, but prong collars are rarely needed.

The correct way of putting on the training collar.

A leather leash with braided construction and no sewn parts assures you that it won't break—no small worry for the city owner.

160

this word! The reason it's said is that phonetically it doesn't sound like any of the other command words. If you say the five basic words aloud you'll hear that they all sound very different. So clear pronunciation of the words *is* important and screaming commands or reprimands is absolutely taboo. There's no quicker way to cheapen yourself in a dog's eyes than to yell command words or scream reprimands. I train dogs in New York City and I never yell or scream. Make the dog listen for the commands.

Two good rules of thumb are: (1) when giving a command or reprimanding the dog, change your tonality (lower it) *not* your volume; (2) if the command is for an active exercise, pitch your voice slightly higher (heel, come) or slightly lower for static commands (down, stay, sit). Remember, if the exercise involves movement, up your voice; if it doesn't, keep your voice low.

In heeling the dog is at your left hand side at your heel. Keep your hands palm down on the leash so that you have the full power of your forearm to give your dog a correction in toward your thigh. Use a metal training collar with pounded flat links for proper action. Unless your breed is short-coated, keep the collar up high around the dog's neck with the rounded rings of the collar rotated under the ear closest to you. Step off, saying, "Tippy, heel."

It is a nice courtesy to step off with the foot closest to the dog (your left foot) so he can see that you're leaving. If your dog lunges or lags give the appropriate correction with the leash. Make it a smart snap, not a restrained choke action. Snapping that leash, popping that collar, zipping the dog the corrections are the keys to good heeling. Restraining the dog will only result in a terrible stand-off between you and your dog.

Use plenty of praise as you strut. When you stop, sit your dog next to you by simultaneously pulling directly up on the leash and pushing down on the dog's rump. You'll find in time that just a slight snap of the lead up and slightly in toward you "telegraphs" a sit down your dog's backbone.

The Automatic Sit

Part of the heeling process is teaching your dog to sit automatically when you stop. This technique can be trained right with the heel. Some dogs just sit naturally when the owner stops and if yours does count yourself lucky—you were spared a sore back. But if yours doesn't, pull up slightly on the training collar as you stop and, if necessary, transfer your right hand to the base of the leash. This will free up your left hand to guide the dog's bottom into a sit as your right hand jerks the collar up. Drill your dog. Take five steps and insist on a sit. Take another five steps. Sit. And so on. *Don't* say "sit"—just get it. If you say the word the dog will learn the heeling exercise as follows: "Heeling means stay by my mistress' or master's side, and when they stop, *remain standing* until they say, 'sit.'" You will then be doomed to saying "sit" every time you stop, which in a city, will be

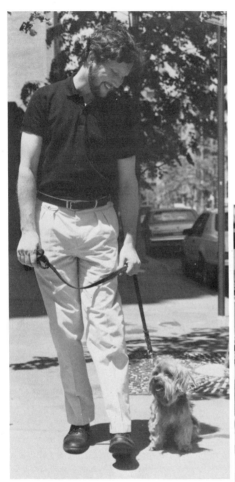

Start out with your left foot to begin heeling.

Teach your civilized canine hallway, elevator and lobby etiquette. Greeting the doorman should be done politely. Lobby lungers are not appreciated.

often. The automatic sit is *not* ornamental for the city dog—it is essential. Insist on it, each and every time, especially at curbs. Be careful about double commands like "Sit down" or "C'mon, heel" while practicing heeling. Remember, "down" and "sit" will very shortly be distinct words meaning desired actions in a short time. Don't confuse your dog. Use "Let's go" as a term of encouragement instead.

Okays

"Okays" are used when you want to release your dog from strict heeling to relieve itself, to play with another dog, to sniff around or to just hang out without heeling. I don't believe that the city dog should pull you to where it likes to eliminate, play or sniff. Instead, I believe in an either/or proposition for the city dog, which means that you heel your dog to the spots where *you* want him to engage in any of these activities, and release the dog from heel with a loudly pronounced, "Okay!" Your palms will be flat down on the leash, but now, turn your left hand around and dramatically push the leash forward, clearly indicating that the loose lead means more freedom. Let's say that your dog is now through eliminating or playing, or let's say it becomes obvious to you that the dog is empty, or the dog is simply garbaging and abusing the "Okay" or there is glass in the area or for whatever reason, you want to move on. You then end the "okay" by bringing your dog back into the heel position, hiking the collar up high and reissuing the "heel" command. Continue on your way.

City Context for Heeling

It is absolutely essential for the city owner to realize that *heeling begins indoors.* You cannot allow your dog to *pull* you out the apartment door, *pull* you down the hallway, *pull* you into the elevator, *pull* you out of the elevator, *pull* you through the lobby and *pull* you out onto the street and *then* ask your dog to "heel." You've already relinquished control and it is far too late to regain it. Worse, if you consistently allow a dog to precede you in or out of the main entrance to territory, you're telling your dog a whole heck of a lot about who owns that territory. Your dog will think, *"I go first, my wimpo owner goes second."* Remember, dogs don't think in terms of addresses, street names, boroughs or neighborhoods. They think in primitive terms of *territory*—and who owns the territory is often dictated by who goes first.

Worse yet, if your dog door-charges three or four times a day you're allowing your dog to take charge. Your dog gets a chance to stake a claim to the territory, with ensuing problems. Quick examples: the dog is allowed to barge out of the apartment or brownstone and has a problem fighting with other dogs. Aren't you setting the stage for fighting by allowing the barge? Another: the dog chews destructively when the owner is not home. If you routinely let the dog crash into the brownstone, crash up the hall and crash into your apartment before you, aren't you telegraphing to him that the home is *his* territory—to chew, to trash, to "rearrange" at whim? Heeling *must* begin indoors, and part of heeling is checking your dog with a training collar correction if he attempts to barge—in or out of territory.

Hallway and Elevator Etiquette

I once had as a student a certain brownstone bruiser who literally dragged his owner down three flights of stairs three times a day, 365 days a year. The owner, to prevent being pulled face-forward and mutilating himself, had taken to (this is the truth) sitting on the polished oak railings and letting his Doberman pull him down to floor one. The railings all connected in this old brownstone with a spiral staircase. The owner was quite proud of his dexterity and even kept the railing polished with furniture wax to ease his descent. He insisted on showing me his feat, and while I admit it was quite comical, the aggression of the dog toward other dogs once it hit the street was most definitely not. This dog was taught Evans-style hallway and staircase etiquette *pronto.* His spiral staircase steeplechase was in fact aiding his feelings that he "owned" the borough of Brooklyn.

I believe firmly that urban dogs should be taught to hold sit-stays on either side of the door. No matter how wild your dog is, no matter how overjoyed he is to be going for a walk *do not* let your dog hurry you into opening the door until you have had the dog sit. Then, and only then do you go through your doorway into the hallway. Now, sit your dog again. The reason? You need to be able to lock-up without a lunging maniac trying to pull you toward the elevator or down the stairs. Pull up sharply on the collar and say, "sit." Do *not* lock your door or proceed in any way until you have these "sandwich sits" on either side of your dwelling's door.

Remember, you are setting the pace for everything that will follow whether peaceful or pandemonium-filled on the street in just a few short minutes. Insist on sandwich sits on both sides of the door.

Now, if you live in an elevator building, walk toward the elevator; if you live in a building with stairs, walk toward the stairs. *Don't* let your dog lunge ahead—give a smart check on the collar with a "No!" and then "Heel!" Remember your tonality and don't scream. At the elevator, sit your dog *away* from the doors. Teach your dog to gravitate toward the wall. There's nothing worse for another tenant to confront than stepping on a dog as they exit the elevator because some inconsiderate dog owner allows their dog to snoop around the elevator door opening indiscriminately. People exiting the elevator often get tripped-up, jumped on or even mauled by such creatures who are allowed to wait for the elevator by pacing around randomly. Wall-train your city canine and issue the "stay" command too.

When the elevator arrives, don't allow your dog to barge into it. Practice giving the stay command (see the next section) and even if you have to miss an elevator, let your dog know that *you* are the one who says "heel" and gives the permission to enter the elevator. Just because an elevator door opens does not mean that your dog is free to jerk you in. Through this elevator etiquette, as formal as it may sound, you are, quite apart from being courteous to your fellow tenants, setting the style and pace for all that is to happen or not happen on the street.

It is just plain rude and discourteous to let your dog sniff, nuzzle or accost other passengers in the elevator. Read on to the sit-stay section and teach this in the elevator as part of the manners you expect. If your dog engages in rude sniffing, jerk the collar hard and say "no sniffing!" Then, loosen the lead to give the dog a chance to do the rude sniffing again. If he does, you're being informed that your correction just wasn't enough. You will have to readminister the correction. Use this same technique if your dog "garbages" on the street. Teach your dog to sit and stay near the wall of the elevator. There's nothing more annoying than to have a dog (the bigger the dog the more annoying it is) firmly plopped down and ensconced in the middle of the elevator, forcing human passengers to go against the wall, scrunched up with their packages and parcels.

You will find, however, if your dog enters the elevator with aplomb, sits against the wall and does not annoy others he or she is welcomed with open arms, genuine affection and even missed when you appear dogless on the elevator. The reputation of an elevator canine Jack the Ripper spreads quickly, though, and the owner is often asked to use the service elevator or the stairs. In fact, in New York, unruly behavior in the elevator and lobby has led many buildings to insist that all dogs, regardless of their behavior, use service elevators or stairs. It's too bad that a few untrained dogs have to make it difficult for all the rest. It could all be avoided with a little training in hallway and elevator etiquette.

If your building doesn't have an elevator, you are still responsible for keeping your canine charger from bowling over fellow tenants who frequent the stairs. Enforce the heel up and down the stairs and please don't get into the common and lamentable practice of letting your dog off the lead once inside the building to run up or down to your apartment. Along the way he can maul or even maim unsuspecting stairway users. Some owners allow this because they feel that running up or down the staircase provides much needed exercise for the city dog and they are right. But try to do your stairway exercise at a time when few others will be on the stairs.

Elevator users in high rises: be sure to teach your dog to negotiate stairs! This is often overlooked. I've been called in to teach many a city dog who is suddenly removed from a high rise, where it rode the elevator and never had to so much as take a step up or down, how to negotiate a third floor walk-up. Expose your puppy to stairs early on, and if your older dog has a problem with the stairs, insist on the heel. Encourage the dog firmly and constructively and at the head of the stairs issue the command, "Okay, Lassie, *heel,*" so that your dog sees that heeling applies to staircases as well. You can fudge on the "only on the left" rule here and let your staircase scardeycat hug the wall for comfort and bracing purposes. Remember with the long-backed breeds, such as Daschunds or Corgis, to take the stairs *slowly.* These breeds are prone to spinal disc problems and stairs can aggravate this condition.

If all this elevator etiquette sounds too Emily Post, let me remind you of "Henry," who lacked all such manners and got on an elevator on his own (he barged out the apartment door). He rode around for some time, jumping up on the floor-selection panel to "pick" his desired floor. He would get off whenever he wanted, run around that floor, crash into any apartment that happened to have a door opening or closing, terrorize the tenants and then get back on the elevator, push a few more floors, ride a bit and repeat the whole process again. Somehow he always got back to his floor. His owner thought this was "cute" behavior and that it demonstrated the dog's intelligence. Unfortunately most of the other tenants thought it was distinctly rude. They served Henry's owner with an eviction notice. The next week, "Henry" broke free and again went elevator-riding, this time getting off at the lobby, scurrying past the doorman and directly into the path of an oncoming car. How very sad. The owner, at least, got to stay in her apartment, and I found out about this incident when I trained her second dog, who follows Evans' Elevator Etiquette eloquently.

The Lobby

Many city dogs lunge through the lobby, intent on getting to the street and being free to defecate, urinate or, if untrained, walk their owners. Their desire is perfectly understandable and perfectly unacceptable, for the lobby of most city buildings is a place of decorum and poise, a place where people stop to chat, to pick up their mail, to receive a package or dry cleaning, to talk to the doorman or to receive a message. A lunging maniac at the other end of the leash doesn't really endear the owner to anyone else passing by.

Do yourself and your dog a favor and for the next week do a five-second "pit stop" in the lobby. Teach your dog that the lobby is a place where you might stop—because, after all, you *do* stop there, for mail, for messages, for conversation. Simply stop and exert a little upward pressure on the leash. This will tend to keep your dog in a sit. Let lobby traffic flow around you, and then proceed outside. Do *not* let your dog lunge through the lobby or you will make heeling outside much more difficult—you will have relinquished control in advance and allowed the dog to taste territory that is not, technically, his.

One victim of lobby lungers is the unfortunate doorman or concierge who must open the door or preside over the lobby. Most doormen love to greet their building's dogs, and some even keep a supply of treats available for resident dogs. But they do not appreciate being jumped on, having their uniforms torn or dirtied or being interrupted in their duties by an unruly dog. Teach your dog to sit and stay to greet your doorman; if he is too busy to say hello, inform your dog, by enforcing a strict heel, that sometimes stopping to say hello is not possible. If your doorman is especially kind to your dog as it passes through the lobby, or does anything out of the ordinary for your doggy friend, you owe that doorman the same bonus at Christmastime as you would grant if he had done you yourself a personal favor. In checking over my records for my last five years as a New York City dog trainer I was surprised to find that a full 7 percent of the referrals I've had for new dogs and owners have been via doormen. I always give doormen my card when I leave a building. After all, they have already seen the *worst* aspects of a city dog's behavior and are often grateful that their lobby is now liberated from a dog who was a nuisance. They'd like all dogs in their building to be so well mannered.

Out onto the Streets

If you've set up an atmosphere of order and control inside your building, taking your heeling act to the streets shouldn't be like entering a war zone—although I'm the first to admit that city streets provide surprises and distractions that can challenge the competence of the best trainers. Let's go over some of the biggest problems one by one. Let's begin with small-fry distractions and build up to bigger ones.

Pigeon-Proofing. First, pigeons. If you are laughing you haven't met New York or Venice pigeons. They are smart. They are quick. They love to tease dogs. Training against pigeons has to be tight, and pigeon-proofing isn't easy. However, from a technical point of view it's all part of obeying the word "heel."

Teach your dog early on that pigeons are not prey. If he lunges toward a bird, snap the collar back hard with a stern, "No." If you can then head through another flock of birds, so much the better. This will give your dog a chance to heel correctly right away. *Doubling back* is, in fact, the key to correcting heeling havoc with most city distractions. Doubling back, that is, and *advance warnings.*

Advance warnings consist of a sentence delivered in a low, authoritative voice: "Okay, Konrad, don't even *think* about it...." Then, at the least, you've warned the dog about your intentions to correct and you will

Pigeon-proof your dog! Snap the collar sharply and say, "No"—then, double back and try to find another pigeon to give your dog a chance to do it right. *Mark Bergman*

Heeling applies even when bikes, skateboards and other moving objects whiz by. Don't avoid such distractions—head *toward* them to practice heeling.

correct with a leash jerk, the shake or even the swat if you have to. At the most, you might be able to glide past distractions like pigeons with impunity. Doubling back helps to secure one more chance to correct if the first reprimand didn't "take."

Manhole Covers and Gratings. Many city canines will spook at manhole covers and panic when they have to walk over a grating of any kind. At first the unsuspecting owner might not recognize what is troubling his companion because such distractions are so common in city walking. When the owner catches on he or she might be sympathetic since the owner might also tend to avoid such interruptions in the pavement of the city to spare himself or herself falls, broken heels or worse. Trouble is, manhole covers and gratings liberally dot most cities and if your pet refuses to walk over some of them, soon it will refuse any and all of them. Of course you should not attempt to get your dog to walk over gratings or manhole covers that are dangerous, but most are designed to accept weight and tolerate pedestrian traffic and you should take the tact that most trainers of Seeing Eye dogs apply: teach your dog to walk over such distractions. Believe me, if you simply try to avoid such obstacles your pet will soon add things to the list of what he or she will not walk over. Soon, you'll be unable to walk a block without the dog erratically breaking heel, jutting in front of you or tripping you up because of fear of a manhole cover, a grating, a puddle, a drop-off at the curb or even a white line painted on the street. Don't let this cycle begin. Teach your dog to be brave!

Begin by delivering that all-important advance warning in your lowest, most growling tone as you approach the gaping "hole" in the earth you know your dog is going to refuse to traverse. Now, go. Just go. Pull your pet forward. Don't worry, he'll go with you if he wants to be where his head is. If necessary, stop, turn and give a slight shakedown, then reissue, "Heel!" and continue. You might want to stop dead center in the middle of the grating and sit your dog. Insist on the automatic sit and just pause. Let your dog see that nothing is wrong with the grating, the manhole cover or other "unsafe" surfaces. Talk calmly yet constructively to your dog. Flash the "stay" signal discussed in the next section and pause there together. Believe me, it's worth the little tension involved. Your choice is a dog who panics at every walk and zig-zags along the street breaking heel constantly.

Bikes, Skateboards, Shopping Carts and Other Moving Objects. Right now I am working with a Westie who lunges for delivery boys who drive pedal-powered push carts that rattle, a Cairn who attacks kids on skateboards and a Norwich Terrier who hates any and all bikes—tricycles and their riders included. I would be less than honest with you if I disguised the fact that many terriers see such objects as prey. Since no one is about to outlaw food deliveries or kids on bikes or skateboards in the cities, the

169

An advance warning as you near a manhole cover makes all the difference in the world to many dogs. Deliver one in a low tone and proceed with heeling.

Some gratings are unsafe for dogs but many are meant to be walked on and are difficult to avoid. Teach your dog to negotiate them by delivering an advance warning including the "heel" command . . . and then gliding your dog into the automatic sit right on the grating. Your dog will quickly see there's no danger.

170

solution is train dogs not to spark at such distractions. This applies even to terriers.

The solution is a low advance warning, coupled with a foray into and toward the distraction, a repeated correction (get physical if you have to) and then *doubling back* reissuing the strict "heel" command. It takes timing, it takes tolerance and it may take a session with a professional. Sometimes city distractions happen so frequently and so fast that a lay owner might find it impossible to cope. That's when you need a trainer. But before you call one in, give it your best shot using my methods.

Most importantly, *stop avoiding* such distractions! When most owners who have such dogs see a skateboard or spot a bike, they head the other way pronto. First, that's no way to live, and secondly, there will be *another* kid on a skateboard or on a bike right around the corner. So what are you trying to avoid? Real life? Instead, you should confidently head *toward* the distractions that send your dog into a tail-spin, issue your advance warning, heel past them, correct if necessary and if possible double back. Believe me, that's the only way to desensitize the city canine that skateboards are not prey, that bikes are not bait. Your alternative choice is to go out only at 3:00 A.M. or move to the country (but I hear they have skateboards and bikes there, too).

The One-Hand Heel

Once you've mastered heeling and your dog is gliding by at your side, sitting automatically whenever you stop and not pulling, you are ready to take one hand off the leash and practice the very practical one-handed heel. Wind your top-quality leather lead around your left hand and make a fist over the leash. Place your other hand in your pocket, or carry your umbrella or packages. Proceed. Get ready, heeling difficulties will suddenly take on new urgency. Your dog will somehow sense the change and will try to lunge, lag, veer or trip you up. That's why it's best to take your dog on a test run for one-handed heeling.

I had a client who didn't. She went to Tiffany's. Her dog was admitted, as many well-trained dogs are in finer shops in New York (as they are in Europe). She shopped and bought an item, a splendid glass piece. Her dog sat like a king in the store, proud, holding a sit-stay, regal, dignified. But the moment the owner hit the street the dog jerked forward suddenly, sensing that the owner only had one hand on the leash, and, presto, the glass piece was on the sidewalk, shattered. That dog is still alive, and he now knows the one-handed heel.

Lunging at Other Dogs

By far the worst problem for the city owner in teaching and maintaining the heel will be the distraction of other dogs. Passing other dogs on the

As you become more proficient in heeling, practice one-hand heeling so that you will have the other free to carry packages or an umbrella—essential if you live in London, Seattle, Vancouver or Portland!

172

street can be a nightmare for many owners. There are various "golden hours" in different cities when the dog population on the streets swells. In New York, the "golden hours" are 5:00–7:00 P.M.; in San Francisco and L.A., the time is slightly later. These are the hours when everyone gets home from work and rushes to take their dog out for a walk. If I can, I *deliberately* schedule sessions with dog sparkers and fighters for these hours, since the streets will provide me with all the doggy distractions I need. Most of my clients, playing the avoidance game, have been waiting out the "golden hours" until the street population of dogs subsides. But they soon find that at 9:00 P.M. or at 3:00 A.M. there is still a dog out on the street—and probably one owned by another owner playing the avoidance game, fearful of having their lunging lunatic accost another dog.

It is important to understand the psychology behind city dog disputes. Here's what happens, from the point of view of the owners: Two owners with dogs in tow meet on the sidewalk, the dogs lunge at each other barking wildly, perhaps also snarling and snapping. Perhaps only one dog displays such behavior. Either way, the two humans are deeply embarrassed and usually offer an excuse. Favorite excuses:

"I'm sorry, he doesn't like males (or females)."
"She doesn't like white fluffy dogs like yours."
"He's old and grouchy."
"He doesn't see very well anymore."
"She just had an operation."
"She doesn't like any other dogs."
He doesn't like New York (or Toronto, L.A., Chicago, etc.)."
"She hates everybody, even me!"

The owner usually whimpers this excuse using marvelous littermate stress tones, and the resulting tonalities inform the dog that aggression is, indeed, indicated and wanted. The dog obliges further and the owner, perhaps repeating the same or another excuse, drags the dog apart from the other team and down the street. Of course each dog is lagging behind, looking over its shoulder and getting in just a few more barks and growls. The owner wipes the perspiration off the forehead and braces for the next dog-eat-dog encounter.

Here's what happens from the dog's point of view. Let me narrate it for you, speaking as a dog: "Well, we're going for a walk again. I wonder who I'll get to eat today? Boy, am I rarin' to go! Why does that stupid owner of mine take so long to put my collar and leash on? He's getting slower every day. I'll just bark and jump around here a bit to hurry him up. It's working. Look at him rushing to get his coat and telling me to just 'Hold on, hold on, we're going.' Don't give me excuses, just move it. Aaaah, that's it, nice and fast. Now comes my favorite part, when I run out the apartment door first and get to do my Tarzan yell, announcing to the world that this hallway, this elevator, this lobby, this apartment building and this city is my supreme territory! Mine to defend, to preserve, to conquer! Just let any other dog come my way I'll show him. . . . Wow, there's one now. . . . What a great fight! What a high! Too bad my owner is pulling me away, but wait, I've still won, look at that other dog running away from me! I am the toughest dog on this block. Next?"

While this is certainly an anthropomorphic rendering of canine thought processes, any canine behaviorist knows that what was said above is technically accurate. You'll notice that in the above scenario, the dog never gets a correction, only restraint. Nor does he ever hear a *command* word, just a whimpered warning that is next to meaningless and that might, in fact, increase his desire to be aggressive. If commands like "heel" and "sit" and "stay" are not taught and enforced, why should the dog do anything *but* fight? In my opinion, if nothing is said, nothing should be expected in the way of good behavior.

If you have a fighter, immediately stop making excuses. That is always the first step in training—not the mechanical step, but the psychological step. Resolve to stop the dog from wreaking further havoc on the street. Tell yourself you will no longer cheapen yourself by walking the streets with Jack the Ripper. Do whatever you have to do but get motivated fast. Train, don't complain.

Begin by teaching the heel in a quiet place, even the hallway of your building. Tighten up that automatic sit. Drill your dog. Take five steps and get an automatic sit. Five more steps, sit; five steps and sit. Get it tight. No yelling. No whining. Keep the collar up *high* with the ring of the collar rotated underneath the dog's ear closest to you. Be sure there is no more than three inches of extension when the training collar is pulled tight. Be sure you have an unbreakable leather leash.

Sit your dog at the door of your apartment, make eye contact and issue a strict warning in a low tone: "Okay, Bruiser, you touch one dog on the street and you're history." Now, proceed. Follow the previously described elevator etiquette to the letter. Prevent any lobby lunging. At your first sighting of another dog tap your dog's forehead, issue that low warning phrase again and go forward. Don't issue the warning continually and don't say it too loudly—otherwise the approaching owner will know your dog is a killer and avoid you, ruining your chance to correct your dog. I often tell my clients to say something elusive like, "Bruiser, look at me—you know how you are," if suddenly brought face to face with another dog/owner team. Remember, advance warnings often make the difference between a lunge or a lull in the fighting. Don't hope that your dog will be good this one time. Of course he won't. He'll probably be worse. Warn, and add a firm, but not loud, "Heel."

If your dog disobeys the warning and the command word you are perfectly justified in correcting him strongly. Use a leash-jerk correction,

Lunging at other dogs can be solved by enforcing a tight heel as I'm doing here. The other dog, though, is most definitely *not* on heel. Here's the wind-up . . .

. . . and the pitch.

To "proof" my dog against the distraction I'm doubling back again. The other dog should be trained similarly and would no longer lunge.

Off-leash street scrappers will often agitate dogs on leash. Point a finger between the two dogs that are facing off and put the leashed dog on a sit-stay fast.

176

the swat under the chin, the shake or all three but make him maintain the heel. Do not stop. Keep moving. There will come a time when your dog can be put on a sit-stay and made to face other dogs strolling by without molesting them, but for now, you need to simply teach your dog to *pass* other dogs in peace. Whatever scrap develops, correct your dog as strongly as is necessary and move along. *Quickly* apologize to the human involved if there is a fight. "Sorry, Sir or Ma'am" will do. Save your time for your dog. Concentrate on the canine. If you make it quite clear that you are training and disciplining the other owner will understand why you can't stop to chitchat. Fact is, his dog might have the same problem.

If you can double back without offending the other owner, do so promptly. The other dog is probably being dragged away at a fast clip, and you want to cash in on this distraction and have your dog pass again, this time in the right way. Say "Heel" again, turn quickly and double back around the same dog. Glide by. Issue that warning again. Now, depending on where you were originally going (before all this transpired you *were* going someplace, weren't you?) double back again and continue on your way. You just got two or even three corrections for the price of one. You just amazed another dog owner. You just taught your dog that he is *passing* other dogs on the street, not chasing other dogs away. There will be another chance to warn, correct, and double back on the next block, if not sooner. But perhaps it won't be so rough this time. Perhaps Bruiser will listen to the quiet but firm advance warning. Perhaps he will inhibit his desire to fight from *within,* opting to obey the command word instead. Perhaps this initial period of heavy *enforcement* from you toward your dog will mellow into an *agreement* between the two of you.

Until that agreement is a reality, don't let your dog play with other dogs. When he is passing without provoking, pick a few select dogs, perhaps some of his old friends (I hope he had *some!*) and give some selected "Okays" for play. Watch carefully for any signs of aggression. They are:

- Ears pricked forward
- "Hardness" of the eyes, firm eye-set, glassy eyes
- Hackles (the hair on the back of the neck) erect

If you see any of these signs, issue your warning, and if the signs do not subside, jerk your dog toward you and issue a physical correction. You can then decide to let the dog resume relations with the other dog or move on and put your dog back on heel. And obviously, no dog fighter should be allowed *any* off-leash freedom in the park or elsewhere. Let me repeat that: *NO* off-leash freedom.

Off-Leash Street Scrappers

You've been working on your problem dog-inciter, and you're doing well. Even if other owner's dogs spark yours, he trots by on heel with perhaps just a nasty stare back. Good for you. But you find yourself still prey to off-leash dogs let to run at large by irresponsible owners. Seemingly from out of nowhere these canine criminals rush out to confront you and your dog. Even the best heeling won't allow you to get away fast enough, and if you attempt to run away with your dog that will switch the attacking dog into a prey response and you will be chased and bitten. What a jam! What to do?

Try this. If it is truly not possible to heel away, sit your dog and issue the "stay" command taught in the next section. Leave the heel position and step around in front of your dog. Stay close in to your dog and keep a little upward tension on your lead to hold the dog in the sit. Attacking dogs like to investigate the face or the genitals of their prey and you've essentially cut off access to those areas by this move. Look around. If you see anybody who looks like an irresponsible owner in the vicinity call out in your rudest voice, "Call your dog please!" Maybe the owner will do so. Maybe the dog even knows the recall. But don't count on it. At the very least the owner will probably hasten to your side and physically remove his dog, allowing you to heel away.

Should you say something to Mr. Irresponsible Dog Owner? That depends on your state of mind, the other person involved, even the part of town you're in. I would hope that you would, but I am too street-wise to say dogmatically to do so. As angry as you may be, it is often best to come on softly yet firmly, "That was very difficult for me, please keep your dog on leash." Of course, if repeated infractions are the case you can get tougher: "Keep your dog away from me, or else!" Or you can simply report the dog and owner to the proper animal control authorities.

Backup Measures for Heeling Problems

Some owners just don't have the timing or the physical strength necessary to deliver effective corrections to a dog that is breaking heel. Nor will these owners suddenly "get" timing or strength by working with a trainer. They may own a dog with an extremely powerful foreassembly, such as a northern breed genetically geared to pull a sled. In this case *you* are the sled. Rather than zip, zip, zipping the collar and delivering useless corrections that the dog has tuned out, or learned to time his lunges in between, try the Pass Around. In this technique you *stop the action* immediately and stand still. Get the dog back by your side and into the heeling position. Now, jack the collar up high around the dog's neck and rotate the ring of the collar so that it is directly under the ear closest to you.

Pass the leash around behind you. You may want to place the lead on, under or above your buttocks. Wrap up the extension of the lead in your right hand — don't let it dangle — and place your left hand palm down near the bolt of the leash. Reissue your heel command and continue. The dog will now have to fight your entire body weight in order to pull. I've seen 90-pound little old ladies control 100-pound Great Danes using this method.

Another backup measure is to experiment with collars. While I prefer metal collars with pounded, flat links, there are other possibilities. There is the snap-around collar, which maintains its function as a training collar but snaps around the dog's neck rather than being passed over the head. This makes for a tighter fit and often more control. A prong collar is necessary only in dire circumstances; with use of the Pass Around technique the need for such a collar is often eliminated.

Summary

This lengthy section on heeling might surprise readers of other training books and even some trainers. The fact is, suburban and rural dog owners don't use the heel command as frequently as city dwellers do. When city owners pick up training books they generally see instructions about heeling that really apply more to the obedience ring, or they find short comments that underplay the exercise. But outside there are manhole covers, gratings, street noises, off-leash dogs, irresponsible owners, tempting garbage on the streets and ten thousand other distractions to heel past. Nobody is saying it is easy, but once you make it happen, heeling can be heaven.

SIT AND STAY

You might find that you taught the sit at the same time you were teaching the heel just by snapping up on the lead. If you're not this lucky, or if you've decided to teach "sit" first (which is perfectly acceptable), signal the dog by using three fingers pressed together and making a curved downward motion over the dog's head. As the dog's rump sinks as he follows the motion of your hand, say "sit."

Attach a leash to teach the stay command. Start from the heel position, with the dog on your left and the leash absolutely straight up and down. There should be a slight amount of tension on the lead. Hold the taut lead with your left hand and bring your right hand down in front of the dog's face with your hand just slightly cupped closed. As your hand nears the dog's eyes, flash it open, fingers closed, and say, "Stay." Step in front of the dog. If the dog moves, give a zip on the leash and repeat. If not, praise and return to the heel position. Now, go half way around your dog, return, and go all the way around. Say "stay" each time you leave the stay signal in your dog's face. Loosen the tension on the lead and widen the distance you go away from the dog. Repeat the above steps until you can walk completely around your dog using a six-foot leash and the dog doesn't move.

That little "flash-flourish" to your stay signal is not unimportant. It makes the signal more dramatic and important. While most trainers use a flattened hand with no flashing movement, I prefer a burst of fingers. I picked up this training technique by watching old clips of Diana Ross and the Supremes singing "Stop! In the Name of Love" and flashing their hands at the audience in their trademark choreography. It was effective for audiences then and it's effective for dogs now—they stop and stay in place—if not in the name of love then in the name of obedience.

Proofing the Sit-Stay

I like a proofing method found in *Training Your Dog* by Joachim Volhard and Gail Tamases Fisher (Howell Book House). They suggest the following to get the sit-stay tight and super-reliable. From the heel position:

> signal and command, "Stay," walk three feet in front of your dog and turn and face him. Your left hand is at your midsection and the right hand is ready to reinforce the stay. With as little body or hand motion as possible, apply slight pressure on the collar towards you. This is accomplished by folding a few more inches of the leash into your left hand. If the dog begins to come to you, reinforce the command by slapping the leash with your right hand repeating "Stay."

This "tug-test," as I've dubbed it, forces the dog to give primacy to the word and the signal and not to the distraction of your pulling him toward you. It forces the dog into a mode of deductive reasoning, making him think out that, indeed, words mean what they say despite distractions. In this case, the distraction emanates from you via the slight tug (don't go over three to five seconds of slight pressure), but out on the streets the distractions will assault you from all sides without your being able to control them. Better to proof the exercise inside first, and then hit the streets for these progressions to a solid sit-stay. By the way, be sure to keep your fingers fully closed when flashing your "Supremes signal." The air holes in an open hand make a slight difference to the dog in terms of overall blocking effect. Don't use your dog's name while teaching the sit-stay and don't praise physically until the "tug-test" is completed. You'll just break the flow of the progressions and switch the dog into a play mode when you want him in the work mode. Run the progressions past your city dog once inside and once on the street. Select a quiet spot at first and then, and only then, build up to Rodeo Drive or Fifth Avenue. Now, put the exercise into context.

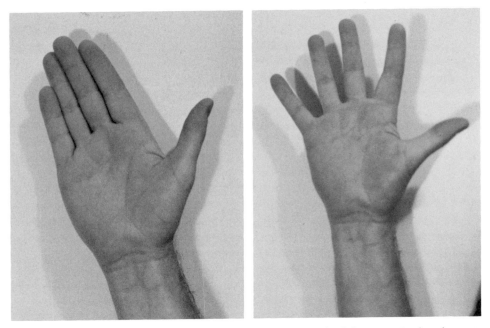

Keep your fingers closed for flashing the "stay," as shown on the left, not as in the photo at right—the air holes make a difference to the dog and make the signal less effective.

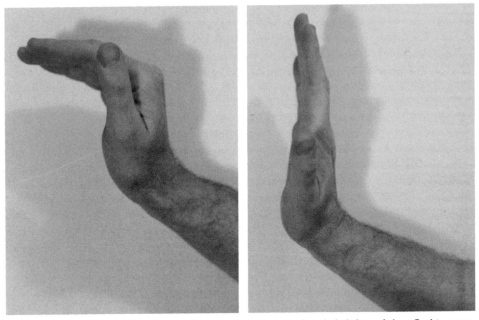

Flashing a "Supremes-style" stay signal means cupping your hand slightly and then flashing your hand flat at the dog.

City Context for Sit-Stays

At first the sit-stay looks rather frivolous. Heeling and the down look far more important and many a city owner considers the sit-stay valuable only at curbs. Besides, with all that flashing of signals and saying "Stay" it is boring to teach—and what if I hardly use it anyway? I sympathize, but I disagree. I agree that the sit-stay can be boring to teach and that the progressions can appear elementary and even exasperating. But they are necessary.

Greeting Guests

There are myriad uses for the sit-stay in the city and the first and most obvious is when greeting people who come to your home. During this process all hell often breaks loose. First the admittance bell is intoned from the street or by the doorman or concierge. This primes the dog that someone is going to come through the door momentarily. The dog then begins organizing his welcome, usually by spinning around the house or apartment at full speed, yapping his head off, chasing his tail and generally going nuts. The owner screams "No! No! No!" but to no avail.

By the time the person actually rings the home's doorbell the dog is already excited. The neighbors upstairs and downstairs are phoning or pounding on the floor or ceiling. You hurry to open the door and admit your guest, hoping that once he or she is inside and settled Screechy will shut up. Sometimes she does. Sometimes she doesn't.

Although the barking, yapping and yodeling usually subside rather quickly, your dog is now scaling your guest's body in ardent passion. Owners unconcerned with what their dog is doing to others will make the usual excuses:

"Well, he's certainly frisky, isn't he!"
"That's funny, he's never done that before."
"Just let him jump on you for awhile and he'll calm down."
"Bend down and pet him, but be careful—he might spring-jump into your face."
"He just wants a little love."

How rude! You wouldn't allow your child to behave this way toward a guest, so why allow such behavior from your dog? Did you invite your friend over for a mauling? Do you expect the grocery boy to keep delivering foodstuffs to a house where he is molested by a dog? What about Aunt Sally's best nylons, now torn to shreds? Stop all excuses. Your salvation is a solid sit-stay.

Here's the correction for jumping up in shorthand. A full description will follow.

1. Whip down hard on the collar, tab leash or leash and say, "No."

2. Pull up on the collar, tab, or leash and say, "Sit."

3. Flash the stay signal in your dog's face and say, "Stay."

You should understand that refusal to sit and stay and spring-jumping on guests is not just an expression of love, it is a form of canine *dominance*. Don't put up with jumping, no matter how "cute" you think it is, no matter how small your dog is and no matter how much guests tell you they think jumping is "cute." I can assure you, they are lying. Outside they are saying, "Oh, how cute, he likes me," and inside they are saying, "Get this creature off me this instant." Since they will most probably not administer the above correction it's up to you to step in from behind and *remove* your canine clinger from your guest's body. Snap the collar up smartly and issue your verbal stay command and the "Supremes signal" for stay. Have the guest pet the dog again, right away. If the dog jumps again, readminister the correction.

The best ruse you can pull on your dog to teach him to greet guests properly is to arrange to have a family member and then less familiar guests show up at the door. The difference between a staged arrival and real life is that you will be prepared to correct your dog. Attach a short "tab" leash for your set-ups so that you will have more than flying fur to grab if the dog breaks the sit-stay. You issue the "stay" command to your dog *before* you open the door. It's perfectly okay during the set-up to slam the door in the "guest's" face (they will understand, this is a set-up) and correct your dog. The point you want your dog to get is that persons are not admitted until the dog is seated and under control.

The arrival of guests is rarely easy for most dogs, but set-ups pave the way to success. You might try a "dry run" set-up without any person at the door. Put your dog on leash and station him or her at least four feet from the door. Don't let the dog crowd the door. You will need that space for admitting your guest. Get your dog into a sit and deliver the "stay" command. Open the door half-way. Correct your dog with an upward snap as he moves. Close the door. Reissue the command and open the door all the way. Correct if necessary. Open the door all the way. Close it. Reissue the command, open the door all the way and ring the doorbell or buzzer. If the dog breaks the stay, correct immediately. Many dogs have been unintentionally trained to freak out when the doorbell rings. If you stage a set-up in a peopleless dry run, you can build up to a set-up with a volunteer and then real people!

The above techniques and corrections apply equally to meeting people on the street or in the lobby. Passersby often make it difficult, especially on owners of smaller cute breeds, because they will greet the dog and then, when it jumps up, actually hold the dog up on its hind legs, supporting the paws. Very few if any will ask your dog to sit before petting it, and every time the dog jumps up on someone and is supported the behavior is okayed. Since you can't train the people of your city not to hold up your dog, you must train your dog. If the dog jumps up on someone who does not know or will not use the three-part correction outlined above, then *you* must step in from behind, grasp the leash to yank your dog off firmly, sit the dog and flash the stay. Only three words should come out of your mouth when you administer the jump correction: no, sit and stay.

A quick summary: the verbal sequence—No, sit, stay; the physical sequence—Pull down, pull up, flash the stay signal.

What too often transpires is a ton of verbiage that just confuses the dog: "No! Off, Tippy, goshdarn you bad dog get *off* that man. Oh, I'm so sorry. Tippy, Off, Down, No! Stop!" No dog can make sense of such oververbalization, so restrain yourself to the three acceptable words and coupled this with the physical sequence of the correction.

Long Stays

Teach your dog to hold the stay for longer and longer periods of time. Issue the command and go out the full extension of your lead. Turn sideways and count to 60. Return and praise. Correct with a "No!" and a snap on the lead if your dog breaks the stay during that time period. Now, turn your back to your dog and watch your dog in a mirror. Keep a hand cupped under the leash ready to snap it up if the dog moves. The purpose of this exercise is to teach your dog to hold the sit-stay even when you appear not able to correct him if he breaks.

The next step is to take it to the streets. Go window shopping and stop in front of a display window that features mirrors or reflects the dog's image nicely. Set your dog up on the sidewalk (leave room for pedestrians) and issue the stay command. Window shop, but watch your dog in the reflection. The faster you correct breaks, the faster your dog is going to learn a rock-steady sit-stay. A technique I often use with my canine students is to set the dog up facing a restaurant window. Most New York restaurants display both the menu and their reviews in the window. I simply pretend to read the menu or the review or both, but of course I am really watching my student's sit-stay in the reflection.

Try to build up to five to ten minutes on your long stays. The time period can seem like an eternity, so pick a place where you can read a review, take in a view or window shop to proof your dog. Remember that this lesson is very important for your dog. You are teaching him that he has to do what you say, when you say it, for *as long* as you say it. This is invaluable practice in teaching him to be patient in stores and on the street, and it also prepares the dog to hold the long down.

Here's a practical use of the "stay" command —greeting guests. Flash your stay signal *before* the guest enters.

For store stays, sit your dog, give the stay and issue an advance warning before entering the store. I say what my mother used to say to me: "Don't *touch* anything!"

Store Stays

You'd be surprised how many proprietors will allow you into their store if you have on heel an obviously well-trained dog. The words, "Don't worry, he's trained," will melt the heart of many a store owner. Of course, if a sign says, "No Dogs" then you have no say in the matter, but if the matter isn't mentioned, try your luck. We Manhattanites take our dogs almost everywhere on errands and with few exceptions dogs are allowed in banks, stationery stores, clothing stores, some delis, dry cleaning establishments, some libraries and even churches. You will find that in densely populated cities like New York, where residents are discouraged from owning or driving a car, access for dogs is improved. There seems to be a realization that people are going to have their dogs in tow and will have no car to leave them in while they shop—as if leaving a dog in a parked car is a good idea, anyplace, anytime. This is, however, a common practice in many other cities where spatial dimensions are less constrained and "car culture" is predominant. Even in these cities, trying to take your dog with you into certain stores isn't against the rules and all the proprietor can say is no.

For solid store stays, issue an advance warning at the store door. Sit the dog, make eye contact, tap the area between the dog's eyes sharply (two taps will do) and deliver your warning in a low, quiet tone. I usually say what my mother used to say to me when she'd haul us into a store, "Listen to me: *Don't touch anything.*" Remember, it's the tonality that counts for the dog, not the actual words.

Within the store place your dog on a stay off to the side of the aisle, not directly in the passageway. Never let the dog wander around aimlessly at the end of the leash. If you do your dog is bound to touch something and knock it over. If you have not progressed to long stays, keep your dog nearby and put a little upward pressure on the lead to hold the dog in the sit. Proof store stays by "accidentally" dropping some unbreakable piece of merchandise and flashing the stay command and signal at the same time. Pretend to be examining merchandise, reading ingredient labels or product instructions. Make your dog think you are otherwise occupied so that you can trick him or her into breaking the sit-stay.

A Big Never

If for some reason you cannot take your dog into a store, my advice is to skip that store and come back another time. Never leave your dog attached to a parking meter, even if you are only going to be inside the store briefly. Your dog could be dognapped. Stealing dogs is a fact of life in many cities and owners must beware. Some dognappers sell their stolen goods to laboratories for research, and others specialize in stealing high-cost pure-bred dogs. Individuals and even gangs will roam the classier neighborhoods of town, spot a dog parked by a parking meter, cut the leash and run. The owner is then called at the number on the dog's identification tag and threatened that the dog will be tortured if a ransom is not paid. Don't risk this!

Don't think I don't appreciate your jam when you take off to do errands with your dog in tow, fully trained, poised, practiced in store stays only to be denied entrance to a store you thought would admit your friend. It's frustrating, and there is that temptation to hitch your dog on the street just for one moment. But it only takes one minute for a leash to be unhitched, too, and how would you feel if that happened? The store that denied you entrance isn't leaving the planet. It will still be there tomorrow. Try this: take a shopping tour dogless and mentally note which stores have "No Dogs" signs and which stores don't. Of those which do not, do you see other customers with dogs? Note that stores in which one tends to make quick purchases (stationery stores, newsstands) tend to admit dogs by default—half the time the store personnel may not even realize the dog is there. Sometimes you will be caught off guard and take your dog to a place where you would *think* dogs would not be a problem, like the post office or a government building. I can assure you unless your dog is a Seeing Eye, Hearing Ear or Therapy Dog you will be turned out onto the street before you can buy a 25¢ stamp or try to get out of jury duty! Scout locations and rescout, your dog will thank you.

Crowds

The sit-stay is wonderfully proofed in crowds. Go to a subway station or a bus stop and just park yourself. Keep your dog in the heel position and maintain some upward tension on the training collar. Give your flash-stay signal and let traffic flow around you. Invariably, someone will stop and offer to interact with your dog. Take advantage of this. Flash your stay command just after you say "Okay" to the interaction. If your dog jumps up, administer the jump correction smartly, and ask the person to pet your dog again.

I like mass transit junctures because pedestrians will often have no choice but to relate with your dog, and you can let your dog see that crowds are a part of city life, to be accepted and moved through, not to be objected to and mauled. Of course, it isn't easy, and if you suffer from crowd fears yourself (as I did when I came to New York) you must be very careful not to telegraph this fear to your dog via faulty paralanguage (bad tonalities) or faulty body language (petting your pet when it exhibits shyness) when in crowds. Despite what you yourself feel, cloak those feelings for the sake of your dog. Remember, the old adage "Shy dog-shy owner" is often true.

Never use the sit-stay this way. Your dog could easily be stolen.

To stoop and scoop your dog's waste more easily put your dog on a stay after elimination is completed and then clean up.

Stoop and Scoop Sit-Stays

It can be difficult—almost impossible—to stoop and scoop the feces of a dog that is dragging you away from or even *into* the very excrement you are attempting to remove. No wonder so many dog owners "cheat" on the laws of their cities and "run away" from elimination sites. The solution, again, is a solid sit-stay.

Wait until your dog has eliminated fully, and then place him or her on a firm sit-stay. Stoop and scoop. It helps if you have staged a fake stoop and scoop session during which you are picking up a stone, gavel, garbage or even nothing, in order to proof the dog's sit-stay. Remember, when you bend over your body language looks pretty subserviant and inviting, and your dog doesn't know that you are obeying the city law and retrieving waste so that you will not be heavily fined. Truth be told, your dog could care less. All he or she sees is a bending human who *appears* to be inviting the dog to come, play, cavort or even stomp on the very feces you are trying to remove.

Before you bend over to clean up, put your dog on a sit and then flash the stay signal at your dog. Fake pick-ups as mentioned above and correct sternly if your dog breaks. It's not surprising that this series of commands is readily agreed to by most city clients, whereas they might object to others they see as "too strict." The fact is, picking up after your pet is most likely the law of the land where you live. While it certainly is no thrill, having a lunging maniac pulling you into and through elimination won't increase your desire to perform this task. You can obey the law and perform this essential service without losing a shred of your, or your dog's dignity by utilizing a solid stoop and scoop sit-stay.

Hot Dog Stops and Phone Calls

New Yorkers have their hot dog stands, Philadelphians their hoagie shops, and in Chicago I once saw Polish pierogi being served off an outdoor pushcart. But if you purchase one of these taste treats and have a wild dog tugging at your arm, you may find that you wind up with more of food *on* you than *in* you. The canine psyche derails in the presence of food. This is one reason I never use food in training commands—orders go in one ear and out the other. Again, the answer is in advance warnings before purchasing food, and in enforcing the sit-stay as the food is prepared and delivered.

When placing a phone call the last thing you want is a little monster mauling you or pulling like a bucking bronco. Even if you have a small pet, it is unwieldy to pick the dog up, man the phone and perhaps write down a number or take a message all at the same time. Practice makes perfect and in this case it is easy to stage a set-up. You can call your own number or an understanding friend and "pretend" to chat—breaking off to correct your dog immediately if the stay is broken. Give the physical and verbal signal and word before you dial, and get ready; many dogs will break the stay as soon as they hear you begin speaking.

If you allow your dog to pester you while you're on the phone at home, don't expect his street stay to be any better. If you let your dog bother you when making calls, or hold or caress the dog then, you are essentially training the dog to expect that kind of attention whenever you pick up that funny thing with the twisty tail. In fact, some dogs seem to perceive the phone as a strange sort of other dog. It has a tail, a curved body and is held close and talked to. I've had more than one client who has complained of having the "tail" of their phone severed from the main body of the machine, and sometimes the receiver itself attacked. Revenge?

Whether it's hot dogs you want to eat or phone calls you need to make, remember that your sit-stay will have to be enforced using only one hand. Be sure you've practiced some one-handed heeling in advance so that the dog knows that you have continuous control.

COME

Before you can teach your dog to come when called, it must fully understand and obey the sit-stay. One command builds on the other. Place your dog on a stay and then unfurl a twelve-foot leash or rope. Put a weight on the end of the lead so that it can be thrown out and away from you easily. Walk directly away from your dog—do not back away—but keep an eye peeled over your shoulder in case the dog breaks the stay command. If he does, wheel on the dog quickly and flash your best "Supremes" stay signal. If the dog doesn't re-park himself, return, scold and try again.

When you get to the end of your lead, turn, kneel all the way down, open up those arms wide, smile widely and clearly bellow "Tippy, Come!" This one time you can yell just a bit. If the dog doesn't move, give a firm snap on the leash to enforce your command. If he does move *do not,* repeat *do not* say the word "come" or "c'mon" again. This is a common owner mistake. The dog will start toward the owner on the word "come" and the owner, in an attempt to encourage the dog, will continue to say the word, "That's it, c'mon, c'mon, c'mon." *Don't* do this. You'll wear out the word "come" and confuse the dog. He's already responded to the command! But *do* offer encouragement during the dog's transition to you: "Good boy, great! That's my boy!" You want that dog running into you gleefully.

When your dog arrives raise slightly, guide your dog gently into a sit, make eye contact and praise lavishly, but not for more than seven seconds. Too much praise will backfire and the dog will switch into the play mode. Instead, immediately place your dog on another stay and try a longer distance recall. Go with the flow! Pattern in the come response by repeat-

190

Use the sit-stay when buying a hot dog...

...or making a phone call!

ing seven recalls each day. Remember: positive body language, positive tone of voice and positive eye contact!

City Context for Come

Obviously, the street is no place to practice the recall. Find a nook or cranny you can practice in safely. Better yet, find three such spaces. Look for long narrow spaces like the sides of buildings, alleyways or entranceways at first, then graduate to the park or other wide-open spaces. The narrower spaces will help to funnel the dog in toward you since your dog will have few other choices or diversions. A common mistake city owners make is to begin recall work in the park. The psychological associations the dog makes between the park and freedom to play, cavort and generally *not* come when called, plus the openness of the area, make many an initial park recall session a disaster. It is better to start in a more confined environment.

Since training nooks and crannies are difficult to find, I've provided a chapter to help you. Don't think that simply training your dog for the recall using the hallway of your building will do the trick, however. The dog might perform wonderfully there but the great outdoors is another matter. You will need the recall when you need it and where you need it, so outdoor practice is essential. Try to minimize the risk factor of the dog getting away from you by selecting a well-enclosed space or by having another person around when you are working on the recall. Remember, too, that even though you are being a responsible dog owner and trying to train your dog, in some cities you may still be violating the leash law simply by dropping your leash to practice.

Couple Recalls

If you are one-half of a couple, be sure to practice some couple-comes. Simply pace out the steps for the recall as described above together. Issue the "stay" command at the same time, flash the stay signal at the same time, walk away together and stoop to call your dog at the same time. Now, try a variation. Station one person on one end of the enclosed area you're working in and the other person 20 feet away. Place the dog on a sit-stay in the middle and call the dog back and forth, back and forth. A long, narrow space will facilitate this exercise neatly.

Remember, if you are having trouble with the recall, immediately deny the dog any and all off-leash freedom. Turn to the section on the problem in this book and try the techniques there. If necessary you may have to call in a qualified trainer (see the section on how to select one) to help you stage set-ups to produce recall disobedience and correct it. Don't sit and suffer because of a dog who runs away from you. Take action quickly and train, don't complain (as my mentor the late Jack Godsil used to say).

For top-flight recalls, remember: *positive* body language, *positive* tone of voice and *positive* eye contact. Use a narrow training space to help "funnel" the dog to you.

To practice the recall issue the "stay" command.

Walk out from your dog, unfurling the leash

Turn, genuflect and call your
dog, praising the dog as he
comes in.

194

If you are one-half of a couple, be sure to practice couple recalls.

There is a *special spot* on your dog's back that can help you to down your dog. Note the placement of the thumb and index finger—that's the spot.

DOWN

The down is taught from the heel position, with the dog seated. There is a spot on your dog's back that is sensitive and analogous to the spot behind your knees. Pressure here can fold the dog into the down position. Put your left hand on the dog's shoulder blades (properly called the scapula) and with your thumb and index finger trace down the scapula to where the spinal column begins. You will find an indentation there into which your thumb and finger will fit readily. For those more experienced with canine anatomy, the "secret spot" is the upper thoracic vertebrae. Push gently forward and down on this spot. Most dogs will go down readily, but if there is resistance, lift one front leg with your other hand and say "Down." Add a hand signal, with the finger of your right hand pointing to the ground, as you say the command.

Secrets of the Long Down

For the city canine a solid long down is the essence of being civilized. Now that you've got your dog going down on command, getting into the actual physical position of all fours flat on the floor, you should know that you are at a very critical and important juncture in your training efforts. The reason this moment is so important is that you can royally goof up right now and train your dog to give you only short mini-downs unless you *insist* on a long down.

How long? Thirty minutes. "Thirty *minutes?*" you might be saying, "My sweet monster has never hit the dust for longer than 30 *seconds!*" Or you might be not just a Doubting Thomas but also a Sympathetic Sam, who feels 30 minutes is too lo-o-o-ng of a down. After all, what if your dog has to entertain, feed or relieve itself during that thirty minutes? My answer: there's 23 1/2 hours left in the day for your dog to pursue those activities and *you* need some quiet time, too. The long down is your way to get it.

Don't expect to get much coaching about long downs if you are taking your dog to the typical obedience class. Unfortunately, long downs are rarely taught in classes. Three- to five-minute mini-downs are routinely taught because these are needed for the professional obedience ring. My response to this kind of reasoning is ring-*schming!* A three-minute down is next to useless in real life. You can *do* something with 30 minutes and the dog can be easily convinced to extend the time once he's passed the 30-minute threshold.

Don't expect to find much about long downs in training literature. There hasn't been much extensively written about this glorious exercise and on how to demand it from the dog. In fact, to my knowledge, the information I'm going to give you here is unique in print.

Starting Out. Don't attempt a 30-minute down until your dog goes

The signal for the down is one finger pointed toward the ground. Assist your dog by easing down on the "special spot" if necessary, lifting a paw, or both.

Proper positioning is important for a solid long down. Place your dog against a wall—not underfoot or in a passageway. Flash extra "courtesy stays" if necessary.

197

down reliably without your touching the *special spot* and/or offering paw assistance. When you are getting the down response to just your finger signal, and when you can flash a "Supremes" stay signal in your dog's face, rise and walk slowly around your dog (keep a hand cocked over the dog's back to correct him if he rises). Then, and only then, are you ready to try out 30 minutes. I stress again, though, don't train too many short downs, releasing the dog with praise, because you may never get the long down.

Selecting a Practice Site. Where you position your dog when you ask for a 30-minute down is important. I'd advise you to avoid placing the dog directly under foot or in passageways. Directly underfoot is a bad choice because if you so much as cross your legs with an inexperienced dog trying to hold a long down at your feet, the dog will probably interpret the movement as permission to move. Also, with your dog camped out at your feet, you cannot make effective eye contact to correct the dog if he breaks from the down. Probably more importantly, you are going to find your hand stroking your dog, which will only make it more difficult for the dog to stay down and not rise and solicit more praise. Be fair to your dog. I'm not saying that your dog can *never* lie at your feet, but if you are counting on a canine to commit himself to a long down it is better to *recess the dog from your body.*

For committed long downs always think in terms of centrifugal force — put the dog against a wall and out of a passageway. Dogs do not like to be told to lie down and stay in a passageway. They know that the passageways are where the humans walk and they are worried about getting stepped on. Little dogs really fret about this, and cats are almost phobic about passageways. All dogs psyche out the passageways in a room the minute they enter it, and when they want a silent snooze will often select a spot against a wall or at least in an out-of-the-way area. Sometimes dominant, bratty, bossy dogs will *deliberately* plop themselves in passageways to make their owners step over them. If you own this type of dictator, it is even *more* important that you place your dog on long downs out of the mainstream of traffic.

Wherever you go with your dog for the lifetime of your pet — even if you are in unfamiliar surroundings — psyche out the room from the point of view of the dog in terms of where the passageways are. See why this exercise if often not taught in a class setting? You need a real *room* to train long downs, but even if this exercise wasn't introduced in class or in the books you've read, select your spot and read on.

Toughlove Corrections. Got your dog positioned in a proper spot? Attach your six-foot leash and string it out from your dog's side toward wherever you'll be sitting. Now, down your dog. Flash your stay signal in the dog's face. Stroll to your seat, but keep a strict eye on your pooch and immediately wheel on the dog and say, "No!" Down! Stay!" if the dog rises. Remember, no screaming. Just darken your voice; change your tonality not your volume. Did you get to your seat and he didn't break the down? Great. Have a seat, but *as you sit* flash another courtesy stay at your dog just so he doesn't misread your body language and think that your sinking down is permission to come. Don't look at the dog, but keep an eye on him. Staring will invite the dog to negotiate with your eyes—which are full of weakness and worry at this point because you really *don't* believe that he is going to stay there for 30 whole minutes, do you?

Well, he is, because you're going to make him. And you're going to make him because you know that even though this exercise looks like a terrible limitation on the dog's freedom right now, this long down will really be his *liberation* if the two of you really get proficient at this exercise. Why? Because you will be able to take your dog many more places because you will know that you can, in essence, park him. You have to be strict.

Here's your corrective sequence if your dog breaks the down (and believe me they all do):

- *At the first break,* say, "No, Down, Stay!" On the word "no" raise your finger up as in a warning, on "down" throw that raised finger down dramatically and on "stay" flash the stay-signal at your dog. No excess verbiage. No screaming. If the dog hits the dust again, fine—but don't say "good." Say nothing. The dog isn't doing anything "good"—he's correcting his response to a prior command that he goofed up. If the dog tries to bolt out of the room, step on the leash and reposition the dog in the same exact spot.

- *At the second break,* repeat the above sequence, but even if the dog drops back into place go and give the dog the shake or the swat. Strict? Yes, but totally humane and in the dog's best interests. If you do not get physical, the dog will simply continue to rise and fall, and you will be continually rising from your seat to reposition the dog. Some dogs will actually come to enjoy being shoved down again and again and making you get up and sit down repeatedly—it's a canine version of musical chairs.

- *At the third break,* repeat the verbal correction and the physical one, and then in silence tie your dog to an immovable object like a chair leg. Tie your tether tightly and *short*—so short the dog cannot rise to sit. Do this in silence. Return to your seat, complete the 30-minute down.

Through this corrective sequence you tell your dog how important this exercise is to you and that you will not give in and let him walk around at will. Nor will you give in and use your crate as a cop-out, or throw the dog in another room or cheapen yourself by yelling and screaming until finally he leaves you alone. You are through with yelling and screeching.

You are through with avoidance, such as casting your dog in another room. You are teaching, not tolerating your dog.

Proofing the Long Down

Proofing is a method of weeding out the kinks of an obedience exercise to ensure that the dog truly understands what the word really means. Proofing requires an owner to set up situations where the dog is tempted to break his down and decides not to, or gets corrected if he does. Proofing means trying the long down in the structure of *real life.* The dog must know that he has to do *what* you say *when* you say it for *as long* as you say it—whatever "it" is, including "down."

Proof your long down against four distractions: movement, going out of sight, food and friends. Here's how:

- To proof against movement, flash a courtesy stay signal from your seat and move to another chair, adding a second courtesy stay as you sit again. I call these extra flash stays "courtesy stays" because they are just that—forms of politeness to the dog so that he doesn't think the stay is over. You'll find you need fewer and fewer courtesy stays because the dog will settle into the down (especially if you do one or more 30-minute downs each day). At first they will be necessary. Try throwing a magazine up in the air and saying and flashing "stay" just as you do. Or "accidentally" spill a dish of candy on the floor with an accompanying "stay." You get the idea. Be creative.

- To proof against movement when you are out of sight, begin by snapping a set of keys on your dog's collar (just use the bolt of the leash). Return to your seat. Now, rise and flash a courtesy stay. Leave the room and flash one more courtesy stay just as you disappear from sight. Listen carefully. If the keys clink, your dog is cheating. From the room you exited to, say, "No, Down, Stay." If the keys stop, your dog listened. If they keep rattling, he's still moving. Return and replace the dog in his spot. Repeat going out of the room and follow the same corrective sequence outlined earlier. Crafty, aren't we?

- To proof against a food distraction, don't try to do your first 30-minute down during Thanksgiving dinner. The canine mind goes crazy around food, so start with a glass of water and a cracker at the dining room table with your dog properly positioned on the down. Eat that cracker *slowly,* savoring every bite. Slurp the water. Get ready to go through your corrective sequence. Remember, at some point you are going to have noisy eaters as guests, if not

200

already in residence. Proof that long down! Don't forget the alfresco dining situation. Proof these by simply ordering a drink or an appetizer at an outdoor restaurant. Be sure to check in advance if dogs are admitted—often they are, at least in the outdoor portion of the establishment.

- Finally, proofing around friends. Most dogs, even dogs who have performed spectacular long downs and resisted movement, food and disappearing owners, will fail miserably to stay parked in the presence of your friends. The dog senses that you are not going to be as strict in front of your friends and that all bets are off. Since you'll really want to use the long down when friends come over—especially friends who may not appreciate being mauled or goosed by your dog—proof the down by inviting over an understanding friend who will sit in total silence as you correct your dog. It usually takes one or two "proofings" but, believe me, most dogs then see that *everyone* is in on this long-down business and the only way to get in on things that happen around the home is to come in, say hello, find the nearest wall and plop down.

Your release word for a long down is simply a loudly pronounced "Okay!" Don't say "come" because we don't want the dog resting on the down but inwardly thinking any minute you'll say "come" and this stupid exercise will be over. Praise your dog nicely after a successful long down. Make him know how very pleased you are that he's done the greatest obedience exercise of all—the one that shows his deepest respect for you as leader, the one that allows you to take him to baseball games, dog shows, libraries, outdoor restaurants, even, in some cases, to church.

The long down is the culmination of all the other exercises. It produces deep dignity in the dog, respect for the owner in the dog and reverence for the dog in the owner. It is the crowning achievement that elevates mere obedience training to the level of etiquette and manners. While you must be strict in teaching it, don't deprive your dog of learning the long down.

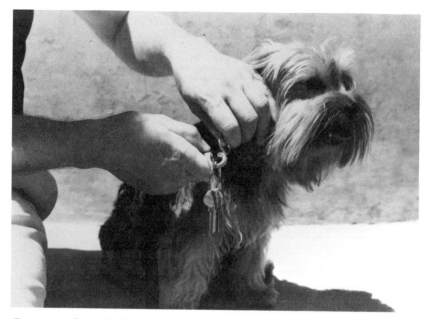

To test your dog on the long down, clip on a set of keys, flash the stay signal and listen from another room. If the keys ring, he's cheating!

The long down liberates you and your dog to move about town as a team. The four-month old Westie holds a down in a bookstore while I catch up on my book-reviewing duties.

12

People, Pooches and Problems

$\mathbf{A}$S YOU TEACH your dog words like "heel," "sit," "stay," "come," "down" and "stay" and explore uses of the words in your city, you will see the words becoming more than mere words, more than commands, more than "obedience exercises." You will see the words you have taught become *manners* in your dog. These words you teach do not simply signify control and domination. They are *gifts* you give your dog, a ticket to freedom you share together so that you can move through the city as a team. You'll also find ways to use the words to help you solve any problem punches your dog may throw your way—and believe me, I've never met a pet without *some* problem.

Take a poll of dog trainers and you'll find that they all agree that in the majority of cases, when a dog is having a behavioral problem it is really the people who are the problem, not the pooch. But it is often easy to diagnose and even solve a behavior problem if it is not *your* dog. It's much harder when the offender is yours because, well, love is blind. But love isn't enough, is it? Otherwise, no dog owner would ever have a problem dog. Again, education, communication and compassion are the keys.

Last night I watched the movie, *The Miracle Worker*. It's the story of Helen Keller, a blind and deaf child. At one point Helen's teacher tells Helen's parents that their love for Helen is the most damaging aspect of their child's existence. Their love is so full of pity that it blocks every attempt at education the teacher makes. It is a love that always makes excuses for the one loved, a love that protects and nourishes but does not teach, discipline or challenge. Ultimately it is Helen Keller herself who transforms her parents' love to a more mature level. I often think problem dogs are in the same jam Helen was, unable to communicate what they really need, fully ready to learn but instead excused and pitied. Offer your pet a love that teaches; help your dog to learn to be good.

Now that you're in the right frame of mind—and your attitude toward resolving a behavioral problem often dictates *how* it will be resolved—let's look at five common complaints: housetraining, destructive chewing, jumping up, not coming when called and aggression. I'll give you as many tips as I can, but remember that if the problem persists you should contact a qualified dog trainer. Ask your veterinarian for a referral.

HOUSETRAINING

Getting your puppy or dog to realize that cleanliness is next to godliness can be accomplished by following the ACCESS plan I outline in my book *The Evans Guide for Housetraining Your Dog* (Howell Book House, 1987):

A . . . is for *Alpha*—that's you.

C . . . is for *Corrections*—that's what you give.

C . . . is also for *Confinement*—that's what you provide.

E . . . is for *Establish.*

S . . . is for a *Schedule* (which is what you establish).

S . . . is also for *Selecting* a dog food that will aid you in getting your dog housetrained.

You know all about how to be alpha already, so remember to establish eye contact formally twice a day as previously described. Correct your dog for housetraining mistakes by quietly taking the dog to the "proof" itself, sitting the dog, focusing his eyes (*not* his nose) on the "proof" and delivering the shake or swat correction. Remember, no screaming and no over-physicality!

Stick to your schedule of walks and select a food that will help, not hinder housetraining. Stay away from unlabeled generic foods, dairy products and super-oily foods. Remember, what goes in comes out!

I've found that most owners who tolerate unhousetrained dogs either trust the dog too soon and too much, granting the dog more area than he can really handle, or they just cheat on the ACCESS plan and then blame

204

Besieged by housetraining mythology and held hostage by a dirty dog? You're not alone!

the dog for goofing up. An exception is the ill dog. If you are having any problem with housetraining, get the dog to a veterinarian! After that, assuming your dog has a clean bill of health, I'd offer you my tips here, my book on the subject and my sympathy! Don't worry though, given time and consistency, most dogs *do* clean up their acts.

Paper Training

While many training books will dogmatically advise you not to start paper training at all, the authors of such tracts are out of touch with the reality of city life. Most city owners *have* to housetrain using papers, and then, if they so desire they have to *de*-train their dogs. Still other owners want to have it both ways—with the dog eliminating either inside on papers or outside in the street. Either/or propositions found in much of the existing literature just don't apply to city owners, who need more options and less linear advice.

The reason most city owners will have to housetrain is *parvovirus.* This particularly nasty and troublesome virus is spread by contact with dog feces, and once acquired is not easily defeated. Most city veterinarians suggest three or four parvovirus shots before placing the dog out on the city streets. Because most city owners do not have private backyards, absolutely free from the intrusion of other dogs, they must keep their pets indoors until the series of shots is completed. It can take one or even two months before you can take the pet outdoors safely, depending on how many shots the pup has already received from the breeder and how many the veterinarian has yet to give. You simply do not have a choice of whether to paper-train or not. You have to. But all the literature says no, no, no. While the literature might be "right" for rural or suburban dwellers, it doesn't apply to city dwellers.

When you place the papers down, try to fit them into a corner so that when your dog goes onto them to defecate or urinate he doesn't "miss" the paper. A three-sided cubicle is best. Divide the available space into three areas, separated by at least five feet: an elimination area, a sleeping area and a spot where the food and water is placed down. Dogs do not like to eliminate where they eat or sleep. Make sure the papers are at least five layers thick and arranged in a neat square. If newsprint stains are a problem, you might try to procure a roll of unprinted newspaper from your local printer.

Many people decide to use the bathroom or the kitchen as the confinement space. Consider several angles. First, you will need to step over a baby gate to get in and out of the room. A cardinal rule in housetraining is don't close doors on dogs. Dogs don't like to be shut away from the rest of their "pack," so get a baby gate. The kind with a tension bar is best because you can adjust it freely. But remember you will have to hike over it each time you go in or out of the room so pick a confinement room that minimizes this hassle. For this reason, many city dwellers pick the bathroom, especially if they have one to spare, rather than the kitchen.

The room should *not* have a carpeted surface. Chew-proof the room as much as possible. In a bathroom this often means taking the toilet paper off its spindle and placing it away from the puppy, who will otherwise grab the end and wrap it around everything wrappable, or just shred the roll to bits. Obviously, pick up all cleaners, scrub brushes and other dangerous items. Place some toys in this area, but be sure they are of a safe variety—no squeak toys with squeakers that can be torn off and swallowed by the pup.

Crating your dog is also a possibility and highly suggested by many trainers, including this one. There is nothing wrong with crating a dog for short periods, since the dog is a den animal. If born in the woods, the dog would have lived in some sort of den, cave or overhang during the nursing stage. The mother keeps this den area spotless by consuming elimination and by forcing the young outside when their stools become too large for her to consume. So pups are genetically geared *not* to soil their den. If you use a crate as a "den" you will automatically have an advantage.

That said, let me note that sometimes city dwellers have bathrooms or kitchens that are so small that the addition of a baby gate essentially makes the area a "crate." If that's the case, why invest in one? Further, there is a small minority of dogs who do *not* crate-train well and need slightly larger quarters if they are to be housetrained. Don't believe the dogmatic statements you'll read in other books that a dog will *never* soil in its crate. That's patently untrue. Some do. It does not mean the dog is stupid. It does not mean that the dog is disgusting. It means that the dog soils its crate, period. Larger, but only slightly larger quarters are the answer in most cases.

If you are to be gone for more than four hours at a time, do *not* crate. You should confine instead and paper-train. You have to. This is the best arrangement for many city owners.

Earning Rooms

How do you open up the house to your city canine? I've devised a seven-day plan, The Evans Edict for Earning the Environment. Here's how it works: Your pet should be confined strictly to the restricted area for seven days, both while you are home and certainly when you are gone. The exceptions to being in the confined area when you are home are as follows:

- the dog is in your arms or in your lap

- you have the dog on leash out on the street or in the house

- you are sitting on the leash with just enough extension to let the puppy sit

- you are in another enclosed room with the puppy under your direct supervision

Those are the exceptions, period. No exceptions to those exceptions, please! Don't trust your puppy too soon and let him wander through the house. You'll only find "presents" left for you all over the house and have to discipline your dog after the fact, which is less effective than catching him in the act, and with some dogs, totally useless.

When your pup or older housesoiler goes seven days without missing the paper, or, if you are not using papers, without soiling in the house, you are ready to grant the dog another room. Why seven days? It's a somewhat arbitrary figure, I'll admit, but after 15 years of training, you'll have to just trust me: it works. You start counting your seven days with the first *clean* day, not seven days total including dirty days when the dog missed the paper or soiled in the house.

Let's say you were using the bathroom and there is a hallway attached. The baby gate would come down on that magical seventh day, and on that seventh day the dog would earn the hallway. The baby gate goes up at the end of the hallway, however. Seven more days pass, and of course you correct your pup for any and all infractions—failed attempts to make it back to the paper or refusal to hold until you can get the dog outside. When you reach the seventh day, you throw open, say, the dining room (or whatever room is next) to your dog and gate the next appropriate door. Are you with me? Good. Now, let's cover the kinks in plan.

Let's say your dog liberates himself from the bathroom and gains the hallway, but on the sixth day of what would have been his second full seven days he lays a load in the hallway, refusing to wait to go outside or make it back to the paper. Should the dog be demoted back to the bathroom and gated in? No. He never loses what he earned. In *The Evans Edict for Earning the Environment* effort is rewarded. He doesn't lose the hallway. But he does get disciplined and he has to clock in *seven more days* in the hallway. Under no circumstances does he earn the dining room (or whatever room would have been next). He earns the dining room only after seven days of cleanliness and next he earns the living room and the bedrooms only after he can show seven days of cleanliness on his canine check-out card. With this method, most households open up to most dogs within about a month, unless you own a mansion (in which case you probably don't live in a city and need to wait for my next book, *The Evans Guide for Rowdy Rural Ruffians*).

Giving Corrections with Connections

If your dog goofs, here's what to do. Do not react to the evidence of elimination. Silently go and get your dog. Sit the dog in front of the mess as

208

described earlier and focus his attention on the "crime." Sometimes tracing a line several times between the dog's eyes and the pile or puddle (you need not touch it, obviously) will assure a correction with a connection. Do not yell. Use a low, growl-type tone of voice and scold for no longer than five seconds. Give a swat under the chin for discipline and immediately trot the dog to the desired area for defecation to make a full connection.

If you are going to march the puppy to the paper for a connection do so smoothly and do not pick the pup up and carry him to the paper. If you do you might be mistaken as giving affection too soon after discipline and worse, the pup might deduce that he only has to use the paper if mommy or daddy *picks him up and puts him on the paper.* That, of course, is not the message you want to convey. Instead, the message is, "Wherever you are in this household, in whatever room you have earned, you take your four feet and you get yourself back to those papers, or else." So trot your dog back to the papers and indicate them by touching them with your forefinger, then confine the dog to that area, return to the mess and clean up. Don't let the puppy see you cleaning up after him, except on the street, where it is okay and where it is the law in most cities.

If you are *not* paper training or have an older dog that has graduated from papers to the streets, deliver the same correction but take the dog outside to the street to make sure he gets a correction with a connection. Your challenge here is to get your dog out onto the street without him thinking, "Hey, this is a neat deal—I poop in the house and then they take me out for a walk!" So, after the disciplinary swat at the scene of the crime quickly leash your dog and get out to the stairs or elevator as soon as you can. (Leave the elimination there—someone else will clean it up, or you can later.) Don't swat your dog again, but give a leash jerk as you wait for the elevator or go down the stairs, growling at the dog in a low tone to keep it fresh in his mind that he is in trouble, big trouble. When you get outside point to the ground in front of the dog's nose and say, "Here, *here* is where you go!" Remember, the words don't matter, it's the emphasis. Turn sideways a bit and wait just 30 seconds, then take the dog back upstairs. There's no use staying out longer and having the dog think he's being rewarded with a walk for letting loose in the house; you simply want to make a full connection after your correction. Besides, he *already* eliminated upstairs and even if he didn't totally clean himself out, he probably will be shaking from the correction and trip down the stairs or on the elevator and be unable to produce whatever substance he may have left inside. Confine the dog when you get back to your home, return to the mess and clean.

Always clean with vinegar and water. A fifty-fifty solution is best. There are scent substances called pheremones in dog defecation and urine, and these substances tell the dog "go here again." They are extremely powerful. When wolves squirt or lay down pheremones in the woods, even rain water, which contains salt, doesn't nullify them. To be cancelled they must be acidified, and vinegar does that. Don't use ammonia, as ammonia is a component of urine and it is also present in smaller amounts in defecation. It will reattract the dog to the soiled spot.

Sink or Schedule

Here's a sample schedule for you to follow if you are home most of the day and able to walk your dog, or if you are lucky enough to have a back yard and can let the dog out for elimination. Schedules aren't chiseled in stone, and you can usually lessen the number of walks as the dog gets older. The dog's "holding" powers develop with age, so you can eliminate walks that do not result in elimination activity:

A.M.

8:00 Get up, walk Munchkin immediately
8:15 Feed and water Munchkin, play with puppy
8:45 Walk Munchkin
9:00 Bed Munchkin down in crate or confined area
Noon Feed Munchkin second meal

P.M.

12:15 Walk Munchkin
12:30 Obedience session: come, sit, stay
12:45 Short play sessions featuring ball play
 1:00 Bed Munchkin down in crate or confined area
 4:00 Kids home from school, do Round Robin Recall (pass dog around in a circle)
 4:30 Feed last meal to have pup empty for overnight
 5:00 Walk Munchkin
 5:30 Umbilical cord Munchkin (sit on leash) for dinner
 6:30 Kids play with Munchkin in confined area
 7:00 Walk Munchkin for elimination, then a short run
 7:30 Put Munchkin in confined area
 8:00 Offer water, then take up for night
10:30 Walk Munchkin, offer two or three teaspoons of water when you return, bed dog down for night in confined area.

This is a good schedule for almost any owner of a young puppy. "But all those walks!" you might say. Yes, there are six walks according to the initial schedule (or six paper pit-stops if you are paper training) and that is a lot of chances for the dog to eliminate. Your pup needs that many chances at first—perhaps even desperately. If you mentally note which walks the puppy routinely chooses to use for elimination, you can cut one, two and even eventually three of the outings on which he consistently refrains from eliminating. But stick to the schedule strictly at first.

Don't start cutting walks from the schedule until you have observed a consistent pattern for more than two weeks. For instance, many dogs will not eliminate during the 5:00 P.M. walk, and you might be able to have the pup go the bulk of the evening "holding it" and take the pup out for the final 10:30 P.M. walk—or perhaps you'll find it best to move that walk to 10:00 P.M. The schedule is not etched in stone. Your pup will determine certain aspects of it by his or her personal style and needs. Your needs and style will also shape the schedule, especially if you are a working owner. Here is a sample schedule for someone who works 9 to 5, Monday through Friday, owns a puppy less than five months of age and absolutely cannot come home from work or provide for anyone to come home at midday and allow the dog access to the desired area for elimination. This owner *must* use papers and should follow this schedule:

A.M.

7:00 Get up, walk Speedy immediately for exercise and/or elimination
7:15 Feed Speedy ¼ of total daily ration, during this time attend to personal care
7:50 Walk Speedy again for exercise and/or elimination
8:00 Short obedience session to remind Speedy who is alpha
8:10 Leave for work. Make goodbye calm. Leave moderate amount of water and confine Speedy in area that includes sleeping quarters, water bowl and elimination papers. Leave radio on.

P.M.

5:30 Return from work, greet Speedy calmly. Release from confinement, but only into "earned" environment
5:45–
6:00 Feed Speedy ¾ of ration, take up water after feeding
6:10 Walk Speedy for exercise and/or elimination
6:30 Umbilical cord dog (sit on leash) while eating dinner
7:00 Play session, including fetch
8:00 Watch TV together
9:00 Obedience session
9:15 Walk Speedy for exercise and/or defecation
9:30 Offer small amount of water, then put Speedy in confined area with papers
10:30 Retire, place Speedy on floor near bed (tether if necessary), or use crate for sleeping.

If you compare the two schedules you will find that they cover the extremes in city dog-owning styles. There are readers who will object to my even outlining a schedule for the 9-to-5 owner who leaves the dog alone for long stretches. They will say that such souls just shouldn't have a dog, period. However, I doubt that my fellow professional trainers will say that. It's reality and we've learned to respect that.

The fact is, people who work 9 to 5 every day do procure dogs and do need to be provided with a schedule. Of course, the situation is not ideal—but it hardly borders on criminal. In the same breath, I must urge all 9-to-5 owners to try to arrange for someone to come in at midday and walk the dog. You'd be surprised how many trustworthy school kids would jump at the opportunity and will be very responsible about the job. In most large cities there are professional dog-walkers for hire. The fact that the dog will probably not eliminate outdoors (the pup thinks it should go inside, on the papers) doesn't really matter; the pup still needs exercise and social interaction. Sometimes group-walking with a dog walker will help to "de-paper train" a dog because the paper-trained dog will see other dogs in the group eliminating outside.

Under no circumstances should the 9-to-5 owner attempt to crate his or her puppy for that length of time. The puppy will be forced to soil the crate. The time period is simply too long. However, you can leave the crate, with its door open, in the confined area and many pups will use it as a sleeping area. In fact, I've known many 9-to-5 pups who will sleep practically the whole time their owners are away, waking up only for a piddle once or twice and then sacking out again. A radio helps to mask outside noises and if kept on soft music (not rock or talk shows) can lull the pup to sleep and help wile away the time.

De-Paper Training Your Dog

Since most city owners, because of parvovirus and other considerations, *must* paper train, they must also have a method for de-paper training the dog. There are two ways of going about this process, a long way and a short way.

The long way is to simply do nothing. Just leave the situation as it is, the papers where they are, and correct your dog using the methods outlined previously if the dog has an accident off the papers. The dog will gradually start to reject the papers. After awhile—and it can take up to five months—the dog will be eliminating very little on the papers and mostly holding until it can reach the street. Males, especially, start to reject the paper once they begin lifting their legs as they desire scent posts to mark with their urine. Remember, as J.R. Ackerly remarked, "Dogs read the world through their noses and write their history in urine." Your dog will not want to write his history inside for "limited readership." He will want to "publish" a special edition on the trees, fire hydrants and street signs of your neighborhood each day. Bitches can take a little longer to reject the papers, but most do in time.

You can take up the papers once you've reached seven straight days when nothing, absolutely nothing, is deposited on them. Again, seven days is an arbitrary amount of time, but it works. Once you take up the paper, it is best to restrict your dog's access to the area where the papers were previously placed. Close the door to that room or place a large object, like a packing crate or trunk over the area where the papers were. If your dog has any lingering desire to use the papers, we want him to stumble upon something placed in his desired spot, and then either make the decision to "hold it" until he's granted a walk outside or make a mistake and get disciplined and taken immediately outside for a correction with a connection.

A shorter method of de-papering is to immediately close off the area where the papers were, and walk the dog ten, even fifteen times a day to give the dog every chance to eliminate outside. You will have to have three or four free days to do these many walks and you will have to be very dedicated and conscientious about those walks. Under no circumstances can the dog be allowed to traverse the area where the papers were. Going near that area will only kick off the gastro-colic reflex and encourage elimination. Since blocking off the area that once harbored the papers will be next to impossible for many owners, especially if the area is a kitchen or bathroom, and because the shorter method of de-paper training takes a lot of effort, I usually advise clients to use the longer method. However, every once in awhile I will have a client who finds the papers (and the droppings on them) repugnant and insists on the shorter method. That's okay with me, as long as you understand how much dedication will be involved.

Terrace Training

Terraces are trendy. Most of the new "luxury" buildings in New York feature postage-stamp sized terraces. While they are not big enough in many cases for two human beings to sit and enjoy the view, they are usually large enough for a dog to use for elimination. Since you paid big bucks for such a feature, you might as well get your money's worth.

First, check to be sure this is permitted in your building and that the terrace has proper drainage. Otherwise your dog will send "presents" or "rain" to the terrace below. Also, be absolutely sure that your dog cannot escape the terrace or hurdle the railing. Installing wire mesh can often make the terrace safe for a little dog, but be careful here, too. Many buildings forbid such restructuring because zoning regulations require the building to look uniform in appearance. Do not use the terrace as a toilet if you have a breed that can jump up and possibly go over the railing—don't risk it!

You can place papers on the terrace or simply clean the flooring. In good weather you can leave the sliding glass door ajar a bit to allow access for the dog, or in some cases you can even install a dog door. But be sure that you are not endangering the safety of your apartment or the other tenants and that your terrace cannot be reached via other ones or via the roof of another building. Burglars are excellent climbers. So are dognappers. Finally, terracing your dog in no way excuses you from daily walks for exercise and socialization. Note the plural — *walks*.

DESTRUCTIVE CHEWING

After housetraining complaints, destructive chewers comprise the second largest group I receive the complaints about. Chewing is a distinctive city problem because of the limited spatial dimensions dogs are forced into, because of lack of exercise and because of the length of time owners are away. Right now, this very minute, there is a dog sitting in an apartment munching on garbage he's stolen from a trash can, and right now, this very minute, there is an owner unlocking his or her apartment to discover just such a mess. Right now, there is also a dog who is being cruelly disciplined for doing what comes rather naturally as a result of canine boredom. A little understanding on both sides would go a long way.

First, let's say it once and for all: dogs do not chew destructively out of "spite." In fact they don't defecate, urinate, bark, yodel or tap dance out of "spite." Bluntly, they don't do *anything* out of spite, because the canine mind doesn't work that way. It is an easy human misinterpretation to claim spite, but dogs don't function that way. Dogs chew out of frustration, loneliness and boredom, but not out of spite. There is no malicious desire to harm, annoy or humiliate you. The dog is not "getting back" at you for leaving him alone. But he might be telling you tons about himself as a pack animal and about the *way* you leave him alone. But get "spite" out of your head once and for all, otherwise it will cloud your relationship with your dog and give you license to overdiscipline your friend. Check your own behavior instead.

Watch those hellos and goodbyes! Overemotional greetings or departures might set up an atmosphere that will encourage your dog to chew. Greet and leave your dog quietly. Otherwise the dog is kept on edge. When you leave take a moment and sit your dog in front of you. Make eye contact, deliver a short speech in a friendly but serious tone ("Okay, Tippy, be a good girl and watch the house, and here's your special toy that you love so much. Goodbye") and leave. Present a special toy kept near the door to the dog. Scent the toy by rubbing it firmly on your palm or, better yet, wetting it with saliva. *Personalize* it for your dog. When you return, take this toy up. It's only presented when you leave and scented each time.

If frustrations mount while you're away, your dog might decide to chomp on the special toy rather than your shoes.

Be sure you are not using toys that resemble human items like shoes, and don't give your dog socks, nylons or yarn as chew toys. Hard nylon bones are great, durable, and if nicked up a bit with a jack knife, take scent well.

It's best to make the environment itself look like it's disciplining the dog, especially since you may not be present when your dog chews. Substances that can be rubbed on wallpaper or coated on chair legs include tabasco sauce, bitter apply spray or cream, cayenne pepper (vaseline applied first helps it to stick) or my favorite, jalapeno peppers. Wear gloves when rubbing the hot Mexican peppers on chewed surfaces.

When your dog is least expecting it, pull a "blitz" on your dog to cure chewing. Here's how it's done. Leave with a proper goodbye for just 15 minutes. Return and check for destruction. If you have "proof" of chewing, you can use the "proof" to convict your dog of his chewing crime as long as you *do not scream at the evidence of chewing before you get the dog to the proof.* Stay home for 15 minutes and then leave for one-half hour, return and repeat the above. Next, stay home for 15 minutes and leave for one hour. Got it? Build by half hours with a 15-minute return between each part of the "blitz." This "blitzing" method forces the dog to accept many hellos and goodbyes (carefully underplayed by you, of course) and makes the dog resist chewing from within. Scent that special toy each time you leave!

You might need a free day or a free evening in order to stage your first blitz. Try to build up to at least one and one-half hours in your first blitz. If you have a double problem with the dog stress whining when you leave you must also discipline for that using the shake or the swat corrections, as stress whining sets the stage for destructive chewing. If you stage a blitz and the dog "fails" a part of it (that is, chews), discipline correctly, stay home for 15 minutes and if possible repeat that part of the blitz again.

Chew proof as much as you can before blitz time. Get out those jalapeno peppers, the cayenne pepper and the Tabasco sauce and annoint everything you even think might be chewed. In severe cases, mousetraps set strategically work wonders. Obviously, don't place bait in them and don't let the dog see you set them. They will not catch on your dog, but they will make the environment itself look like it caught your dog in the act.

Your dog should not have full freedom of the house if he is destructively chewing. Make him earn the house by imposing The Evans Edict for Earning the Environment, which is described in the section on housetraining. Use the seven-day plan as described, and try to stage a blitz as you grant each new room or area. If you want to be absolutely safe, you can crate your dog, but not for more than four hours at a time, which will automatically rule out crating for many city owners. Even if you did crate, sooner or later you'd have to pull a blitz on the dog anyway to liberate him or her from the crate. I know many owners who use the crate as a cop-out, never giving the dog *any* freedom, *any* license, and then are royally upset when the dog does damage in a situation where the crate wasn't allowed—like a hotel room that is trashed or a neighbor's home destroyed.

Again, I have nothing against crates—they are wonderful teaching tools fully connected with the dog's den background. They can be misused as a cop-out and a crutch, however.

Dogs do not like separation, but owners have lives to live and can't be home 24 hours a day. Understandably, from the dog's point of view as a pack animal the pack leader is supposed to be home, but even a mother wolf leaves the den occasionally, if only to take care of her own physical needs. You are entitled to as much and more. Get over those guilties! Don't bawl your eyes out, blitz! Teach your dog that you are the alpha, that *you* are the one who comes and goes at will, that sometimes Fido goes with you and sometimes he doesn't.

Be especially careful about Sunday night. Why? You might have overloaded your dog with love during the weekend and the contrast on Monday, when it's back to work, might prove to much for the dog and lead to chewing or trashing. So, on Sunday night, act a little cool and perhaps give your dog an obedience session to minimize contrasts and maneuver toward Monday. Remember, you can't change the fact that you have to go to work on Monday, but you can lessen the impact on the dog by spending a calm Sunday night (or whatever night is correct for your schedule).

Don't try the opposite tact of overloading the dog with so much love on Sunday night so that he will "forgive" you for leaving on Monday. You're mixing human emotions into dog thinking. Such a ploy will backfire. The dog will not appreciate the extra love on Sunday night, in fact, he'll be even more frustrated on Monday when you leave because the contrast is just too great.

Finally, remember, in extreme cases you simply *must* consult a qualified private trainer for help with chewing difficulties. Don't just shed tears over trashing or curse chewing. Get help. The cost of a private trainer (you do not need a class for this problem) will most likely be less than that Oriental carpet Rascal is targeting right now.

JUMPING UP

We've already covered the correction for this problem to a degree, but let's recap. Put a short "tab" leash on your dog and let the dog wear it for the next seven days. It should be one to three feet long, depending on breed size. If your dog jumps the correction is three-fold:

- Grab the tab and whip it down *hard,* say, "No!"

- Pull up on the tab sharply, say, "Sit."

- Flash your best "Supremes" stay signal in the dog's face, and say, "Stay."

Memorize this physical and verbal sequence. If you don't you will probably engage in oververbalization that will only confuse the dog: "No, Tippy, off, down, stop! Sit, stay, No!" No dog can make sense of that verbiage. If the dog is jumping on someone who does not know or will not do the correction, *you* must step in from behind the dog, grab the tab, whip it down hard and deliver the correction. And no excuses—just take it as a given that most people will not help you in your efforts to stop jumping. Instead they will hold the dog up ("Oh, isn't he *cuuuuute?*") and complain of ripped nylons later. *You'll* have to step in to correct and teach your dog to sit for praise. You can't change other people, you can only train your dog.

NOT COMING WHEN CALLED

Examine the tips provided earlier and if you are having a chronic problem with your dog running away you *must* call a six-week moratorium on any and all off-leash freedom for your dog and practice formal recalls during that time. Do at least seven a day, for six weeks. There is no quick fix. It takes a dog a long time to forget about running away from or around but not *to* the owner.

Give your dog time to forget old ways and learn new behavior patterns. During this six-week period, whatever you have to do, do not place yourself in a situation of saying the word "come" and then not being able to correct the dog if there is not a correct response. Every time you said the word "come" in the past and the dog stayed where he was or ran the other way you were unintentionally training your dog that the word "come" meant nothing. Now you have to reverse that. It takes time.

Once the six-week moratorium is up, practice in a confined area with the dog wearing a tab leash. Do three formal recalls and then act nonchalant and let your dog wander off. When he's not suspecting it, pull a sudden recall on the dog. Drop to the ground on one knee, open your arms and call your dog. If he delivers himself in front of you, go on to working in a larger area. If not, go get the dog, even if a chase is involved, give a good shake correction and repeat one formal recall. Now guess what? You got it. Six more weeks of no off-leash freedom. It probably won't come to this if you've invested the original six-week period in training a good recall.

Remember, the six-week moratorium applies whether you are in the city or in the country.

AGGRESSION

My advice on this matter is short and not-so-sweet: If you own a growling, snapping, biting dog you are in deep trouble. Immediately employ a qualified *private* trainer to work with you *in your home.* Don't delay. While the problem is serious and will not get better in time without training, aggression is often easily treatable by a qualified professional. Do not take the dog to class. You need private, one-on-one instruction. "But he's just growling . . . " you might say. As I tell my clients, a growl is a bite that just hasn't connected yet. Owners of aggressive dogs often live in a dreamworld of denial concerning their dog's behavior and some even secretly want their dogs to be nasty. A trainer can guide you out of the trouble and terror of living with a canine terrorist.

The trainer might advise you to neuter your dog. Do it. It might help. The trainer may also suggest a regimen of drugs. Give them. But be absolutely sure that the trainer is also working with you on the *specific instances* in which the dog is aggressive. This is usually done via "set-ups' '—deliberately concocted events in which the bad behavior is elicited from the dog so that it can be corrected. Most of all, don't be hopeless and don't take your dog to the shelter and dump the problem on unsuspecting staff there. Train, don't complain. Remember, one session with a private trainer often works wonders with aggressive dogs.

Even before the trainer can get to you, try the following:

- Stop *all* treats.

- Don't let the dog go in or out of the main entrance to the apartment or home before you. Consult the section on heeling. Go together, and enforce *strict* hallway and elevator etiquette as described in that section.

- If your dog is on your bed, *at all,* get him off. Allowing him up there makes you look like a littermate not a leader.

- Get the dog to your veterinarian immediately to rule out any health problems. Poor health or pain can spur aggressive behavior.

- Don't give the aggressive dog *any* people food.

- Limit praise. Make the dog earn it. Tell him to sit if he solicits praise. Don't give it for nothing.

Most of all, don't just sit and suffer or live in fear of an aggressive dog. Call a trainer. If you are reading this book, most probably you live in a city, and my experience is that most American and Canadian cities have at least one, if not many more, professionals skilled in treating aggressive dogs. Call your veterinarian or the nearest veterinary school if you need a recommendation.

Trying to diagnose or treat canine aggression in print is next to impossible and, at worst, unethical. The contexts in which dogs are aggressive (and almost all aggression is context-specific) are too complicated to dissect in a book of this scope. Add the complications of city distractions to the aggression problem and one can readily see the necessity for competent one-on-one guidance.

Finally, this is not meant to terrorize you into training, but mentioned as a very real possibility: you could lose your dog unless you act quickly. In a city context, aggression will often be twice as pronounced and twice as often displayed. The excitement, spatial dimensions and stimuli that will set a dog off into an aggressive reaction are more than abundant in a city. There are laws being concocted and passed in many large cities that will effectively limit an aggressive dog to one, and only one, serious bite. After that, it's death row. You would have to euthanize your dog or leave town to an area with more liberal laws. City dwellers have *had it* with biting dogs. The "Pit Bull" terror and sensationalistic reporting on that breed and on dog bites in general hasn't helped matters, but all of that is really beside the point. Let's talk about *you* and *your* dog—in this case your growling, lunging, snapping, biting dog. What are *you* doing?

Dog Eat Dog: Interspecies Aggression

The solution to on the street aggression between dogs can be found in the section on heeling. Follow those instructions to the letter. If your problem is within your household and you are living with dogs who fight with each other here are some tips:

- Issue an advance warning when the dogs even *look hard* at each other. Watch the dog's body language. Ears up, hackles raised, tails straight out spell trouble. Don't wait for growling to begin to insert your advance warning.

- Don't cheapen yourself by screaming at your dogs. If the warning is not heeded, get physical, using the swat under the chin method, unless a fight is in progress, in which case you will want to simply get the animals apart, and then discipline one at a time.

- Put tab leashes—short one- or two-foot leashes—on your fighters and let them wear tabs whenever you are around. This gives you something more than just collars or flying fur to grab if you have to separate the dogs or discipline them for not heeding your warnings.

219

Owners of fighting dogs must learn to watch canine body language carefully. Here are two dog-level views. These two dogs are greeting each other affectionately . . .

. . . while the dog on the right here is clearly terrorizing the other and should be disciplined with the swat and/or a stern collar correction.   Courtesy of *Chip Simons*

- Discipline *both* dogs. Don't play the losing game of trying to figure out who started what. Chances are, through subtle body signs and piercing stares the dog who *didn't* growl overtly "started" the fight. It takes two to tango and they were *both* fighting, so both should be disciplined—perhaps the "innocent" party with the shake and the "guilty" party with the swat.

- It is very important that you do *not* separate the dogs after a fight. Keep them in the same room together on down stays or tie one in one corner and the other in another corner. If they try to scrap again while holding the down or tied up, discipline again, harder. If you separate the dogs, which many owners do just to preserve their own sanity, you are only playing into their hands and making them more determined to fight to the finish next time. If the dogs don't yet know the long down, teach it. See the appropriate section in the obedience exercises.

A dog fight in an apartment can be like descending into hell, because the spatial dimensions don't allow for any escape. The neighbors upstairs and downstairs will probably be pounding on the floor or ceiling yelling at you to shut those dogs up, and adding to the general commotion and confusion. If the situation is beyond your control you must call in a private trainer fast.

Be careful about breaking up a full-scale fight by inserting your hand between the dogs. One or both dogs may attack you. Here is where the tab leashes can be of help. If you have no tabs on, get a broom, a mop, even a chair and bring it down hard between the two embattled parties, and after an incident like that, call a trainer.

OVERBARKING

Other than an aggressive dog, nothing will get you evicted from your building and possibly from your city faster than a yappy, overbarking dog. The most common misconception owners have about correcting barking is that if they do, the dog will sit in stone silence as the Brownstone Burglar breaks in. So, they let the dog bark at anything and everything, including noises on the street, sounds in the hallway, even sounds on TV. Many owners then try to soothe the dog out of the barking with seductive tonalities, mimicking littermate sounds so that the dog deduces that, indeed, something *was* wrong with whatever noise he reacted to. The dog is then determined to bark more quickly and longer next time.

I've been in the apartments of clients who literally cannot move without setting their dogs off on a barking jag. One woman made all her phone calls on the street because the minute she picked up the receiver,

"Max," a West Highland White Terrier, would fly into a barking rage. When people called her, she didn't answer until she had put Max in a closet, where the dog would bark continually. When the call was over (most of her calls were kept short) she would open the door, but Max would sit shivering, refusing to come out, unless of course the phone rang again, at which point the whole cycle repeated itself.

I had this client "umbilical cord" Max to herself for the next week (in other words, attach a six-foot leash to Max, the other end to her body and go about her day). If Max barked at all—even a whimpering sigh (that's a *bark* in my book)—he was to be given a strong leash correction, and if necessary the swat under the chin. His diet was to be changed—he was to eat twice, not once a day—and under no circumstances was he to be put in the closet.

I then called the operator, disciplining Max firmly when he saw me pick up the receiver (warning him in advance, of course). I asked the operator to call me back right away to test for a problem in the line (so, I lied!). The operator rang back and I took my time answering since I had to rediscipline Max, but much less so this time. Already he was getting the idea. My client then felt confident enough to work with Max in the same way and so I went down to the street and began calling Max's owners, chatting for longer and longer periods of time, understanding perfectly that the client may have to pause to "discuss" phone etiquette with Max. By our fifth call, silence reigned. In subsequent sessions we worked on noises in the hallway, securing the help of the neighbors for similar set-ups, TV noises and street sounds. Max progressed beautifully. He didn't really want the stress of barking like a lunatic, anyway.

If your dog is barking when you are away from home, the solution lies in pulling a "blitz" on the dog similar to the one described for curing destructive chewing.

- Get a toy, a nylon or rawhide bone or other such indestructible item and make this a special toy for the overbarker. Keep this toy up, and offer it only when you leave. Take it back up when you get home. The purpose is to give your dog something to do with his mouth (hopefully) other than bark with it.

- When you leave, sit your dog, make eye contact, give a warning and present your toy with a toss. Leave a tab leash on the dog, and tie a knot in the end of it so that when you *explode* back into your home or apartment (which is exactly what you are going to do) you will have something more than flying fur to grab in order to discipline the dog. The knot will help the tab not to slip through your hands.

- Now leave, and if your dog even whimpers (whimpers should be considered barks) get back into the house quickly. Leave the door fixed so that you do not have to waste time unlocking it again. That will only delay the correction. Close off rooms so the dog can't run too far. As you reenter, bang your fist on the door and head toward your dog. Discipline with the shake and/or the swat and quickly resit your dog, remake eye contact, reissue your warning and rescent and rethrow the toy. And hurry up about it—because you are going to leave *again.*

- Some owners will have to work hard to get the dog not to whimper even for five seconds or five minutes once it realizes that you are leaving. But persevere, and try to build up to a blitz. Leave for 15 minutes (proper goodbye, scented toy, etc.), and return for 15, then leave for one-half hour and return for 15 minutes, leave for one hour and return for 15 minutes, leave for one and one-half hours and return for 15 minutes, and so on. This blitz technique teaches the dog that you are the one who comes and you are the one who goes and no amount of protest barking will con you into returning to soothe or comfort, in fact all protest barking will do is cause you to return, wreak havoc and then leave again.

Guilty owners often have trouble staging effective blitzes because they are secretly mad at themselves for not being home twenty-four hours a day to be with Popsy. Let's face it. People need to work. People need a social life, too. That means you might have to go out to work, come home and go out again. Within reason, your city dog just has to accept that. Get over your guilt. Your "guilties" aren't doing anyone any good.

When you get into the longer periods of the blitz, you should sneak around, snoop around and otherwise sleuth to find out if your barker is cheating—being quiet for awhile but revving up after a certain period of time. Don't think that because you disciplined and your dog got to, say, the half-hour point in the blitz that you are home-free. You most definitely are not. Sleuthing is in order. Go out and then come back an hour later, but take the elevator to the floor *below* yours. Get off and sneak up the stairs. Listen. Any whimpering, whining, barking or yodeling? No, fine. Yes, discipline.

Another method is to tape your intercom button down with masking tape and then go downstairs and listen in on your own apartment. If you have staff in your building the concierge will be only too happy to let you use the phone to listen to your own apartment—he's probably been receiving complaints about the dog and will welcome the chance to help you train. Still another method, not quite as effective, is to turn on a tape recorder and record your home using a long-playing tape. Although you have to listen to the tape again to see if Bossy barked, you can fast forward it to see exactly where his control breaks down—which will give you a pretty good idea of when to sneak up those stairs on your next blitz.

VERY LOUD NOISES

When I first came to New York City, every noise frightened me. Garbage trucks sent me shivering. I avoided construction zones. I held my hands over my ears for police sirens and hospital ambulances. I hated jackhammers. I identify fully with the city dog under stress from noise. I also know that the only way to adjust to city noise is to discipline oneself, or be disciplined into facing it, sizing it up, and eventually dismissing it as the nuisance it usually is and not the threat it can be perceived to be.

A dog can be desensitized, but the dog must have the confidence and support, and if necessary the disciplinary hand of its owner in order to obtain this goal. Here are some tips:

- First, teach a good, solid heel and sit-stay. You can do nothing to solve noise-shyness unless your dog knows these words.

- Helped by the heel, the dog can then be guided past people, places and vehicles that make loud noises. Avoiding such areas is the worst, most dangerous tact to take because the dog will just add other noises to the list of sounds he doesn't want to deal with. Instead of avoiding situations that are noisy, go *toward* and *into* such areas, enforcing a strict heel.

- If your dog freaks, give a leash correction and in a low, stern voice say, "No, that's enough, heel"—and continue on. If possible, double back and go through the noisy situation again. Remember, no amount of soothing the dog will make the situation any better. You'll only sound like a littermate in trouble with a whining tonality and the dog will get worse. Besides, the dog can't hear you anyway because of the noise, right? But he can feel that training collar jerk, the shake and he can hear your lowered tonality if you give the warning before the noise begins. If it's too late for that, lean down and "growl" in the dog's ear.

We can't change the fact that cities will be full of unexpected, weird, obnoxious, irritating and often unnecessary noises. Since this cannot be changed the dog must adjust. It's really not that difficult. By following the above procedures noise-shy dogs can develop into dogs that are confident and poised, and who heel through the streets with aplomb.

Sometimes avoiding city construction zones just isn't possible. If the area is safe for you, it should be for your dog. Enforce a tight heel and do not try to soothe the dog out of noise-shyness.

13

Where to Train in City Spaces

YOU MIGHT BE SICK of me by the end of this book because I am going to lecture you mercilessly about the value of training and the need to teach your doggy denizen manners. I'll try to be funny about it and hopefully you'll read on, master the exercises and go out into the street to find a training area. You are then going to get angry at me all over again, because unless you know the secrets of finding city training spaces, you are going to feel walled-in by skyscrapers or beseiged with traffic. Thus, this chapter.

I know what you're going through. When I came to New York I tried training right on the sidewalks. After you get pushed aside, shoved rudely and even pummeled by passersby you start to get the not-so-subtle hint that your training efforts are not especially appreciated when Sadie's sit-stay blocks the pedestrian traffic. Attempting a down-stay on a New York sidewalk can be in many areas like ordering up a canine pancake. The solution is to find training nooks and crannies where you can safely train until your dog is street-smart and ready to move into the flow of city life as a regular pedestrian.

The first training ground that many city owners think of is the neighborhood park, but frankly the parks are usually the *last* places I choose as city training grounds for several reasons:

- Distractions abound from other dogs, other people and other animals (notably squirrels, pigeons and rodents). It is better to train in an area with few distractions at first and work up to training with distractions.

- Many dogs feel that the public park is a place to play, run, fantasize and relax—not a place to *obey or work or learn*. In the minds of many dogs the city streets represent obedience—walking nicely on the lead, not pulling, greeting strangers nicely and being polite. But the park means *freedom* from all these restraints, and two blocks before they even reach a public park some city dogs go into a state of exhuberance and forgetfulness that will not aid your training efforts. You might not be able to bring the untrained, inexperienced dog down to earth sufficiently to train decently. Later on, you will and in fact *must* train in the park, but not now.

- Since many training exercises (for instance, the recall) involve dropping the dog's leash and having the dog perform off-lead (or at least with a lead dragging along with the dog) you will be more liable to fines if your training ground is the public park. The ticketing officer will not care that you were trying to train the recall.

For all these reasons, I prefer small areas that are enclosed, easily entered and exited, distanced from city distractions as much as possible, and that have concrete flooring. If the area is enclosed by walls or fencing, there is less chance that your dog will bolt away from you during training, and if he does, you can catch the dog right away. Enclosed areas also make it less likely that other dogs or other animals are going to be hanging around complicating the training process at a time when the dog cannot handle distractions. Concrete is preferable because it provides good footing for your dog and generally is not as distracting to dogs because it holds scent far less well than grass or gravel.

With these requirements in mind I want you to go for a walk—preferably dogless—and scout your neighborhood for training terrain. Is there an alleyway nearby that is not full of garbage and sufficiently well-lit to assure you of safety? How about small, enclosed spaces at the base of skyscrapers? If you have buildings in your city that feature grand staircases (museums, concert halls, government buildings) you might check out the top or sides of the staircase. Often there will be enclosed areas here, if not enclosed completely then enclosed on two or three sides. (By the way, great urban staircases can be wonderful for exercising your dog and teaching him or her to climb stairs. Remember—if you live in an elevator building, don't forget to expose your dog early on to stairs.)

BONUS TRAINING TERRAIN

Ready-made training grounds can be tracked down in Chicago, New York, Toronto and several other cities with a simple phone call. For instance, in New York, there are now more than 200 plazas in the city. They are most often the result of a deal made between the city and the apartment house or office tower developer. In exchange for building higher or in greater density than zoning regulations permit, the developer promises to donate some space to the public as a park. The space can actually be quite small in space. I call these areas "parkettes."

A call to your city's office of zoning or parks department will get you the locations of such areas. If you cannot get an actual list, simply scout out such areas yourself. Although some such public spaces are disguised as "private" usually a plaque or sign will denote their true purpose. Often an explanatory sign is *required* to denote the space as available for public use. Some donated "parkettes" will be well known and heavily used, such as the public palza at the Citicorp Center in New York, or the public spaces at the base of several Montreal skyscrapers, but many will be empty and make excellent training territory. In many cities following the incentives-to-developers theory popularized in New York, the donated spots will be found at the base of taller "luxury" buildings in high-rent districts.

Remember, however, that many "freebie" parks are allowed to open in the morning and close at sunset. Often there will be a gate you open and close to enter the area. This is perfect for our training purposes, but not so hot if you arrive, dog in tow, and the gate is locked. Of course, if there is a "No Dogs" sign posted, you are out of luck. However, with the exception of having to stay open for 24 hours, most of these zoned-in parks have to provide the amenities expected at local public parks including drinking fountains, proper sanitation and upkeep, and open admission to leashed dogs.

When you locate your training spots be sure to vary the location of the training from day to day. This means you should find at least *three* training grounds. Otherwise your dog will think that coming when called is just a cute thing that is performed only in the alleyway near Southstreet Seaport, or only at the base of the CN Tower or under the Arc de Triomphe. That won't do, so rotate your training areas.

Using your own back yard (if you have one), your building's courtyard or your apartment building's hallway is acceptable, but conditions there can never approximate the lure and distractions of foreign turf. Remember, you will need obedience from your dog *when you need it,* not when you *don't* need it, and it's really no great tribute to your training skills if your dog does a perfect recall in your enclosed backyard or hallway and runs away in a public park. You simply must find three training territories that meet the basic requirements, and then "graduate" your dog to public parks, to the beach, to the woods and to any other locale that you frequent.

IN-HOME TRAINING

Do not forget to have training sessions in your home. Certainly you will practice most of your long down-stays there, as well as most of the other static, nonmovement exercises—but don't forget to do recalls in your home as well. You don't want your dog to think that training and obedience is an outdoor affair and that the interior of the house is his playground. Training is really a way of life with your dog that applies everywhere.

To move around and train effectively in your apartment or home you might have to move some furniture or clear an area. That's a small sacrifice for a well-trained dog. There's another problem with in-home training I've noticed with my clients. Funny as it may sound, they feel highly artificial training in the home. Since the dog may leave them unbothered indoors, going its own way and plopping itself someplace and really not being much of a bother, the owner might wonder why it is necessary to "bother" the dog with training sessions indoors. Precisely because when guests come or the dog has another excuse to act up you will have wanted to practice indoors so that the dog knows that commands must be obeyed *everywhere,* home turf and strange situations.

As you graduate your dog from zoned-in public plazas or secret alleyways to the parks and the streets, you are ready to go to stores. If you live in a "car-culture" city like Los Angeles, the temptation will be to park your car *and* your dog. How will your dog learn to behave in a store if you never take him into one and practice the dog's obedience? If you live in a place like New York or Tokyo, you'd be crazy to drive anywhere (except directly out of town) anyway. So your choice will be to teach your dog store manners or leave him alone in the apartment.

Don't go barging into Tiffany's with your terrible tyke until you have mastered the sit-stay and your dog holds it rock steady. You've heard about that bull in the china shop? Your untrained, unproofed dog could wreak havoc and do damage that will make the bull look like an amateur. I had a client who took her happy-go-lucky Labrador into a store that sold fine crystal. She thought he was trained, and indeed he was—he knew how to hold a beautiful stand-stay. The owner put the dog on command and gawked at a decanter-goblet display. Customers in the store began to approach the Lab in a steady procession, patting him, making a fuss over him and generally "oohing" and "aahing" about his stunning face and appearance. This, of course, made the Lab very, very happy and the happier he got the more he wagged his long tail and the more precious crystal smashed to the ground. Yet, the dog never once broke his stand-stay. The bill ran close to $250,000. High price for a good stand-stay.

Obviously the Lab should have been on a *sit-stay* if he was in a crystal shop at all! Follow the progressions for a good, solid sit-stay that I outline in the obedience session and "proof" the exercise in stores that do not sell breakable items before you enter more dangerous territory. Stationary stores and newsstands are perfect. Here are some further tips for insuring store sociability:

- Don't proceed into the store without issuing a warning to your potential canine crasher. Sit your dog at the entranceway to the store, make eye contact and in a low tone of voice deliver your warning. "Look, Fido, don't *touch* anything." One warning goes a long way. Tap the region between your dog's eyes—it's a powerful spot

- Follow the guidelines outlined in the obedience portion of this book. Recess your dog as far from passageways as possible so that other customers can get by and so that your dog doesn't feel uncomfortable holding a sit-stay where there's a chance of getting stepped on.

- Do not use the stand-stay or down-stay in stores. Using the first is foolish (witness the Labrador above) and the other position is simply rude—nobody wants to step over a sprawled-out dog who is monopolizing the aisle.

- Don't hesitate to quietly correct your dog. You can be physically firm but verbally very quiet and few will know. Deal with the disobedience swiftly and firmly and if possible put the dog back on a sit-stay in the same spot as before. Remember, it is a privilege to be allowed into a store with your dog, not a right. Since many dogs think all training bets are off and that anything they learned before just doesn't apply in stores, swift, firm corrections are often unavoidable. The correction, if strong enough, only has to be delivered once, in *one* store and your dog will know that obedience and manners apply *everywhere*.

CHURCHES AND CATHEDRALS

One final tip on searching out training spaces: Don't forget the outside of churches. I routinely train on the rampways of St. Patrick's cathedral, and I don't think there is anything disrespectful about this. In Cologne, West Germany, I observed a professional trainer putting a German Shepherd Dog through its paces at the foot of the famous cathedral downtown. The *Dom* in Cologne is in fact surrounded by pedestrian areas where traffic is not allowed, and the Gothic architecture of the ancient cathedral allows for many nooks and inlets where one could practice easily without bothering anyone. There are similar areas around Notre Dame in Paris and the Notre Dame replica church in Old Montreal. Just be sure to issue your commands quietly as you wouldn't want to disturb the prayers or meditation of someone inside.

14

A New Leash on Life

IN MOST MAJOR AMERICAN and Canadian cities there are stringent leash laws that may or may not be stringently enforced. Most of these laws dictate that one's pet be attached to the end of a leash and that the other end be held by a human being. Some laws even dictate the length of the leash, and some regulations state that the dog must be on leash or "under the immediate control of the owner." Just what "being under control" means is not always made clear, but usually it means if the dog comes when called, it is under control. Owners, of course, love this loophole as they can then apply their version of what having their dog under control means. For some owners this means that the dog comes when it is called, the first time, every time; for others it means that as long as the dog is not mauling, pummeling, chasing or biting other human beings or dogs then anything goes—even if the dog disappears from sight. "Oh, he always comes back—usually takes about 20 minutes," was the explanation one person gave me when I questioned her in New York's Central Park as her dog bolted out of sight. Just what the dog does during that 20-minute out-of-sight period didn't seem to matter to this woman. To her, out of sight, out of mind applied beautifully to her sense of "responsibility" concerning her dog.

This lady was guilty of the "magical thinking" that affects many dog owners and even some parents. (Psychiatrists say *especially* parents.) The thought line goes like this, "Tippy is such a joy at home, why he doesn't have a mean bone in his body, and he never misbehaves. Why would he do anything out of my sight that he wouldn't do in my own home where he is an angel, a sweetheart, a doll?" And so off comes the leash and off goes Tippy, running happily out of sight.

If you want to have a dog in a big city you have to obey the leash law, period. If you have to know why, just think it out for a moment. If your dog is not on leash he is *ipso facto,* out of your control. I don't care if he is obedience trained—every dog has his day and every dog will bolt and run given just the right opportunity and circumstances. More than that, your dog is not socially or genetically geared to the hermit life and he is in fact geared to seek out and engage in social interaction with his own species. I don't care if he *is* friendly to all other dogs—what if the other dog is a canine psychopath? I also don't care if your dog is loving to other people. In cities there are hordes of people who are not so lovable. First and foremost, people who do not like dogs and are afraid of them need to have the assurance that they can walk down the streets without getting mugged or bothered by an unruly (not to mention biting or dangerous) dog. In case you've forgotten, our dogs are *guests* in town; the city itself belongs to the human residents. Secondly, any large city and many smaller ones have odd individuals who by virtue of their economic or mental state act in irregular ways. In New York, for instance, there are thousands of homeless individuals, many of them ex-mental patients, who camp out on city streets talking to themselves and often exhibiting paranoid symptoms. Because their vocalizations and body movements are not ordinary, even very sound dogs will spook when they come into contact with such souls. The indigent person then quite rightly becomes quite indignant and trouble can result.

Other victims of the leashless dog's enthusiasm or lack of manners are toddlers, preschoolers, the elderly, the handicapped and those who lack sure footing because of illness or even inebriation. Yes, even drunks have rights over leashless dogs. In short, a dog without a leash attached to its collar and without the other end attached to an observant human being is a potential menace and, technically, breaking the law. However, it will be you, not Fido, who pays the fine for breaking the leash law.

At this point some readers might be saying I am simply a cop in disguise, bent on keeping dogs hemmed in, constrained and shackled. This is the criticism most often voiced by members of the I-want-my-dog-to-feel-free school of thought. These people will not be impressed by the arguments already set forth, nor will they be convinced when beloved Rover narrowly misses careening taxis, buses, or trucks. Sometimes the freedom ethic is so pervasive that these dogs will not even wear a collar by which a pedestrian could grab them and save them from the path of an on-coming car. Frequently such free dogs wear sixties-style bandanas or kerchiefs slung around their necks or other such adornments that indicate that they are free to "do their own thing." The "owner" often does not see himself or herself as an alpha figure to the dog, but rather as an *equal.* The dog is "free" and that's all that counts. Heavy fines are the only measure that will

Homeless individuals will be especially frightened of an off-leash or unruly dog. Teach your dog to be polite and to hold a solid sit-stay...

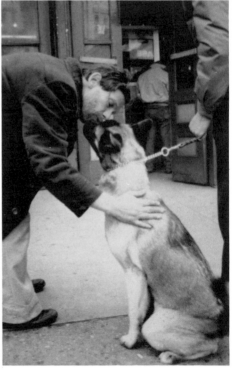

...and to accept love and praise from all who approach with a sincere heart. Just think—this Akita probably made this man's day.

force such souls to take the bandana off and put a real collar on, and attach a leash to that same collar and the other end to their hand.

The irony is, the leash can give your dog a new lease on life in the city—*if* you get over any hang-ups you might have concerning its use and use it creatively. In the section that follows, "Work That Body," we discuss the benefits of sustained, aerobic running for city dogs. This type of exercise must be done on leash. In fact, it cannot be done properly off leash. The joy, the true freedom and exhilaration your dog will feel after such exercise makes it clear that the leash can be more than just a restraint.

A 20-foot leash can be used quite creatively to exercise your dog by using a training technique horse trainers use frequently. It is called *lunging* and is a method of getting the horse ready for the rider, but also of exercising the horse at the same time the horse is taught obedience. To teach your dog to lunge, select a quiet area, preferably an area that is rounded and enclosed. You will need a 20-foot lead. A retractable type is fine. The rounded area will help guide your dog in a circle as you let out more and more leash. You might be able to find a garden area that is rounded or an area at a playground. I know one owner who taught his dog to lunge by using a large children's sand box late at night.

Stand in the middle of the area and let out about five to seven feet of leash. Hold the leash in your right hand and start turning toward the left *as* the dog takes the leash out. Turn very slowly at first and let out more and more lead. If the lead tightens, just keep turning to the left and slip your left hand to the bottom part of the lead and your right further up the lead to ease it gently to the left. Encourage your dog with happy praise—a distinctive sound helps, such as clicking your gums, saying "Go for it!" enthusiastically, whatever you feel is appropriate. Keep moving your dog around and around in a circle and try not to bring the dog in to you at all. If your dog simply stops in its tracks, smile, leave the leash limp, but do not praise the dog. Wait a second, and then give the leash a light snap to the left and begin encouraging the dog again if he moves. If the dog really gets on a roll and starts trotting around the circle, let all the leash out and let the dog rip.

Be sure to plant your feet firmly in the middle of the circle until you have to begin rotating, and then be sure to simply take quarter steps to the left and not to let the dog pull you out of your basic position. Sometimes having a helper skip or run in front of your dog with a liver treat can help the dog to get the idea of running around in a circle, but the helper should hop out of the circle as soon as the dog is rotating. You can get your dog ready for lunge work by practicing the Round Robin Recall, as described in *How To Be Your Dog's Best Friend*. In this technique the monks suggest forming a circle with three or four humans and passing the dog around, on leash, from participant to participant. This gives the dog the idea that running in a circle is a good thing, especially when enthusiastic verbal praise accompanies this exercise.

236

Remember not to use any soothing or worried tone of voice in an effort to get your dog to run around in the circle. Your dog will simply think that something is wrong and freeze. Also, get ready because you are going to get very dizzy when you exercise your dog this way! Finally, if you know somebody who has a dog who is lunging successfully, place your dog behind his or her dog and yourself next to the owner in the middle of the circle and rotate together. Chances are your dog will develop a running relationship with the dog that already knows the routine and they will become racing buddies. Also, if the two dogs become too active or unruly (running together tends to bring out the devil in many dogs) you will each have leashes on your dogs to give a corrective tug to calm the dogs down.

I'm often asked by my clients if it is all right to let go of the long lead and let the dog drag it, for instance in a park or playground. That's a tricky question. On the one hand, technically, you're breaking the law in most cities; on the other hand, it seems like a harmless violation of you are within a few feet of the dropped end of the leash. A far better solution would be to find an enclosed place to let your dog romp. Such places are around—playgrounds, alleyways, service entrances to apartment buildings, and other nooks and crannies around town.

Remember also that if you are a city-country person you should let your dog drag the leash for the first day of its country visit. For many city-country dogs the swift transfer from on-leash city living to off-leash country freedom is just too much to handle and as soon as the lead is snapped off, it's time to head for the hills—or the local highway. Ease your dog into the country freedom gradually. Let the dog drag the leash for one day, surprising the dog with sudden commands to "Come!" and then giving the leash a smart snap if there is no response. Practice standard recalls using the sit-stay and the come, always orienting the dog *toward* the house or residence you are living in, and do these on leash. Again, even in the country the leash can be your dog's lease on life. Once a lead is attached it is *yours* —your to put on and take off, yours to manipulate your dog with and yours to drop, if you wish. If your dog bites or touches the leash, give a strong snap forcing the lead out from the dog's mouth and say, "No!"

In short, there's nothing wrong with a leash unless you humanize its use and feel sorry for the dog who has to wear one. Society paints an ugly picture of leashes with talk of "leash laws" and "leash regulations," and the most common comment from country dwellers criticizing the idea of dogs living in cities is, "I'd never keep a dog in a city; I'd have to keep him on a *leash* all the time." Smart city-folk know that creative use of the leash makes it the dog's lifeline—its lease on life.

WORK THAT BODY!

"I exercise Tippy every day," moaned Mrs. Travolinni, "but she never loses any weight." For the umpteenth time the distraught dog owner was telling me Tippy's problems, most of which centered on Tippy's weight. Tippy had lost interest in almost anything other than eating. Her idea of exercise was to go outside with her owner, walk around the block a few times and then immediately come into the apartment, go to the kitchen and sit for a treat, which was usually forthcoming.

If you ask a typical dog owner what they do to exercise their dog, they will probably answer, "Toss a ball," which means the dog retrieves the ball and maybe, just maybe brings it back. If he doesn't, and decides to munch on it or even digest it, that's the end of the "exercise" for the day. Another typical response is, "I walk her," which means the dog is walked at a slow pace around the block. Once. That's not enough.

The city owner who is away at work all day and thinks that the pet is busily exercising itself in the apartment is usually mistaken. If you were able to train a video camera on the dog for the duration of the time you are away and monitor the dog's movements, you'd probably find that the height of the dog's activity comes when the owner says goodbye (dog jumps up and down, wags tail) and when the owner comes home (dog jumps up and down, wags tail). The rest of the time the dog is just lying around.

If you want to improve on this lazy situation, the first thing you have to resolve is that you are going to allot some time into exercising your dog. You then have to section out two ten- to 15-minute periods a day. That's all it really takes to give your dog a new lease on life through exercise. Your goal can be to help your dog lose weight, tone up, live longer or just form a deeper bond with you, and you'll wind up gaining all these benefits even if only one is your goal.

First, set up a program of roadwork for your dog and you. Roadwork differs from plain exercise because in roadwork you literally go out and work the road. There are several ways of approaching this project. The best way is to run with your dog on leash at a light jogging pace. If you own an exceptionally large breed, you might have to pace yourself at a faster rate. Find out the background of your breed. Is it a trotting breed, a coursing hound, a galloping breed? For instance, a German Shepherd dog should not be forced to gallop in the mistaken notion that more can be accomplished in a shorter period of time that way. The Shepherd is a trotting breed and will exercise the proper muscle groups only if run at a trot pace. If you are not experienced with the way your dog's gait should look, ask someone who knows the breed or attend a show where they are gaiting the dogs correctly. In the case of Shepherds, though, this may be difficult, for exhibitors are racing these dogs around the show rings at jet speeds. Similar situations exist within other breeds too, so do some careful research. The dog will also indicate to you when a comfortable gait has been reached—you can "feel" it together.

It is important to run with the dog *on leash*. This accomplishes several things, often overlooked by dog owners. First, you are able to regulate the dog's gait more effectively. Secondly, the dog, obviously, cannot stop, unless you do. The value of *sustained* exercise is tremendous. If you just take the dog out and begin to run with the dog off lead, sooner or later (usually sooner) Fido stops to smell the roses or more interesting items. You call back to the dog, trying to keep moving yourself and keep him moving, but the momentum has already been broken. Off lead, the dog can decide to quit, whenever he wants to. Besides the physiological momentum being broken, the psychological build up is also aborted. The dog views the exercise session as just another walk, albeit at a faster pace, but basically a walk with all the elements of a walk important to him—stopping to sniff, urinating, investigating and so on.

If the leash is connected to the dog, you can use it to encourage the dog to go that extra half mile. You can use verbal encouragement and praise, or you can give the lead a light, playful snap forward to encourage completing the course.

Watch your dog as you jog, and pace yourself into the program, beginning with just one-quarter mile for an overweight or elderly dog, at a slow pace. Work up to your breed's proper pace gradually, over a week's time. Be sure to consult with your veterinarian before you commence any roadworking program and check your dog's pads periodically to be sure they are in good condition. The best running surfaces are beach sand that is not too soft, grass, dirt roads that are finely graded, and after these gravel or macadam. Be especially careful about hot pavement in the summer, and if bike paths are available, use those instead of the shoulder of the road. Run in the cooler part of the day—early morning or late afternoon.

Roadworking off a bike or car is also a possibility if you are not able to run yourself. If you use a bike, begin quite slowly by walking with the bike between you and the dog. Arrange the leash so that you can easily snap it away from the bike, and use a stern warning phrase if the dog veers too closely to the wheels. You should be able to feel out whether your dog can handle being roadworked off a bike by the way he responds when you are simply walking the bike between you and the dog. If the dog shows an abnormal interest in getting in front of the bike or coming too close to the wheels, and does not correct himself when warned away or corrected with the leash, forget this type of roadworking and get out your sneakers. Most dogs, however, adapt quite nicely. Of course, very small breeds cannot be worked off a bike, as the speed will be too much.

Roadworking off a car, if possible in your city, usually takes two people and is not recommended until you have inauguerated a steady program on foot or off a bike. When doing car work, try to use a hatch-

A good dog walker can be the solution to the exer cise problem.

A program of roadwork benefits many dogs—even if it means driving out of town. Close communication between handler and driver is essential, super-slow speeds a must and, obviously, roadwork is only for larger dogs.

back style car so that the person handling the leash can feed it out of the back and sit on the edge of the car. Run the dog on the side *opposite* the side where gas fumes are emitted and be sure your muffler is in order and pollution control devices working properly. If you use a pick-up truck, you can run the dog off the side and avoid the rear completely.

Many professional breeders and trainers roadwork their dogs off a car, but the idea can horrify the layperson who envisions an accident. For this reason, never try to roadwork alone, and be sure that your driver is skilled and can brake immediately. On most vehicles, the gas pedal need never be touched; simply putting the car in gear will move the car at the right pace. You need to get out of the city and find a completely deserted road, and you have to have a dry run, without the dog, on the road to check it out in advance. Because of all these limitations to roadworking using a car, most dog owners will just skip it and bike or run. I mention it for the sake of breeders and others who may have large numbers of dogs, all of whom need exercise. As one breeder put it, "I have 13 resident dogs, all of whom I'm actively showing. I can't afford any spongy constitutions or out of shape dogs. I could never roadwork them all on foot, and with a driver and one helper, I can get all 13 out within the course of a day by doing two at a time. Luckily, I have a half-mile long driveway!"

However you decide to do roadwork, try to set up your course so that you and the dog are running toward home in the final stretch. This has a great psychological impact on the dog (and on you!) and as you near the home stretch, shout encouragement to the dog. Have a short "cool down" period before you go back into your dwelling. Don't worry whether the dog can pick out your apartment correctly. Believe me, the homing instinct is very strong and your dog will know when home comes into view. Besides, as you hit the home stretch and begin whooping it up with heavy verbal praise, the neighbors get a terrific free show.

Here's an interesting innovation on tossing a ball for your dog. Use two balls. Start the game by revving the dog up by high verbal praise and then throw one ball. When the dog gets it and looks at you, as most dogs will, immediately display the new ball and indicate it with attractive praise and gestures. Two to one the dog will let his mouth fall open at the sight of this new stimulus and then you throw the new ball and run to retrieve the old one. Keep this up at an absolutely frantic pace and work the dog out by throwing each ball a greater distance each time. Have a third ball in your back pocket as a hedge against not being able to get your hands on one of the others fast enough. This game is also a wonderful solution to the problem of the dog who retrieves one ball and then won't bring it back. If your neighbors don't mind you can use the hallway of your building.

You can play monkey in the middle with your dog using a ball in pretty much the same way as above. Station your dog in the middle of two persons and use the sit-stay if the dog knows it. Then, begin to toss the ball back and forth, keeping it from the dog for at least five throws, no more, then let the dog get the ball. If you simply keep tossing the ball back and forth, you will only frustrate the dog, and he will quit.

These exercises encourage the dog to use different muscle groups than the ones used in pure roadwork, and each time the dog skids to a stop, brakes, picks up pace or jumps, he uses important muscles and stretches the ligaments in a different way.

When I say to praise the dog during roadwork or during ball games I mean *praise the dog* — go absolutely crazy with verbal praise and your dog will push through with the exercise just for you. Why are some aerobic instructors more popular than others? Because they praise their students lavishly and don't let them give up physically *or* psychologically. You have to do the same for your dog and your praise, light and soft, should begin when you produce the leash or ball inside your house and rise to a high when you are just finishing your exercise.

Perhaps the most pleasureable side effect of what I call "hot exercise" is the incredible bonding it produces between you and your dog. My breeder friend told me, "When the dogs and I go out for roadwork it's about 5:30 A.M., the coolest part of the day — and we are free, absolutely free to be with each other for that 20 minutes. And I believe the dogs know it. Even though they are running, they are focused on me and I'm all theirs. It's quality time between us — no phone interruptions, no doorbell, no TV, no stress. Just us on the road in the cool morning air." Another owner who jogs each evening with his dog in New York's Central Park told me, "When we complete our run I take Prince over to the water fountain for a drink. After he drinks, without fail, he looks up at me with a most curious and loving look. We have a real moment of communication then — it reminds me of the track meets I used to run in school. You'd run with someone real hard, and when you made the finish line, you'd congratulate each other, sling your arms around each other and go off for a drink of water. It's comradeship born of relief and a shared endeavor. I swear when we walk home that Prince would put his arm around me, slap me on the back and tell me how well I ran if he could. It's the most important part of our day."

15

Let's Get Carried Away

IN THIS BOOK I state that big dogs can live happily in the city and that your dog need not be tiny to adjust to the city. But, let's face it, a large number of city owners *will* opt for small- to medium-size dogs and understandably so. Yet, a surprising number of such owners fail to educate their charges on proper procedure for being picked up and carried. Too many owners put up with squiggly-wiggly woofers whose antics resemble more that of an earthworm than a trained city canine.

The fact is, if you own a small dog in the city you are going to have to fetch Fido constantly. There are going to be many instances in which it will be impossible to leave the dog on the ground. One owner of a miniature Dachshund said to me, "The breeder told me not to allow 'Princeton' to walk up the stairs of my four-flight walk-up since Dachshunds are prone to disc problems; but whenever I pick him up, he is so restless it's all I can do not to *drop* him let alone get him up to my apartment." In this case the dog was already one year old and had, indeed, developed a slipped disc problem because the owner has just given up hoisting the unruly pet up the stairs. "Princeton" had never been corrected when he first squiggled and squirmed and so the jostling with the owner had become patterned in.

Teach your puppy from day one that however you decide to carry him or her, it *must* be tolerated. Don't allow *any* feistiness in the matter of carrying. Just treat squirming and squiggling as if it were totally taboo. Many Europeans know they will be taking their small dogs from place to place and decide early on that getting carried is to be an accepted fact of life. Americans, on the other hand, often feel that a dog will willingly *walk* everywhere, but this isn't the case for the city owner. There will be many cases and situations in which you will either be expected or will want to hold your dog for short or even long periods of time. Your puppy must be taught early on that *you* are the one who decides when he or she will be held and in what way. Sound strict? Not at all. Do you want your dog to go places, see things? Then you'd better teach him to let himself get carried.

COMBATTING FEISTINESS

Feistiness is the worst enemy of easy carrying and is often associated especially with terriers. Perhaps this is because they would prefer to be close to the earth (remember "terrier" comes from the Latin *terre* — "the earth"). Many terriers complain about being held and about different holding styles. Trouble is, terriers make good city pets and for their own sakes they will need to be lifted, hoisted and otherwise removed from their beloved earth.

Despite the genetic component here (most Toy breeds are easier to teach in this area), don't give in. If your dog struggles while you are holding him or her, immediately and rudely jut the pup or dog out from your body and give the dog a strong shake. The shake should be curt, almost rude, and include a low warning phrase such as, "No! Hold still." However, be careful not to get loud. Keep your voice low and dark and then bring the dog back into your body and repeat the same style of holding you were attempting when your dog objected.

It is important that your shake-correction not be over three to five seconds and include some eye contact—and that you quickly place your dog back in the objected-to position. If you get more squirming and squiggling repeat the shake correction and don't hesitate to put your dog on the ground and give even a swat under the chin for disobedience in this area. It is best, though, to remain standing, correct with the shake, repeat the stimulus, correct again and *teach,* rather than *tolerate* your dog's desire to be released from your grip.

Don't feel guilty that your city canine wants to be on the ground, free to do his own thing. The fact is, that's not real life in a city, and while you're being strict on carrying might be viewed by the dog as a limitation on freedom, discipline in this area will be, in fact, your dog's liberation because if you teach your small- or medium-size dog early on that all styles of carrying are to be tolerated, you will be able to take your dog many places otherwise forbidden to an on-leash dog. Another plus is that your strictness in disciplining feistiness will allow you to pass your dog around to friends and neighbors, all of whom will have different carrying and holding styles and touches.

All this strictness is not to say that there aren't definite styles of holding that dogs prefer and are most comfortable with. In different cultures, there are different interpretations of which methods allow canines to be carried away most enjoyably and effectively. Let's examine some.

BRITISH STYLE:

Many Brits like to tuck their small dogs under one arm, supporting the dog's underbelly with their inverted forearm. The hand is opened widely and the palm of the hand cradles the dog's breastbone and sternum. This method of carrying allows full freedom for the other hand and arm and might be seen frequently in London because of the frequent rainy weather. I've also seen this style of carrying used in Vancouver, British Columbia, Seattle and Portland—all cities noted for moderate climates but lots of rain. Residents of these towns often appear to have umbrellas permanently grafted onto one hand, and so it's easy to see why "British style" holding is popular. Then, too, many rainy-town residents simply don't want their dogs soaking up rainfall while walking or prefer not to hassle with slapping on the dog's raincoat for every outing. It is also an excellent method for those who do not have facility with their other arm.

While this type of carrying style has definite advantages, there are problems. First, many dogs are distinctly uncomfortable being held this way. Often the dog will panic because it does not feel adequately supported. However, with a little practice most adjust. The owner should snuggle the dog in closely to his side so that the dog can lean against the human frame and not have to balance precariously on one arm. Be sure your hand is opened wide over the dog's chest, too, as this provides support and tends to stop the dog from lurching forward at the sight of other dogs or similar attractions.

This really isn't a good carrying style to use if your dog is bigger than a Cairn Terrier. It also isn't a good support system for a puppy. Puppies are far less adaptable to this type of carrying because they will squirm off the arm very easily. But for the experienced dog who is calm about being carried this style can be quite workable.

CHIPMUNK STYLE

Every dog looks great held "chipmunk style." Here the dog's bottom is supported with one hand, fingers spread wide. The other hand is cupped under the front legs and cradles the chest. The dog's front paws are draped over this hand and the dog is turned outward toward the world. While this is not a practical way for a puppy or dog to be carried for any extended length of time, it is an excellent carrying style for some specific situations.

First, because this style of holding makes the dog look so appealing—the viewer's attention is immediately drawn to the dog's face and paws—I often suggest that puppies be shown by breeders to clients in this matter. It is also a great way to restrain a puppy or older dog if a second party needs to do intricate facial cleaning or grooming. The paws can be easily manipulated in this carrying position also, and this facilitates clipping the nails on the front paws by an assistant. The puppy's back can be drawn in close to your chest for added support.

Anyone who has done television or movie work with dogs knows that chipmunk style truly makes the dog the star of the show. Presentation of the dog's face to the camera is made easy and, because the head and neck are not being restrained, the pup or dog is free to strike all the comical and lovable poses his heart desires. For the dog or pup who is a born "ham" and happens to possess pleasant facial features, chipmunk carrying tends to melt even the most frozen hearts.

Finally, chipmunk style is the carrying style to use if you are taking puppy photographs. The puppy can be easily hoisted up to eye level, and great "cheek-to-cheek" photos can result. Interestingly enough, when held in this fashion the dog's eyes usually do not reflect back to the camera and the resulting photograph does not show a dog with "electric eyes"—a drawback that ruins many a dog photo.

INFANT STYLE

This is the best style of holding when you want a Corgi kiss or a Bichon Buss. Hold your dog cradled in your two cupped arms, supporting the pup's head much like you would a human infant's head. It's easy to tickle your puppy's cheek this way, draw the dog closer to you and share affection. It's also a holding position that allows loving eye contact. Because of the flipped over position and exposed belly, the dog will view being held this way as being submissive—so don't be surprised if older pups or dogs object to being "treated like a baby." Still, it is a method of carrying that you should teach your dog to accept precisely for those reasons. The carrying position itself can be a loving way of expressing dominance—and that's not necessarily a contradiction in terms in my book. With dogs, love *is* discipline and vice versa (your mother must have told you that a zillion times, right?).

FRENCH STYLE

If you visit France, especially Paris, you are going to see dogs everywhere: on the streets, in the shops, at the outdoor cafes, in theaters and riding in cars. A common mode of carrying—although it is not really a form of holding—is to simply perch the animal on your lap and teach it to stay. The dog will often be in a sit-stay stance or it might be curled up in the

I call this style of holding "British Style" because it leaves one hand free to do something else, like make a point with a finger while lecturing or, like many Brits, carry an umbrella.

In "Chipmunk Style" the paws are draped over the hand and the dog held upright. It is a great position for posing for photographs or for introducing your dog to others.

"Infant Style" is a popular holding style and allows for loving eye contact.

owner's lap. While the British, and even some Americans and Canadians might wince, it is not at all uncommon to find dogs seated "French style" at a dining table in a public restaurant and even being fed some of the master's or mistress' tidbits. Personally I think this is a cultural phenomenon that should be respected. I do not even consider it indulgence, if the dog is trained otherwise and not a nuisance. Nor do most French dogs take advantage of such situations. As one Parisian woman explained to me, "I offer her (a Toy Poodle) some of my meat course, but I would never *dream* of allowing her to have dessert—too much sugar! Nor does she beg. I have seen dogs less well behaved *under* the table then mine is *at* the table." Well, to each his own.

This is a practical style of holding not only in Paris. If you are, for instance, waiting in your veterinarian's office with your small puppy or dog and do not want your dog molested by roving *untrained* canines (not to mention cats, reptiles, and other species that have arrived for treatment), use this carrying style.

Teach French Style this way: sit your dog on your lap facing out from your body. Put the leash *under* your posterior. Measure out just as much leash as the dog needs in order to sit comfortably, no more. Keep one hand on the leash and with your other hand flash the "Supremes" stay signal in your dog's face (see the chapter on obedience exercises). Don't hesitate to give a smart leash correction down and in toward your lap if your dog attempts to make a leap from your lap.

This style of holding was also widely popular and frequently seen with dogs and their owners on the brownstone stoops of Brooklyn when I lived there. Then, as now, dog owners and others would "stoop-sit" on hot summer nights to "take the air." Dog owners learn quickly to teach their dogs to "stoop-sit" as they do. It is always interesting to me how the cultural mores of a given community influence the training of man's best friend.

KOSHER-STYLE

No matter how I caution you on the above mentioned styles of carrying your dog, I must say that I can hear objections from fellow professionals who dictate one and only one method of carrying—the "kosher" (right) method. The "right" way of holding a puppy or dog is to hold him against your chest, one hand supporting his hind legs and one supporting his back. It is, in fact, the inversion of "chipmunk style."

This is indeed the "correct" way of holding a puppy. A variation is to hold the puppy belly down, draped over your two outstretched and cupped-inward arms. It is the best method to teach young children, who are more likely to drop a dog. It is the first way to teach your puppy or older dog to be carried, but I would prefer that you teach *all* these styles of holding early on, even if your dog will physically outgrow them. That's why I put

248

"Kosher" style last. I have never been the type of trainer who dictates "the *only* way to do it," nor do I approach canine (or human) life with an attitude of "do it this way or else."

No one style of carrying is right for all. If we insist that only is only one correct way we are denying many aspects of why and how dogs need to be picked up and transported: physical handicaps, weather difficulties, cultural mores, the size and shape of a given dog and the desires of the owner. However, there *are* definite no-no's when it comes to carrying methods.

- Never carry your dog by the top scruff of his neck, whether to discipline it or to otherwise transport it. Sometimes there is confusion about this point because owners hear that dams carry pups this way. That's true, they do—especially when they discipline their pups. They lift and shake them—sometimes quite vigorously. The drawback is that we are not dams. One thing she did not know, as brilliant as she was in her disciplining, is that we would take her puppies and introduce them into *human* society. If you shake from the top scruff or lift there you might make your pup or dog hand-shy. It's better to come from *underneath* for a shake correction (see Chapter 13 on "A is for Alpha") so that you avoid this trap.

- Never pull or lift your dog by its tail. This need not be mentioned, one would think, but it frequently happens, especially among children playing together. Parental supervision is a *must* here. Remember the longer and fluffier the tail (and the more it curves upwards) the more children will be tempted to grab it and lift the dog off its hindquarters. Sometimes all the kid wants to do is cuddle the puppy (even using a *correct* holding style that has been seen) and thinks this is a route to stop the dog and get it to receive affection. Again, you must supervise. Saying "no" from afar, even if it stops the activity, does not necessarily teach the child correct dog decorum. Instead, bring the child and dog together, manipulate the tail in the *wrong* way (be sure the child is watching) and say, "No." Then, show the right way to carry. If the child is too small or weak to lift the dog, just forbid hoisting the animal at all.

- Never lift a dog by its ears. While it would seem that no intelligent person would not attempt to lift a dog this way, embarassingly enough, just a few years ago a president of the United States hoisted his beagles into mid air in this fashion and photographs of such "humane" treatment were widely circulated. Your dog might have huge ears but your Beagle will balk if you belittle it by lifting it by the ears. Again, children (as well as presidents) have to be cautioned about this misguided carrying technique.

CARRYING CASES

If you live in an urban area and travel at all, sooner or later you are going to make the acquaintance of a carrying case (unless you own a Bull Mastiff, in which case maybe you won't be traveling that much after all).

There are several types: cloth, hard plastic, leather and canvas. By far the most popular are the cloth models, which can be slung over your shoulder and can really look quite fashionable. Just be sure the model has a good strong flooring insert so that your pooch isn't forced to scrounge about for good footing. If you use a model that is slung over your shoulder, carry it *level* (looking at yourself in a mirror will help), otherwise the ride can be very unpleasant for your dog.

The hard plastic models are less fashionable and more bulky and yet really *de rigeur* on planes, if you want to travel with your dog in the cabin. While some airlines will let you slip onboard with your dog in a canvas or leather slung-about carrying case, they really are obligated to insist on regulation airline cases. These are made of hard plastic and are usually designed to fit in the space underneath the seat ahead of you—never in the overhead compartment. This will usually mean measurements of 12 inches wide, 17 inches long and 7½ to 10 inches high. If I leave you a little vague on that last height measurement, I'm sorry. In calling the airlines, I got many contradictory measurements. Some European airlines allow larger crates.

Some airlines that the case could be ten inches tall, others said that if it was over 7 inches tall it would not fit under the seat and you would have to check your dog as baggage. All American airlines agreed that the case had to be FAA approved, which means it must be made of hard plastic. The number everyone kept touting (in case it helps) is FAA-approved Model 050 Cabin Kennel.

One thing is certain: the airlines are *not* programmed to be tolerant about pets these days. In a highly competitive atmosphere, financial considerations are very important and the comfort of passengers and pets is often passed over. Airline personnel clearly recognize that once a dog is in the cabin, there will be little or nothing they can do to control its behavior. If the dog wants to defecate, urinate, scream, bite, shriek, hurl itself about or go on a rampage, there will be little they can do about it *except* keep the creature confined in its FAA-approved Model 050 Cabin Kennel. What *you can do* is train your jet-set pet to get carried away without going crazy. Here's how.

First, get the FAA-approved case (be sure to check with the airlines as to *exact* measurements) and bring it home. If the airlines won't sell you one, get the measurements and order it from a pet store. Don't do it the other way around, because, frankly, procuring a kennel from the airline is often the better way of handling the problem since then you *know* that the measurements are acceptable for their aircraft. The drawback is that you'll probably have to go out to the airport baggage station to buy the kennel, and then bring it home to accustom your dog to it. *By no means* should you agree to buy the kennel at the airport and think that you can just pop your dog into it without complication. The dog must be allowed to become accustomed to it.

Open up the kennel at home and let the dog sniff it. Feed the dog in the kennel. Put his toys and a nice blanket in it and make it homey. Let it lay about pre-trip and don't leave it off to the side and then draw it out right when you're packing. Leave it exposed even if it is awkward for you.

A week before your flight, start putting your dog into the crate. Leave a leash on your dog and string the leash through the wire grating on the top or side. Sit in a chair and slip the crate under it. Tuck your leash under your rear end. You have to mimic the aircraft environment as much as possible in advance. Otherwise your dog will act up on board and it will be unpleasant for you. The leash will be there for you to yank—hard—if your dog starts to vocalize. When crate-training correct *all* whining, don't wait for high-pitched shrieks or howls but instead correct even low-key stress whining. Accustom your dog to being in the crate for 15, 20 and then 30 minutes at a time.

Leaving the leash on makes all the difference in the world. You then have a direct "lifeline" into that crate and into your dog's brain and your dog will know it. Beside being able to correct the dog, I feel the dog senses the connection with you and it helps the dog to take flying with more poise. Snap that lead *hard* if you get any vocalizations, because you will, understandably, not be able to add a stern verbal component to your correction during an actual flight.

Some airlines will allow you to take your dog out of the crate pre- and post-takeoff; others will be quite strict and insist on crating before, during and after deplaning. Again, as with measurements for crate size, the regulations vary.

Much of what will be allowed or disallowed will come down to the whims of the flight attendant(s) on board. From long experience in flying with pets both on board and in the hold, and importing dogs from foreign countries, my tips are:

- Don't make a big show about having a pet in tow. I'm not saying cloak your carrying case, but it never hurts. If you don't, fellow passengers are bound to make a big fuss over Fido and that might not make your flight easier.

- Board at the last possible moment. Check at the gate, not at the main station, and get on board on the last call. Remember, in this day and age you might be on the ground for awhile as the plane taxis around or because landing is delayed at the destination airport.

- Do not feed your dog five hours before the flight, if the flight will be less than four hours long; do not feed at all if it is an international flight. If you are concerned about weight loss, *stuff* your dog one day before the trip. Limit water, too.

- The takeoff and landing are toughest on your dog because his ears will pop, just as yours do. Some kids are very sensitive to this and some dogs are too, and some dogs will start to scream, which doesn't add a peaceful atmosphere to a time when airline personnel want tranquility (see why they don't want them on board?) Do not use *any* soothing tones of voice during takeoff or landing as this will tend to connote to your dog that, indeed, something *is* wrong.

- If veterinarian prescribes a tranquilizer, use it, but give it right before boarding (remember that wait you might experience before takeoff?).

- Finally, remember, you, not the airlines, might be your biggest enemy in terms of traveling—any stressed tones of voice pre-, during or post-takeoff will be immediately decoded by your dog as signals that something is wrong with the upcoming or ongoing experience and a freeze or flight reaction will promptly occur.

The city Shepherd escapes to the country and a favorite stream. Aaaaah, peace at last.

16

City/Country Canines

I AM WRITING THIS on the deck of a beach house that I rented in order to get away from my home/office and have the privacy necessary to write parts of this book—especially this section on city dogs who migrate in and out of the city into the countryside. The beach house has been a perfect place to do the "field-work" necessary for this chapter. From the deck, I can see the boardwalk that leads down to the surf. On weekends there is a parade of day-trippers loaded down with all the necessary beach paraphernalia—beach blankets, coolers, umbrellas, sunscreen, radios and, of course, dogs.

A young couple with a puppy just arrived. The dog is pulling its owners down the boardwalk and they are chuckling about how "Munchkin" is anxious to get to the beach. The dog is hardly a "munchkin"—it is a giant puppy with an extremely powerful fore-assembly taking its owners for a walk and entering territory before them. That's what I see as a trainer. What I smell is trouble.

When a dog pulls you on leash, its exhibiting dominant behavior. We like to make jokes about dogs taking humans for walks, but it is not so funny once you realize that the behavior is an attempt to dominate the situation *and* the human who of course "hurries up" as the dog issues "commands" by tugging wildly on the leash. Dominance on-leash leads to dominance off-leash—makes sense, doesn't it? Also, if you let a dog precede you in or out of a main entrance to territory, especially new territory, you're telling the dog something pretty powerful about who owns the territory. The dog says, "I do—after all, I'm going first and you are going second. In fact I'm *pulling* you into the territory. This beach is mine, baby!" Get ready for trouble.

Of course the young couple can't see this and shouldn't be expected to without proper education. All they know is that they come to the beach every weekend and it's the only time "Munchkin" gets to really run and play. "Munchkin" appears to be about five months old, just the age when puppies start to lose their natural propensity to hang around their owners and follow them. Many novice owners mistakenly believe this following desire "proves" that their dog knows how to come when called, when all the dog is doing is following natural puppy instincts to stay close to an alpha figure. But this dog, descending down the boardwalk steps into the sand, appears to me to be entering puberty and a new, independent state. Now I really smell trouble because down the beach I see a big, free-roaming dog.

I had the misfortune of running into this canine hooligan two days ago as he cavorted along the beach molesting anyone he perceived as getting in his way, including me. I was taking a stroll surfside and he started circling me yapping and lunging with "playful" nips at the sand and at my ankles. The owner was some distance away and quite oblivious to the dog's behavior. He probably thought it was "cute." One can feel extremely vulnerable when wearing only a bathing suit, and there wasn't much I could do except to stand still, not stare, and watch the dog's body language. The owner finally grappled with his dog (the dog wouldn't come to him, of course) and apologized.

But here was the same dog, patrolling the beach once again, and the new puppy was about to be released to cavort also. I sat frozen on my deck as the owners unsnapped the lead and invited their puppy to "go play with the big dog." The puppy shot down the beach into the fangs of the canine monster who already "owned" this section of sand. The pup managed to escape the first mouth-hold, and its owners were calling it frantically. The pup looked at his owners bewilderedly, then back at the approaching monster who was coming in for the kill. The owner of the larger dog was running toward the scene, but was a good quarter of a mile away. The puppy's owners were racing toward the two dogs, now fully entangled, all parties screaming hysterically.

I have never felt more like Clark Kent in my life. I jumped up from the typewriter (ironically I was writing about dog fighting) into the house and grabbed two leashes and a broom. I sped down the boardwalk toward the dogs. The puppy had already sustained a puncture wound in the neck. Blood spurted on the sand. All three owners were screaming wildly but whenever they attempted to grab the dogs and separate them, the dogs, in their frenzy, would attempt to attack *them* (this is quite normal in dog fights, as allegiances go right out the window). When I reached the scene I

256

said, "Let me help, I'm a dog trainer!" and without waiting for a reply brought the whisk end of the broom down between the two *hard*, jumped back to spare myself attack, then jumped in and swung the broom in the attacker's face. He backed off toward his owner and I tossed a leash at the owner and said "Leash him!" I did the same to the other owners and once both dogs were under control, examined the puppy, who had a deep puncture wound that would require veterinary care. Both owners were alternately thanking me and seething at each other. Yet both parties were at fault. Both later dropped by my beach house (at my invitation) and we examined what went wrong. I found myself working on my vacation as I explained territoriality, interspecies fighting, puberty, independence, dominant behavior, the correct way to wield a broom in an emergency and a host of other concepts.

Out of this potentially tragic situation came some considerable good. I was able to counsel both dog owners about the realities involved in bringing city slicker pets to the country, and later both owners saw me for sessions at my office in Manhattan. In fact, it turned out both owners lived on the Upper East Side and their dogs are now friends. You see, the dogs didn't "hate each other," as is commonly assumed by many laypersons— they hardly had time to get to *meet* each other let alone hate each other. Nor was one dog at fault and the other innocent. Instead, the dogs reacted negatively to each other because of the *context* in which they were thrust together. In fact, almost all interspecies aggression and aggressions toward humans is *contexual*. Dr. Peter Borchelt, an animal behaviorist practicing in New York, explained:

> Aggression, as any other behavior, is context-specific. This means that the probability, magnitude, latency, duration or any other measure of aggression is to a greater or lesser degree dependent on the situation. *Thus, a dog could be extremely aggressive, or extremely likely to be aggressive in one situation and nonaggressive in many other situations.*

That's why the two dogs are now friends. It's a different situation and the owners are now in control. On the beach they were totally out of control, had signaled to their dogs that they didn't *want* any control, had unintentionally turned the territory over to their dogs to claim, possess and defend and had unwittingly set the stage for a dog fight. If you want to avoid such a mishap with your dog, I'll share some of the tips I shared with that terrified threesome.

CONTROL METHODS

The first thing you must dispel from your mind is the idea that your city dog can go out to the country and simply be turned loose immediately. Yes, I know that you are happy to be in the country yourself. Yes, I realize that your dog leads a hindered, on-leash existence in town. Yes, I realize that you may have a bad case of the "guilties" and those country weekends are partly a gift to the dog as well as to yourself. Still, I do not want you to open the car door when you arrive at your rural destination and let Rover rip.

Instead, take a more structured approach to letting your dog earn country freedoms, lest he wind up in the jaws of another dog, run over by a car, drown in a lake (no, they do not all "swim naturally") or lost in the woods (again, no they do not have a built-in compass).

If your dog is a puppy, you can cash in on the pup's natural propensity to hang around you, but don't bet on this desire after four months of age. By then your dog will be entering a more independent stage of life and will be more likely to wander off. If you're still enjoying puppyhood together feel free to play with your pup in the yard. At this age, unless he's a member of one of the giant breeds and extremely precocious, you'll most likely be able to catch him if he heads for the hills. However, you should practice some structured recalls in the back yard (see the section on the recall in the obedience portion of this book).

Post four months of age you absolutely must keep your dog under control in some way. There are several methods. You can install an aerial chain so that your dog can run around without escaping. Don't use the "stake-out" model as these increase barrier-frustration and encourage barking at strangers and other dogs that come nearby. The aerial chain is best installed so that it hooks into a nearby tree and ends at your back porch. In that way you can easily hook up your dog in the morning and just let your dog run and exercise or eliminate.

"Invisible Fences"

Another method is to purchase an "invisible fence." They usually entail installing shock fencing underneath your boundary perimeters. The track record seems good with such products and the shock is light. However, I will warn you that some dogs are smart enough to hurdle the shock area, or just determined enough to run through the electrified area to "freedom." Again I must say that running away is usually *relational*—if your dog feels so strongly about running off that he will trespass an electrified area that tells you a lot about (1) how much he wants to be around you, (2) the incredible power of whatever stimuli attracts him or (3) both. Whatever the

case, the "invisible fence" might be a *possible* answer for your dog but not necessarily.

Fenced-in Yards

The fenced-in country yard is a far better alternative, but even here some pets learn amazing jumping skills to hurdle them. The fence should be four feet high for dogs of toy size, six feet high for dogs of medium size and eight feet high for dogs of large or giant size. Some owners might be able to fudge a bit on these height requirements if they tilt the top of the fence inward toward the area occupied by the dog.

A fenced-in yard is an expense, but it invariably ups the value of the property and is often needed anyway if you have children or plan to have them. Once the money is spent, you don't have to install another fence (unless you were foolish enough to cheat on my height regulations) and you will love the ease, convenience and freedom from worry that a fenced-in yard provides.

It is impossible to dictate what size the yard should be, since this has more to do with breed size, the level of exercise needed by your dog, and, of course, what you can afford and how much land you own. It's best to check with other dog owners in the area with dogs the size of yours. Remember also that many communities have regulations as to the *type* and height of fencing, so check the local laws.

COUNTRY COMFORTS–AND SOME CONFLICTS

If you are a city/country owner, first, my congratulations. I'm glad you can afford such a set-up for your own personal peace and the happiness of your dog. But you must find ways to *minimize the contrasts* between the city and the country. If you don't, I can promise you that your dog will lose whatever training he has when he gets a whiff of that country air and he will promptly get himself, and possibly you, into deep trouble.

Please take my advice about minimizing contrasts seriously. In my five years as a city trainer, with many clients who own country homes, I know what I'm talking about. Some typical scenarios:

Kathy and Jim

Residences: Upper East Side luxury apartment building, 17th floor; East
    Hampton beach house with large unfenced yard
City/Country Canine: "Onions," a Cairn Terrier

Kathy and Jim leave the city each Friday during about half the year for their Hampton house. Onions, their Cairn Terrier, knows when Fridays arrive because on Thursday night Kathy starts packing up items that will be needed at the country house. If the packing is done Thursday night, she and Jim can load Onions and the provisions Friday morning and speed out of town around 5:00 P.M. (or, if they are lucky enough to get off work, even earlier on Friday afternoon and beat the evening "rush").

Thursday night is really the beginning of a weekly attempt to "beat the rush." Kathy whirls around the apartment hurling things into an open trunk ("I've never been an organized packer"), as Onions follows her throughout the apartment, yapping and snapping at her heels. Kathy interprets the dog's behavior as anxiousness to get out to the country, and says Onions "knows" they are going. Indeed, she does. Trouble is, Onions doesn't tell time and thus doesn't know departure for paradise won't be for another 24 hours. Besides, she's probably not 100 percent sure she'll be going along. After all, there was that time four weeks ago when they put me in that boarding kennel and didn't take me to the beach. How is Onions to know that Kathy and Jim hosted Kathy's parents' 50th wedding anniversary at the beach house that weekend, and had decided (probably wisely) what with over 100 people strolling in and out of the beach house, with all available doors open to maximize space, it was better to settle Onions in a kennel for that particular weekend? Fact is, she doesn't know any of this.

Technically, I suppose Kathy does have several alternatives. She could:

1. Sit Onions down and explain that she is packing the night before to beat the rush the next night but they really aren't going tonight.

2. Apologize to Onions for boarding her during the anniversary party and reassure her that she is indeed going to the Hamptons this weekend.

3. Realize that the dog wouldn't understand any such explanations, stop running around packing in a crazed frenzy, put Onions in another room and let her out when packing is complete.

What noted author William E. Campbell (*Behavior Problems in Dogs*) calls the "Whirling Dervish" act deeply disturbs many city/country canines. "Whirling Dervishes race around the house getting ready, winding up their pet's misbehavioral mainspring. . . . " He says such behavior "wires" a dog and produces a state of high anxiety. I've noted in my own writings that overemotional hellos and goodbyes keep dogs on edge, even if the "goodbye" is vaguely suspected ("Will they board me again?") or delayed ("Why aren't we getting in the car and going *now?*").

The reason I was called in for the initial consultation with Kathy and Jim was that Onions, like clockwork, would defecate on the apartment rug between 9:30 and 9:45 P.M. every Thursday. The owner carefully noted the time. The stool was often runny. The accident was really not Onion's fault. Her owners wound her up to a fever pitch, causing stress-related diarrhea, and Onions would just let loose. Thursdays were nights of wild racing around followed by a letdown.

When I figured out the patterns and explained it to the owners, Kathy, in a bit of a huff, asked why Onions couldn't just learn their schedule. "Let her learn she has to wait one more day," she commented. Speaking for the dog, as I tend to do in consultations, I mentioned that the "schedule" was only in effect less than half the year, sometimes didn't apply to Onions at all anyway and that dogs tend to live only in the present. It would be far easier, and much more productive for Kathy to pack alone while Jim walked Onions, or at least put Onions in another room. Because I try not to make judgments on clients' lifestyles I didn't mention other helpful hints like buying double of everything so that packing would be minimized, or *not* trying to "beat the rush" at all and instead packing *during* it. As it turned out, this city/country conundrum was easily solved.

Michael and David

Residences: Upper West Side apartment building, 4th floor walk-up; Fire
    Island Beach house
Dog: "Frank," a Bearded Collie

In this case, several city/country complications developed. Michael and David shared a house on Fire Island, a 32-mile long sand bar in the Atlantic that is only, at the most, a mile wide at any one point. The ecology of the island is fragile; it is basically held together by vegetation growing out of sand dunes, and so no vehicles are allowed. People get around by walking on elevated boardwalks and truck in provisions using little red wagons. The beach is magnificent, the sky expansive, the weather usually clear and not humid, and Fire Island is only an hour or so from New York City. Sounds like a city/country dog's paradise, doesn't it? Well, it is, and it isn't.

Michael and David's Bearded Collie, Frank, lives a restricted life in New York, and, being a member of an active herding breed, doesn't always take to the strict heel he has to hone to walk the streets of Manhattan easily. In short, he pulls. When he gets to Fire Island, the leash comes off and Frank goes frantic with joy. Since there is no traffic, Michael and David don't have to worry about Frank getting hit by a car and the worst that can happen is a collision with a little red wagon. But there's a problem in this. When Frank returns to the city he pulls on the leash for the next two days worse than usual, and he darts out at oncoming traffic, fails to sit at the curbs and bolts toward any puddle or pond he may see. "From Tuesday to

Friday morning, he's decent on leash," David told me, "but Sunday afternoon and all of Monday are hell."

Part of the problem is that Frank finds it difficult to "come down" from his Fire Island high. Since he doesn't have to worry about traffic out there, when he returns he just may see the streets of Manhattan as boardwalks and the cars and trucks as little red wagons—both easily negotiated or dodged. On Sunday and Monday—the two days after David and Michael return each weekend—Frank is still on Fire Island time. The solution is to *minimize the contrasts* between Fire Island and Manhattan. When first arriving at the island ferry, Michael or David should heel Frank onto the boat and enforce a sit-stay. Frank has had obedience training, so this should not be difficult. Frank might object at first, since he probably considers commands and obedience work something that he has to do only while in town. The owners will have to *insist* on some obedience as they arrive at their second home just to minimize contrasts. I also suggested some basic heeling work and recalls on the boardwalks and especially on the beach so that Frank comes to realize that coming when called applies *everywhere.* Saturday can be an "off" day from obedience for Frank when he can dig in the sand, bound the boardwalks (under supervision) and play with his pooch playmates. But before leaving on Sunday Frank should be given another short (ten minutes) obedience lesson, practicing all the commands he knows, heeled to the ferry, asked to hold a sit-stay while crossing to the mainland and then put on his usual strict heel upon arriving in the city. Again, this kind of system helps the dog to snap back into a working frame of mind, and teaches the dog that obedience applies everywhere—to a greater or lesser degree. The "off" day is not really seen by the dog as a totally "off" day—it's just more "off" than "on."

Michael and David reported that with these flourishes in Frank's routine, heeling on Sunday afternoon and Monday was no longer a problem, and, in fact, Frank's heeling skills improved overall every day of the week. This is because heeling had become a *way of walking* with Frank, indeed, a *way of thinking,* not just something the owners tried to turn on and then turn off.

There were some auxiliary problems in this situation as well. One was a health concern. Fire Island is riddled with ticks and fleas. Paradise has its problems, too. One particularly nasty tick causes Lyme disease in humans and another causes Rocky Mountain Spotted Fever. The bite of ticks infected with *Rickettsia rickettsii* is extremely dangerous to dogs in this region and it looks like the disease is spreading. Be absolutely vigilant about examining your dog if you walk him or her in wooded areas of the Northeastern United States. Michael and David didn't, and Frank caught a case of this hard-to-shake disease.

Be equally vigilant about heartworm medications for the city/country dog. Be sure not to miss a day of giving the preventative because mosquitoes (the insect that passes the disease) are plentiful in the country and your dog will be outdoors more often. Don't count on repellants or the wind to ward off mosquitoes—be *sure* to give the preventative each day. There is now a *monthly* heartworm pill, but it is not advised for all breeds. Check with your veterinarian.

The Kratzmiller Family: Brad, Ellen, Jennifer and James

Residences: Rittenhouse Square, Philadelphia, and any "upscale" campground they can find
City/Country Canine: "Spot," a Dalmatian

The Kratzmiller family live in a very ritzy area of downtown Philadelphia and they like it. But they are also nature lovers—well at least Brad is. His wife, Ellen, is "getting into nature more" but wants to do it at her own pace. This means that instead of really roughing it and camping out with a tent, the Kratzmillers load themselves and their Dalmatian "Spot" into a recreational vehicle (RV) when they head for the hills. They have several problems with their city/country canine.

First, while Spot rides quite nicely in the family car, when he gets into the RV he thinks he is on an obstacle course. He bounds over the seats and couches, jumps up on the stove (once he turned on a burner accidentally) and thinks nothing of pawing open the bathroom door, flipping up the toilet bowl seat and helping himself to way too much water, which makes him more liable to urinate. The fact is, Spot just can't adjust to this much space and he is a traffic hazard to boot.

The solution, of course, is a crate. I advised getting the collapsible kind so that when the family arrives at their destination it can be folded up and put away until the return trip home. Since Spot had never used a crate before he immediately started to holler when placed in it. The solution here is easy. Attach a lead to the dog's neck (preferably to the dog's training collar) and string the rest of the lead through the crate grating. At the *first* whimper or whine, give a stern leash correction. Don't wait for the barking to become violent. Better yet, before putting your dog into the travel crate, sit your dog, make eye contact and give a warning in a low (not loud) voice: "Okay Spot, I don't want any barking in this crate and I *mean* it." Remember the words don't necessarily matter that much—it's your low, growling tone. This advance warning will let your dog know that you are serious and will correct if barking begins. It worked with Spot. He now rides peacefully, playing with his toys and dozing until the Kratzmillers pull into their campground.

The Schnieder Family: James, Karen, Tiffany and Jeffrey

Residences: Downtown San Francisco, California, and house overlooking
   the ocean, Big Sur, California
City/Country Canine: "Chico," a Chihuahua

The Schnieder family had a housetraining problem. They had read
my book, *The Evans Guide for Housetraining Your Dog,* and had recognized themselves in a key sentence from that book: "When humans humanize housetraining havoc happens." They called me long distance for help. I
usually make it a practice not to attempt to counsel dog owners on the
phone but I broke my rule because it was obvious that the solution to the
problem was quite simple.

When the Schnieders were in San Francisco, four-month-old Chico
the Chihuahua was papertrained, but when they reached their country
home, Chico cheated. The problem? Quite simple on the surface but hard
for the Schnieders to snoop out. In the city, Chico had one location for
elimination, in a side bathroom off the master bedroom. He was fastidious
about making it to his paper. Since the city apartment was on the fifth
floor, there was no opportunity to eliminate in a yard, although occasionally Chico would use the street as a bathroom (which was fine with the
Schnieders).

In the country home, Mrs. Schnieder decided that the enormity of
the dwelling—it was a palatial home overlooking the ocean—dictated that
Chico have more than one bathroom with papers and instead decided to
place papers down in the bathroom on the first floor, the bathroom on the
second floor and in an entranceway called "the mud room." This was not a
good decision. Chico promptly began leaving "presents" all over the house.
Frustrated because she had actually tried to do the little dog a favor by
providing several options, the owner called me. "What's wrong with him?"
she asked.

The trouble is, if some dogs are provided with "options" they abuse
them. If an owner places several paper pitstops it can confuse the dog since
what is essentially being said is, "Dog, *here* is okay to eliminate, but *here* is
okay too, and *here,* and *here,* and *here,* etc." This tacit approval by the
owner of many elimination choices confuses many dogs who, quite reasonably from their point of view, attempt to add *more* spots. There must be
one, and only *one* spot for elimination in any one household; if that spot is
hard for a dog to navigate toward, access to that spot must be guaranteed
by confinement in that given area. See the housetraining section for more
details.

I mention the Schnieder's story here because housetraining difficulties are one of the most common problems city/country owners unintentionally foster. The owners forget consistency, confinement and corrections.

264

After all, everything is supposed to be perfect in the country, isn't it? It's another instance of how human mythology causes country craziness in canines. Chico cleaned up his act quickly when demoted to the upstairs bathroom the next weekend, and he speedily earned himself the master bedroom, the hallways, stairways, downstairs and practically all of the Big Sur area—always making it back to that one special spot for you-know-what.

The Victors: Allan and Allison

Residences: Bronxville, New York, and a house they rent for the month of
    August in Vermont, deep in the woods
City/Country Canines: Frenchy and Frazzle, two Labrador Retrievers

The Victors and their canine pals were only in the country one-twelfth of the year, when they retreated for the entire month of August to a cabin in the Vermont woods they had rented for the last seven years. Their two Labs had greatly enjoyed the country cabin for the last two years and spent August 1985 and August 1986 lolling about in the grass, playing with sticks and swimming in the swimming hole. They were puppies the first summer and terrified to go far from the house. Even the second summer, when they were in puberty and becoming more independent and venturesome, they rarely skitted out of the vicinity of the house "except to chase a rabbit or some silly bird," as Mrs. Victor put it.

But apparently the dogs had studied up on their hunting skills during the bulk of 1987 because on the second day of their Vermont vacation Frenchy and Frazzle disappeared for twelve hours. The Victors went crazy combing country roads, notifying the cops and all the neighbors and calling for the dogs until their voices gave out. Night settled in and after four hours of searching roads in the darkness they drove home, parked the car and stumbled toward the house. There on the front porch, sprawled out like two drunks, were a disheveled Frenchy and a very frazzled Frazzle. Between them was the carcass of a chicken or a duck—it was hard to tell at that point. Both dogs had blood on their muzzles and were panting heavily.

Another surprise awaited the Victors inside. The surprise was a message on the answering machine from an irate farmer cussing a blue streak and vowing vengeance on "those damn dogs." What had for two summers been roly-poly puppies enjoying the Vermont hills were now two hounds from hell with a bounty on their head.

The greatest myth about country dogs—and city owners buy into the myth wholeheartedly sometimes—is that the dogs should be free to come and go as they please. City dogs that are cooped up at home most of the year and have no experience with farm animals (who have rights, too) are turned loose to roam at will. The Victors should have seen the signs of trouble with the rabbit chasing and bird-baiting the dogs were up to the previous summer. The dogs should have been reprimanded, but instead the Victors laughed at two city slickers getting a taste of country life. They got a taste, all right—of country chicken. The old myth that once a dog has "tasted blood" it is very difficult to stop further predation on animals seems, in my experience, to be true. Frenchy and Frazzle will have no off-leash freedom during the summer of 1988. The boys will be walked on leash, and an aerial chain will be installed for selected periods of exercise. And they will study recalls and be boundary trained during that summer.

The upshot was that the Victors were hated by local farmers. The story spread fast. By the time the Vermonters spun the tale Frenchy was a killer Doberman, Frazzle was a pit bull and they had raided the entire chicken coop and killed off the whole population—and *your* coop was next. The Victors payed off the farmer, promised to keep their dogs indoors and hung their heads in shame. But back in Bronxville they had still another surprise in store.

Back home they let their dogs run in the park. While both dogs had always sparked squirrels, they now took off after them with new-found vigor. Before they simply treed the squirrels, now they attempted to climb the trunk and finally Frenchy nailed one. The Victors began to pay the city wages of country sins. What happened in Vermont was bad enough, but now *this*. Yet, from the dog's point of view, it was all understandable.

If you have a problem with predation, your first priority should be to *get your dog inside*. Stop *all* off-leash freedom. Do not trust the predatory dog. Do not hope against hope that maybe the call of the wild will beckon less loudly today. Your dog will be gone in a flash, especially if they have already had a kill. Remember, dogs who run away have someplace they want to go. You will have to face the fact that your dog may never again be able to enjoy an off-leash walk with you down a country road. You've cashed in your chips if your dog has had a kill, in my opinion.

An ounce of *prevention* will save you plenty of useless corrections later on. When your pup is young and he chases animals, scold him, preferably *before* the chase is on, at that moment when he gets that wild look in his eyes. Use a low tone, make eye contact with your dog and warn him to stay put. If you are too late and the chase is in progress, don't waste breath screaming at a dog in hot pursuit of game. Your dog is in the Twilight Zone then and won't even hear you. Better to reprimand just after the game has (hopefully) eluded its hunter, with eye contact, a shakedown and a stern (not loud) sentence. Your dog must feel that you will be so displeased about his chasing animals that he inhibits the impulse to chase from within.

Remember that city dogs, who some owners would never suspect of being capable of predation, can be quite good at it. They really enjoy the thrill of the chase and if they have been allowed to spark squirrels at home, they will chomp a chicken in the country. Trouble is, those city squirrels can move faster than country chickens. Do not allow your dog to lunge at squirrels or pigeons in town. You are only setting the scene for predation in the country. Conversely, do not allow predation in the country and then expect your dog to come back to town and stroll nonchalantly past squirrels. My advice to you is to discipline all such tendencies—regardless of breed-type—and provide your dog with enough exercise, massages, fetching, play and quality time so that predation is the last thing on his mind.

SUMMING UP

You can see from these case histories that city/country canines are prone to severe behavior problems unless their owners are awake and aware of potential problems. To recap, be sure that you *minimize the contrast* between the city and the country for your dog. Give your dog an obedience lesson as soon as you reach the hinterlands. Don't wait for your pooch to go haywire and forget everything he's learned. And when you return from the countryside, tighten up the obedience that has probably slacked off, even if you've been out of town for a day or less. *Structured lessons* are mandatory in both settings!

Finally, bravo to you that you care enough about your dog, and obviously yourself, to escape the pretensions and nonsense of much of city life and get back to basics. I would say, at the risk of sounding corny, that this drive is the "dog" coming out in you—the natural man or woman that wants to flower and is so close in kinship with the dog, who does everything naturally. Just be careful to avoid the pitfalls that confront the city/country canine and you'll both enjoy a lifestyle that is rich and satisfying.

17

Guard Dogs, Attack Dogs, Service Dogs

I'LL WARN YOU in advance: This section will include an attack on attack training. Many city owners think they need an attack-trained dog. Few really do, and even fewer owners are capable of handling such a dog. If you're thinking of putting this type of training on your dog, you should ask yourself some serious questions. First, why do you want such training? Will you be able to really control the dog if you have it attack-trained? Do you have insurance that covers plastic surgery for any harm your dog does to others? What's in this type of training for the dog? Probably not much. There's probably more in it for you. Or so you think.

Don't get me wrong. I fully realize that living in a big city can be dangerous. I have a scar on my face to prove it. I've been mugged and slashed with a knife. But I didn't run out and get an attack-trained dog. Even if the same has happened to you, it might be illegal to own such a dog in your city. Check the law carefully.

I guess I'm attacking attack-training because I have seen learned aggression backfire on too many lay owners who do not know how to control such a dog. Then they call me. Learned aggression is, in my opinion, one of the hardest types of aggression to "train out" of a dog because it is "trained in" so completely. Often the owner has to euthanize the dog or just get out of town. I feel that the mere presence of a dog can prevent crime, and if the dog is an "image" dog like a German Shepherd or a Doberman, so much the better.

Rather than get yourself into a situation where learned aggression is uncontrollable, try bluff techniques if you feel threatened. Teach your dog a good, solid sit-stay. If you feel threatened, enforce the heel and then glide your dog into a sit. Give the command clearly and make it clear to whomever is threatening you that your dog is *trained*. What goes through the head of many potential criminals is, "Hmmm, obviously this dog is trained and listens to the owner. I wonder what *else* this dog knows?" The undesirable deduces that just perhaps the dog is attack trained. Not sure, they back off.

You can enhance this perception by holding the leash back toward your body as if you were "restraining" your killer dog. Placing a hand on the dog's chest at the same time can make it look like you are holding the dog back. It doesn't hurt to say, in a voice loud enough to be heard, "Not yet, not yet," while you seemingly position the dog for a vicious lunge. This ruse keeps many an intruder at bay.

SUPER SERVICE DOGS

Service dogs employed for your protection by the police are a completely different matter and I highly endorse the use of K-9 Corps dogs. I have been active training them and their handlers and can tell you that the dogs are sound, reliable, can switch in or out of aggression quickly and, more importantly, their handlers are professionally trained to properly handle and deploy the dogs. Studies have shown that these officers and their dogs are more effective as a working team than dogless officers, especially in crowd control, calming riots and narcotic and bomb detection. You have probably seen such dogs patrolling your city's streets, walking smartly at heel. Be thankful, but do not bother these dogs when they are working. They do not expect to be patted or fawned over and you should not touch them unless specifically invited to do so by the officer. However, you need not be afraid to talk to the officer if he or she is with a dog, just don't bother the dog.

If you are prone to crime and try to outwit a professional "police dog" you will probably fail. The dog will find your bomb before it goes off. The dog will quickly sniff out your drugs. The dog will locate and apprehend you in a deserted building. The dog can do all these things in half the time it would take a foot officer. That is exactly why most large cities have very active and very much valued K-9 Corps. Baltimore's is legendary. St. Louis has a great K-9 Corps also. New York's K-9 Corps dogs are *truly* "New York's finest."

Nor should you ever bother a Seeing-Eye dog. They too are working and will switch to a "play mode" and out of the "work mode" if bothered by passers-by. Unless the blind person specifically asks for help, do not bother

270

Try a bluff technique if you feel threatened. Teach a solid sit-stay and issue the command clearly to make it clear that your dog is trained. With your right hand "restrain" your killer dog from lunging, and say "Not yet . . . not yet."

Guard dogs are fine with me, as long as they are handled by city or state police. These dogs are highly trained and professionally handled.
Courtesy of Fidelco Guide Dog Foundation

the team. My blind clients tell me that this is the most bothersome aspect—often the only negative aspect—of owning a guide dog. Too many people think it is their "right" to say hello to the guide dog. Don't do this.

If you see a team on the street and notice that the handler is being strict with the dog, don't criticize. The sightless handler has been trained at one of the guide-dog schools and is perfectly competent to handle his or her dog. Sometimes discipline is necessary for the guide dog as the dog's responsibility is huge and the dog must keep his mind on his work. I know it's very common for sighted people to stop and stare at guide dogs and their blind handlers, and I'll admit that it is a wondrous, glorious sight to see these brave teams weave through the city streets. I never fail to marvel at the courage, poise and skill of the team. Some people stare because they enjoy watching the dog work and they figure the blind person can't see them staring anyway, so why should it matter? It does matter. Even though the guide dog is trained to ignore you, direct eye contact might cause him to lock eyes with you even for a critical second, which might be long enough to cause an accident. Also, it really does put the blind person on-the-spot. Since one of the reasons they got a guide dog was to integrate themselves as fully as possible into normal society, staring doesn't help. After awhile most city dwellers get used to the teams. I still sneak peeks because I must admit I am so full of admiration for such handlers and their dogs. Finally, and this should be obvious, *never* let your dog relate with or bother the working dog, unless specifically invited to do so by the handler.

Still another type of service dog, less noticeable but no less valuable to the city owner, is the Hearing Ear dog that alerts his owner to dangerous city sounds on the street or simply serves as a canine alarm clock each morning. What is a Hearing Ear dog? Not so long ago the same question was asked about guide dogs for the blind, and today they are universally understood and respected. That same acceptance will eventually be granted to Hearing Ear, or signal dogs that are specially trained to alert their owners to significant sounds. Much has been accomplished by organizations like the Hearing Ear Dog Program in West Boylston, Massachusetts. It serves as the setting for *Sound Friendships,* by Elizabeth Yates (The Countryman Press). The author traces the story of Willa and her dog, Honey. We are with this charming pair from the first time they meet at the school, throughout their fascinating training and beyond, when Honey's skills save Willa not only time and trouble, but also, in one instance, her life.

A hearing Ear dog is not just a substitute alarm clock or a paw to hold. Although they are highly trained specialists, these dogs are still dogs, and they require all the loving attention and discipline that other dogs require. Sometimes they try naughty things, much to their guardians' surprise—or even concoct a romance for an owner, as Honey manages to do toward the end of the book.

Honey is a dog that even appreciates the value of a dollar. During a

East Side, West Side, all around the town—Donald Gomez commutes each day on the New York subway from his home in midtown Manhattan to his job at Harlem Hospital.

A smooth working team, Donald and "Deata" can go safely anywhere in New York. Never bother a guide dog when working. You might cause the dog to break concentration. Courtesy of *Fidelco Guide Dog Foundation*

273

briefing session at the school the instructor says, "There's something more you should know. The Internal Revenue Service has decreed that any moneys expended on your dogs for licenses, vet fees or food, are all tax deductible." At this, Honey starts rapidly thumping her tail on the floor. Smart dog!

The students in the program come to realize the wisdom of their dogs and they are taught to trust them. "There will come a time when the dog will give you a command," they are cautioned, then told to be sensitive to this moment, which may be pivotal in their relationships with their canine helpers. How many of us would be willing to trust our dogs so completely?

These dogs wear a distinctive harness or collar, often yellow or orange in color, and they also should not be bothered while they are working. They are listening for their owners. Do not distract them.

A canine alarm clock, Hearing-Ear dog "Molly," alerts napper that it is time to get up. Courtesy of Hearing Ear Dog Program

18

Dogs and Decorating: A Pet Project

"ONLY IN NEW YORK," I thought as I peered in at the Dalmatian reclining regally on a $2,300 black leather sofa on the ninth floor of the famous Gimbel's department store. No, the dog hadn't broken into the store and crash-landed on the furniture. Nor was he the charge of some preoccupied shopper. The Dalmatian was part of the display itself, entitled "For Pet's Sake"—four showrooms that were open to the public last summer and swamped with viewers eager to pick up decorating tips for their pet-infested homes. The Dalmatian was there to prove a point: You don't have to shortchange the looks of your house just because you have a dog.

Think about the status-quo decorating scheme common to apartments and houses owned by "dog people." I've been in homes that literally resemble kennels—cages everywhere, hair coating everything and everyone, excess hair floating in the air, terrible odors and even worse decorating arrangements. Then there is the "cutesy" look so common in the homes of "committed" dog folk: statuettes of the favorite breed, trophies everywhere, pillows embroidered with little doglets, doggie decals stuck on the windows. I guess the idea here is if you can't beat them join them, or a strange reasoning that dictates that loving dogs automatically means decorating your home in poor taste.

Distress over this status-quo and pure creativity spurred the innovative Gerda Clark, vice president of Gimbels, to design "For Pet's Sake." The settings prove "you can be practical as well as beautiful," says Clark, who derived many of the ideas for decorating around dogs from her own experience. She is the proud owner of eight dogs and eight cats. The dogs include two Australian Shepherds, a Dalmatian and assorted others.

"A dog is not an accessory," she stated flatly, "and I don't like them treated as such." To Gerda, the display makes a lot of sense since a dog is a member of the family. "When small children are on the scene, we have to decorate in a certain way, and with dogs it is no different." But while parents long ago found ways to have children around and still maintain elegant living conditions, dog owners in many cases just buckle under the hair, odor and destructive chewing with the feeling that they can do nothing else. Often the solution lies in proper selection of materials.

For instance, the flooring in the "Dalmatian" room was seamless ceramic tile. This surface facilitates easy clean-up. There are scent substances in a dog's urine and defecation pheremones. These substances tell the dog to frequent a given area again for elimination—they are like canine calling cards, hangovers from their wolf ancestors. These pheremones can travel deep into cracks and crevices, if the floor has such openings. They cannot be easily cleaned up or killed because the cleaning solution usually doesn't penetrate the crack. There is no such problem with a ceramic floor or other crackless surfaces. If you start from the floor up and reason out in your mind the materials you want to decorate with—remembering to "think dog" all the time—you can put together a striking room that will allow you to live in style with your dog. But you must "think dog" and then "decorate dog"—and no, I don't mean decorate with those cutesy embroidered pillows!

Here are some of Gerda Clark's tips for decorating with your dog in mind:

- You don't have to stick strictly to black or other dark upholstery colors to hide dirt. Hair often shows up more on dark colors.

- Avoid nubby, textured fabrics, which tend to trap pet hairs and can encourage scratching and pawing.

- Artificial plants make more sense for dog owners since so many plants are poisonous to dogs. If you have any real plants, hang them out of reach, but remember, some dogs climb.

- Avoid grasscloth, burlap, wallpaper, upholstered walls and other elaborate wall treatments since they are easily damaged. Stick to simple paint jobs that can easily be redone.

- If you have paintings that reach anywhere near a dog's mouth range, either elevate them or use hard-edged or metal frames.

Many dogs cannot resist a frame that protrudes from the wall, practically offering itself as a chew item.

When I heard Gerda talk about this last point I immediately thought about my countless encounters with dogs who chew destructively and the many homes I've visited as a trainer and behaviorist—and the type of materials used in decorating in those homes. Often the dog began chewing something inviting, like the fringe on a sofa, and within time started in on the sofa itself. Of course, there were almost always other reasons for the chewing, such as lack of training, boredom and loneliness, but the fringe or other such item often acted as the catalyst for the chewing. In my experience, if a dog has a place he can start on, he will. I often advise my clients to get down on their hands and knees for ten minutes and "think dog"—look around the room carefully and think about what you'd like to chew. Chances are, it will be something protruding or hanging, and if that something has a little "give" and snaps back, so much the better. You probably won't head toward metal items to chew, because if you're thinking dog you know you don't like to chew metal. At the Gimbel's showroom, Gerda Clark had included a tasteful chair of metal and leather. Other items included a plexiglass desk (most dogs wouldn't chew that and it can be cleaned easily), an acrylic chair (nothing interesting here from the dog's point of view and acrylic doesn't even hold scent) and a black marble cocktail table (try taking a hunk out of *that*, Fido!). The emphasis everywhere was on clean, smart lines, hard, nonporous surfaces that are easily cleaned and do not retain human scent or dog odor, and an absolute lack of frills or fringes. It all worked beautifully, and it can for you, too. Your starting point is to get down on your hands and knees, dog level, and start thinking dog and start decorating dog.

Once you have your materials and items picked out, you can take your decorating one step further by thinking from a psychological and behavioral point of view. For instance, anyone who lives with dogs knows how enamored they are of coming up to you when you are relaxing in your favorite easy chair, presenting themselves and waiting to be petted. Except in a truly neurotic dog, the type who demands attention 24 hours a day, this is not a habit we want to break, so why not encourage it by selecting armless furniture or furniture that facilitates petting? Gerda Clark chose a black leather chair and sofa with sloping armrests. It was a pleasure to sink into the luxurious chair and pet the Dalmatian, but the furniture was also bulky enough to prevent the dog from hurdling itself into my lap. Even if the Dalmatian slobbered, it was easily cleaned.

Many dog owners claim that sofa or couch materials are not that important because they have their dogs trained not to jump on furniture. Trained or not trained, let's be realistic. If you are gone for a long time, a great many "trained" dogs will get up on the sofa or chair and then quietly get off when they hear your key in the lock. The tell-tale hairs are there on that nubby fabric, waiting for you to pick them off, one by one since even the strongest vacuums don't seem to remove dog hair from such fabrics. Be realistic about your dog's training, because just as every dog has its day, every dog has its couch, whether they are supposed to or not.

Your decorating ideas should flow out of an overall concern for your pet and a desire to live peacefully with your dog. "You shouldn't get burnout over your dog," said Gerda Clark, and with the right choice of materials, you won't.

If you already have your home decorated and can't change items and furnishings, "dog decorate" as well as you can, and don't add any new items that are not realistic from the dog's point of view.

For myself, the display at Gimbel's inspired me to redecorate my studio apartment and I hurried home full of ideas, anxious to see if I could budget in some new furnishings. An Akita I was boarding heard me rattling my keys outside the apartment door and I heard him jump off my couch to greet me at the door, smiling wildly. While vacuuming the couch I noticed that "I Love German Shepherds" decal on one window and immediately ripped it off and fed it to the vacuum.

19

When Your Dog Dies

WHEN YOUR DOG DIES you should call someone to talk. Right away. You might talk to your veterinarian. He or she might already know. Perhaps they attended the pet if the dog was ill or had to be euthanized. I know many veterinarians who receive two, three or even more calls each day. Many people call me at such a time. This always surprises me.

I guess I think of myself as the "big Meanie" in the life of so many dogs. The strict trainer who is called in to restore order when it has broken down and the owner and dog are feuding. Often I enter a household at the precise moment when the owner loves the dog the least, when the dog is acting up so badly that the owner wishes it were dead (sometimes). So it is strange to me when so many past clients call to share with me the precise moment when they love their dogs the most, when they have died. "You were the one person who really knew his full potential," one woman said to me, sobbing. "You trained him and you knew his *mind* and his abilities, everyone else just loved him." I'm so honored by such calls, but years into the dog fancy, and having lost several pets myself, I still stumble a bit for the right words. Will you forgive me if I do here, too? I hope so, because this is an emotional topic for all dog owners.

Nevertheless, to get through your grief, to *work it through* successfully, it's vitally important to take a hold of your emotions and "use" them constructively. Don't just sit there and suffer in silence! Call up someone who *knew* your dog, and preferably someone who has lost a pet themselves. They'll understand. Go out for coffee. Bring some snapshots of your lost friend. Sit at a back table and have a good cry. You're a city owner, you have an advantage. Everyone will be too busy to look. If I sound flip, it's intentional. You have to keep your wits about you right now because otherwise this death could destroy you. And I'm not exaggerating. I've seen many owners stumble around in grief over a dog and miss work, break down in public, even walk into traffic because they did not work out their grief and tried to hold it all in.

The reason they held it all inside was often that they suspected their friends would laugh at them for feeling sad over the death of a dog. Rather than trust anyone, they just kept silent. Depending on how dog death was dealt with in their family circle, they may feel that they have to take a stoic approach to the death of an "animal." In some cases they are surprised at the depth of their feelings, perhaps having taken the dog for granted for so long. Others are guilty because lack of training might have resulted in a terrible accident that caused the dog's death. One man called me recently, sobbing deeply into the phone, "Oh Job, Trickster is dead. He ran in front of a car out in the country. I know I didn't practice the recall enough like you told me . . . now he's dead and it's my fault."

Another service you can perform for yourself, besides visiting in person or over the phone with an understanding friend, is to studiously *avoid* the topic with persons you feel or *know* will not understand. Maybe you'll want to avoid that person, period. That's up to you, but my point is you do not have to subject yourself to stupid comments from insensitive louts who haven't been where you're at right now. You know the type of person I'm talking about:

> "Oh, c'mon now, it was only a dog, get ahold of yourself!"
> "Well, he'd been sick for a long time, you'd think you'd know he was gonna go . . . I mean really!"
> "Don't you think you're over-reacting?"

You don't have to share your feelings with these people. You can parcel out your emotions just as you parcel out your time, if you try. Remember, though, the people who don't understand might be your friends on many other levels, but on this particular, very personal level, they aren't. They should be forgiven that, until experience teaches them to respect all forms of grief, all forms of friendship, all forms of life. That's really the *root* problem in unsympathetic reactions to pet death. It's our attitude toward animals in general. Our condescending, Cartesian, superior attitude. Some people think that animals aren't "worth" our grief. More accurately, many people have been taught that.

Unteach yourself, *deprogram* yourself and others by dealing with your loss responsibly and as constructively as you can.

280

ANOTHER DOG?

I'd wait. About one month, for several reasons. If you get a pet on the rebound you might compare too much. Secondly, the scent of the old pet needs to decrease in your home or apartment. It might bother the new dog. Remember, each animal is an individual, and your new pet, callous as it may sound, really couldn't care less about the deceased one. He or she will want to be number one in your mind and heart. It takes time for that.

In the interim period your memories of the old pet will fade a bit. Don't feel guilty about that. It is quite normal and even healthy. You'll also become more anxious to have another dog, and if you have children they will start to agitate faster for a new one than your heart will. Don't blame them either. Kids often process grief more quickly, especially pre-adolescents, and they want a dog in their life *now*.

If you have another dog at home and one just passed away, take some time to clean all the areas where the old dog slept, hung out, ate or eliminated with 50/50 vinegar and water. The acid will eliminate the pheremone scent substances that the old dog left on those surfaces by licking them or even through the sweat glands in his paws. I know it sounds harsh, but I've found such a cleaning helps many dogs to adjust. Dogs see with their noses and if the lingering scent and pheremones are still there the present occupant might wonder why he smells, but does not see, the former. Some dogs get very upset by this and start to grieve themselves. They go off their food, mope around, refuse walks, stress whine and mourn. A week of this is okay, in my opinion, but after that, clean. I do not know how dogs deal with the loss of a fellow dog. But I feel that the best way to ease any possible grief on the part of a living dog is to erase the scent of the old one. I do not think the living dog finds the old scent "comforting." I think they find it, after some time passes, agitating and disturbing, knowing what I do about the olafactory powers of dogs and how much scent means to them. Seeing might be believing for humans but for dogs smelling is believing. Why let the living dog "believe" the dead dog is still alive?

As a side point, I'll tell you that such a cleaning is not easy for the human who has to do it. Once, while at the monastery, a four month old puppy I was raising fell ill and died. I had whelped this dog. But I had two others under my care. When I cleaned, I cried the whole time. The hardest part was washing her blanket—this pup loved her blanket almost like Linus—and her food dish. But I felt it was best for the other two, who were less lively than usual and depressed. I have to admit it was therapeutic for me, too.

BURIAL

For those interested in pet cemeteries, you will find them scarce and expensive in cities. I personally feel that they are waste of already scarce land in many cities, and I think part of what dogs teach us about nature as a whole is to respect limits and natural ecology. There are other ways of decently disposing of your dog that are more practical for city owners.

Many veterinary hospitals maintain crematoria where you can cremate your pet and obtain the ashes. You can then scatter the ashes in the country or perhaps near a favorite spot in town that the dog liked. Check on local regulations about spreading ashes in rivers or the ocean, however. When I have lost a pet I have cremated him or her and always use the ashes as fertilizer. Sometimes people tell me they think this is "gross." I don't think so at all. I like to think that a life that was will be able to give life to a life to be.

An editorial that appeared in the *Portland Oregonian* became one of its most popular ever. Readers ask for it to be reprinted again and again and it wonderfully answers the questions a reader had written to editor Ben. H. Lampman asking, "Where shall I bury my dog?" Here's a segment:

We would say that there are various places in which a dog may be buried. We are thinking now of a Setter, whose coat was aflame in the sunshine, and who, so far as we are aware, never entertained a mean or an unworthy thought. This Setter is buried beneath a cherry tree, under four feet of garden loam, and at its proper season, the cherry strews petals on the green lawn of his grave. Beneath such trees, such shrubs, he slept in the drowsy summer, or gnawed at a flavourous bone, or lifted head to challenge some strange intruder. These are good places, in life or in death. Yet it is a small matter. For if the dog be well remembered, if sometimes he leaps through your dreams actual as in life, eyes kindling, laughing, begging, it matters not at all where that dog sleeps. On a hill where the wind is unrebuked, and the trees are roaring, or beside a stream he knew in puppyhood, or somewhere in the flatness of a pasture land where most exhilarating cattle graze. It is all one to the dog, and all one to you, and nothing is gained, and nothing lost—if memory lives. But there is one best place to bury a dog.

If you bury him in this spot, he will come to you when you call—come to you over the grim, dim frontiers of death, and down the well-remembered path, and to your side again, and though you call a dozen living dogs to heel they shall not growl at him, nor resent his coming, for he belongs there. People may scoff at you, who see no lightest blade of grass bent by his footfall, who hear no whimper, people who may never really have had a dog. Smile at them, for you shall know something that is hidden from them, and which is well worth the knowing. The one best place to bury a good dog is in the heart of his master. . . .

SCRAPBOOKS

Another "therapy" I've used to ease myself out of grief, and that I recommend to others, is to pull out all the photographs you have of the pet that passed away and make a birth-to-death scrapbook on that dog alone. Some owners already maintain such a record, and even then I suggest getting a *better* scrapbook and rearranging the photographs in a special way. Take the best photograph and have it nicely framed. Put it in an honored place. You can also make a donation to your local humane society or to the Morris Animal Foundation, 45 Inverness Drive East, Englewood, Colorado, 80112, an excellent organization that does research on canine diseases.

EUTHANASIA

The magazine I write for, *Dog Fancy,* once did a poll of readers and found out that half the respondents had been forced to put their dogs to sleep. I was surprised the percentage was not higher. It's a slap in the face to many dog owners, but most pets no longer go out and die under the chestnut tree at age 22. Rationally, most of us know this, but dog owners, like everyone else, are great at denial. With advances in veterinary medicine happening so quickly though, most pets will live longer lives, but their owners might have to choose to let them live or die. This brings us to the whole question of the quality of the pet's life.

There can be, in my opinion, no set guidelines for all cases. Each dog is an individual, and each owner has known that dog *in health* in a way that no other person has. You must weigh how happy you think your pet is, how much pain he or she is experiencing. Most of all, if the issue is health, you must listen intently to your veterinarian *and* your trainer. When I say listen I mean listen and *interpret.*

Why do you have to "interpret"? Isn't listening hard enough? Yes, but the fact is many professionals will not tell you that you *must* euthanize your dog. Ethical guidelines for veterinarians discourage them from making blatant statements about what a client should or must do concerning euthanasia. Instead, the emphasis is on guiding the client to see the reality of the pet's situation and letting the owner make the decision. This is as it should be. So when your veterinarian gives you a nonspecific answer to your direct question of whether you should or should not put your dog down he or she is not being evasive or playing games. They are following strict medical ethics guidelines. However, most often an owner can read between the lines, so to speak, and from a careful explanation of the procedures that are involved can get an idea of just whether the veterinarian thinks it is time to say goodbye. If you have a very good relationship with your veterinarian you might be able to tell simply from the look in the veterinarian's eyes. I did, once. The puppy had parvovirus, a terrible case of it. He was on the exam table between the veterinarian and I. I had a deep relationship with this doctor. I looked at him. Our eyes locked. We both knew. I nodded, and the puppy went peacefully to sleep.

I recount the last story not to make you sad but because it brings up the important area of trust in making these decisions. Trust yourself, trust your veterinarian and your trainer, and don't blame yourself later. Your blame won't do anyone, including your lost dog, any good. Get on with life and get a new dog into your life if possible, after a respectful waiting period.

The nature of the euthanasia process itself is important to understand. Sometimes owners fear that it will be painful, or, as one woman said, "I thought my dog would still be alive, just paralyzed." Of course this is a fallacy and you should know from someone who has assisted in the process time and time again that dogs do not suffer and simply go to sleep. The injection is essentially an overdose of a sleeping pill, nothing more. Whether you decide to be at your pet's side when it is euthanized is a very personal decision. Talk to your veterinarian and decide together. For some people this helps, for others it makes matters harder.

If you have to euthanize your dog for behavioral reasons, your feelings of guilt may be very deep. You might blame yourself for failing to secure proper training early on, or for "spoiling" your dog and tolerating bad behavior. You might feel that the pet store or breeder gave you a dog that was genetically defective and was impossible to train. What I would say, as a trainer, is that if the problem was so serious that it brought you to this juncture, you are probably doing the right thing.

At the same time I would urge you to reevaluate your owner skills and leadership skills *before* procuring another dog. Don't simply blame the dog for the bad behavior and exonerate yourself. Most dog behavior problems are partly people-problems, too. Sit down in your grief (or relief, whatever is the case), and list what went wrong. What do you want to do *differently* with a new pet?

EMPTINESS

Don't be surprised if the city seems very cold, sterile and empty after you lose your dog. It is bound to feel that way. Remember, other than your houseplants and the local park, your dog was probably your main touchstone with nature. That's a lot to lose. The concrete jungle can feel pretty lonely after such a loss. Try getting out of town and into the countryside. That's healing. Or go to the zoo and watch the live animals, especially the wolves, if your zoo has any. That's healing too. I personally feel that feelings of loss over a pet run more deeply in city owners than country ones, simply because urban dwellers do not have the soothing balm of trees, fields, forests, mountains and wide-open sky that the country owner enjoys.

FURTHER HELP

If you find yourself depressed after two months, you might really need further help. Perhaps the loss of your dog has brought home to you other losses in your life. If that's the case, professional help might be necessary. I'd also suggest a book to help you through this period of supreme frustration, anger and possibly guilt.

Jamie Quackenbush, MSW, and Denise Graveline have written *When Your Pet Dies* (Simon and Schuster), a sensitive guidebook that will help you confront and deal with your feelings after the death of your dog. Quackenbush is a social worker who specializes in pet bereavement counseling. He begins by explaining the concept of bereavement, then takes us through the steps that most owners must pass through to accept their dog's death. You may already have heard of, or have faced, these steps: guilt, anger, depression, and finally, hopefully, acceptance.

To reach acceptance, Quackenbush recommends reminiscing about your pet to put the dog into perspective and take the edge off its death. Other chapters include, "Does Anyone Else Feel This Way?" and "I Thought He'd Be Around Forever." Other sections deal with making the decision to euthanize your pet, coping with the shock of accidental death and dealing with people who misunderstand your grief.

In the latter section, Quackenbush shows great sensitivity to the owner's plight, which includes enduring such boorish comments as "Why don't you just get another one" or "Oh, c'mon, it was just a dog!" On the first comment, Quackenbush notes that the person who made the statement "hasn't grasped a vital point: No relationship is replaceable." He points out that friendship takes time to build and develop. You were not just caring for a commodity, something easily replaced—but chances are that the friends who make such comments view dogs as replaceable items. His advice? Just ignore the comments and, if necessary, explain that each relationship is individual.

To the comment, "Oh, c'mon, it was just a dog!" the response should be silence, with the realization that this person probably sees dogs as possessions, playthings or, at worst, nuisances. Such a person "probably never had an animal companion or never cared much for the pets he had!"

The worst comment of all is, "Well, that's one less thing to worry about." Quackenbush says that those who make such statements may have only heard you refer to your dog as a burden or a continual chore. They misunderstand the death and might think you will feel relieved. This is also likely to occur if you have had to euthanize your pet because of a severe behavior problem.

While Quackenbush doesn't excuse insensitive friends and their unintentionally cruel comments, he doesn't coddle the distraught owner either. In fact, he advises that grief must be worked through at a steady pace, lest you fall into the "Poor Me" syndrome and redirect your bereavement at some other feature of your life that you just can't face. It's easy to fall into this trap because "you can get more attention from others if you present yourself as a victim of cruelty and thoughtlessness. But that kind of pity, or any other pity you receive from other people, won't make you feel better—it just reinforces the dangerous cycle for yourself!" You will then not only be unable to work through your dog's death, but will also unintentionally (or even intentionally) use your dog's demise as a way of focusing attention on yourself. Hardly a tribute to your dog! "That's why I caution so many pet owners not to feel sorry for themselves . . . The only effective way to feel better about your pet's death and finally put it into acceptable perspective is to work through your own feelings," not coddle yourself or stop living because your dog died.

This is sound advice from a sensitive author writing from a wealth of direct experience with sad owners. This book is an excellent gift for someone who has recently lost a pet (don't hesitate to give it; you will be helping immensely) and a good book to have around even if your pet is healthy. This is a moment every pet owner must face sooner or later, and it can only help to be a little better prepared.

20

A Closing Note

I HOPE I'VE PUT TO REST forever the notion that owners just can't have dogs in the city happily. Of course you can. It just takes twice as much work! Well, so what? What's a little extra effort for such friendship, such devotion, such a *balm* to the city's stresses? I keep thinking of that skeleton in Israel—the one I told you about at the beginning of this book. That woman or man embracing the puppy in the grave. How touching. And they lived in a city. Apparently it was destroyed; probably an earthquake. What a way to go, I'm thinking, with a puppy in your arms.

What a way to *live,* really live in a city—with a dog! I feel that city inhabitants *without* dogs are the deprived ones, not we dog owners. They are the ones who are missing out. Their defense (a rather flimsy one) is to call us "crazy." But as education progresses, even nondog owners will see the incredible value of dogs in a city. The work that is being done in nursing homes, prisons, reform schools and other institutions with dogs attests to the healing power of dogs. Dogs have more to give in a city than anywhere else.

My hope for you as an individual owner is that you truly enjoy your dog, that you have wonderful times together, that you "talk" to each other in your own special way and that you move through the city with poise, grace and, yes, a certain amount of wit and style. Most of all, I hope that you will be a responsible pet owner, cleaning up after your pet, training him or her, socializing your dog to all comers, teaching him manners.

You know from what you've read how much I love dogs. You now

You did it! You've trained a civilized city canine. Enjoy each other, and remember, regardless of where you and your dog live, the best of times is *now*.

know how I got over dog-hatred and city-hatred. I've been publicly honest with you; now you be privately honest with *yourself. Are you doing your very best by your city dog?* Tell the truth! Sit down and reflect. Of course that walk yesterday should have been longer. Of course you should have disciplined that housetraining infraction. Of course you should have taken Tippy to the video store—they accept dogs—when you selected last night's film. Tell the truth!

One last request: go give your dog another big hug for me. Tell your civilized city canine that you read a book that's changed your (and his) lives. Slobber. Love it up. *Thank* your dog.